−7.

13

THE CANADIAN HOUSE OF COMMONS

CANADIAN GOVERNMENT SERIES

R. MacG. Dawson, *Editor*

THE CANADIAN
HOUSE OF COMMONS

REPRESENTATION

BY

NORMAN WARD

Assistant Professor in Political Science
University of Saskatchewan

TORONTO
UNIVERSITY OF TORONTO PRESS
1950

FOR BETTY

PREFACE

A STUDY of representation in a democratic legislature must be directed towards two major ends. The actual membership of the legislature, including such matters as the qualifications of members and the manner in which they are remunerated, is one obvious subject for examination. Of equal importance are the laws and practices governing the selection of members. The electoral system must be broadly viewed as embodying not merely the machinery that begins to move when a government decides to test its popularity at the polls, but also the devices by which constituencies are established and altered, the franchise which determines the extent of the electorate, and the provisions which are intended to control corrupt campaign tactics and otherwise prevent perversions of representation.

Most of these topics as they relate to the Canadian House of Commons have their origin in the British North America Act, 1867. That statute created the elective branch of the federal legislature by the simple assertion that "There shall be One Parliament for Canada, consisting of the Queen, an Upper House styled the Senate, and the House of Commons." Subsequent clauses of the Act established the privileges of the two Houses (s. 18); the number of members each was to have (ss. 21 and 37); the constituencies which were to return members for the first Parliament (s. 40); the electoral machinery and franchise which were to be used until Parliament decided otherwise (s. 41); and the officials who were to have charge of the machinery (s. 42).[1]

The British North America Act, so far as the House of Commons was concerned, did little more than establish that legislature as a going concern. The House of Commons was declared to exist, and arrangements for the first general election were made. But for all subsequent elections the whole representative system, from the periodic adjustment of constituency boundaries to post-election trials for cor-

[1]Sections of the British North America Act, 1867, relating to representation in the House of Commons are found in Appendix A.

vii

ruption at the polls, was provided for in terms which gave
Parliament a wide discretion to alter it at will. For all
practical purposes, the electoral machinery was thus placed
in the hands of the government to be the subject of whatever
legislation might be expedient. If (as was obviously the
case under Sir John A. Macdonald, the first Prime Minister)
the Government's attitude was that the electoral system
afforded not only a means of holding elections but a way
of winning them, there was no legal or constitutional obstacle
to hinder manipulation.

The first few decades after Confederation were consequently years of bitter struggle over election laws. Not
infrequently, as in 1882 and 1885, government bills on the
topic occupied the attention of the House of Commons for
weeks on end, to the neglect of other aspects of the nation's
business. The mere introduction into the legislature of a
bill concerned in any way with representation long remained
a signal for tempers to rise and standards of parliamentary
decorum to fall. The result was that genuine reform of the
electoral machinery in the public interest was a literal
impossibility until well after the turn of the century. That
honesty in elections became possible, and even profitable,
was the result at least as much of forces beyond the reach
of legislative enactment as of positive federal policies conscientiously adopted and administered.

The chronicle of this development, as it can be observed
in several major sections of the electoral system, follows in
these pages. In the first chapter the general nature of
representation is discussed. The alteration of constituency
boundaries after each decennial census, ostensibly to adjust
representation in the House of Commons in accordance with
population changes across the country, is analysed in Part I.
Membership in the legislature is examined in Part II. Part
III covers the electoral machinery, both in its narrow aspect
as a technique by which members of Parliament are returned,
and in a broader sense as a large organization which includes
the franchise, electoral corruption, and election expenses.
Part IV comprises the conclusion. There is one important
and intentional omission: it was found that the relationship

between the member of Parliament and his constituency could not be accurately assessed without a wider knowledge of the private member's work and status in the legislature than came within the scope of this study of representation. The position of the private member will, it is hoped, be analysed in a later volume on the House of Commons.

This book has not been completed without considerable assistance. My friend and teacher, Professor R. MacG. Dawson, first supervised its production as a Ph.D. thesis, and then edited the text for the press; to him I owe a debt which goes back in time far beyond the beginnings of this volume. Other members of the University of Toronto faculty have read the manuscript and made comments which resulted in revision of some sections; several of my colleagues at the University of Saskatchewan have offered helpful criticisms. The text has also been read with painstaking care by Dr. E. A. Forsey and Professor A. R. M. Lower, and to them I wish to express my thanks for catching many errors and inconsistencies which had not crept into the text, but had been inserted boldly therein by me. The former Chief Electoral Officer of Canada, Jules Castonguay, together with his successor, Nelson Castonguay, was most helpful throughout the preparation of the chapters which are connected with his activities. The Maurice Cody Foundation, by the award of the Maurice Cody Research Fellowship for 1947-8, made it possible for me to spend a full year in research, and in addition generously financed a sojourn in Ottawa. I am indebted to the University of Toronto Press for valuable assistance from its editorial department and for financial support from the University of Toronto Press Publications Fund. Finally, my wife has contributed more to this study than could be made clear in words.

N.W.

University of Saskatchewan

A NOTE ON THE SOURCES

For the sake of convenience, I have used these abbreviations for frequently used sources:

Debates: *The debates of the House of Commons of Canada.*
Unless otherwise noted, references are to the bound revised editions; or, for some years prior to 1875, to the printed *Parliamentary Debates of Canada* which are the only extant records of their kind. For the years 1867-9 and 1873-4, I have used the bound collections of newspaper clippings in the Library of Parliament referred to as *Parliamentary Debates* (Scrapbook Hansard).

Journals: *Journals of the House of Commons of Canada.*
Statutes: *Statutes of Canada.*
R. S. Can.: *Revised Statutes of Canada.*
Sessional Papers: *Sessional Papers of the Parliament of Canada.*
S. C. R.: *Reports of the Supreme Court of Canada.*

The personal papers referred to, with one exception noted, are in the Public Archives of Canada.

CONTENTS

CONTENTS

APPENDIXES

PART I

INTRODUCTION

CHAPTER I

THE NATURE OF REPRESENTATION
IN CANADA

REPRESENTATIVE government is so much a commonplace that it comes as a surprise to learn that precise definitions of it are extremely rare. In fact, much disagreement exists about what representative government is and what it is supposed to be. John Stuart Mill, for instance, believed that a single legislature *could* represent a nation and, being happily ignorant of twentieth-century psychology, was able to argue that representative institutions could be improved by taking thought about them. G. D. H. Cole, on the other hand, has stated that the representation of a whole population by one body is impossible; Parliament, he says, represents everybody for everything, and therefore nobody for anything. His way out of this *impasse* is to urge the creation of an apparently indefinite number of representative assemblies, each of which would discharge one specific function.

Further disagreement has arisen over the relationship between representation and election. Mill and Lord Brougham, writing a century ago, assumed that these two matters went hand in hand, so that a representative could truly represent only if those represented had a share in his election. The same assumption underlies many modern schemes of electoral reform. But the *Encyclopædia Britannica* points out, and rightly, that election is not an essential part of representation; the Pope, for instance, represents all Roman Catholics for various purposes, but the rank-and-file members of the Church have no voice in his appointment. Many parts of the government of Canada, such as the Cabinet, the Senate, and the administrative and regulatory boards, have a representative aspect which they have obtained in some other way than by direct election. Even the civil service may be included, and the occasional complaints of members of Parliament from Quebec that French Canadians do not hold their fair share of federal offices suggest that the civil service,

3

to some citizens, is not as representative as it ought to be. An American observer of government in Great Britain has written of the British public service: "In view of its representative character, it has possessed the confidence of the ruling middle class. Because it was both competent and representative, it was an undoubted success."[1]

Representation is thus clearly a term susceptible to conflicting interpretation. This, in one sense, relieves us of responsibility for we can select the interpretation which suits our purposes. A sentence of John Stuart Mill's, although nearly a century old, can be quoted with approval as a definition of representation in the Canadian House of Commons: "The meaning of representative government is, that the whole people, or some numerous portion of them, exercise through deputies periodically elected by themselves the ultimate controlling power, which, in every constitution, must reside somewhere." Perhaps this comes closer to description than exact definition, but it will have to do. "The idea is," wrote an American scholar who found himself baffled in his attempts to define representative government, about which he had written a book, "that the people, while not in person present at the seat of government, are to be considered as present by proxy."[2]

The general nature of representation in the Canadian House of Commons having been settled, it is permissible now to ask what each individual member of Parliament ought to represent, and what he does represent. "No man," G. D. H. Cole has said, "can represent another man, and no man's will can be treated as a substitute for, or representative of, the wills of others."[3] According to this theory, what is ordinarily called "representation" in the case of a member of Parliament is merely the substitution of the member's will for the wills of many citizens. R. M. MacIver, a champion of representative government in its liberal democratic form, is perhaps not far from admitting the same thing when he postulates that representation implies both direction and control, the fulfilment of the people's will. And the will of

---

[1]J. D. Kingsley, *Representative Bureaucracy* (Antioch Press, 1944), p. 281.
[2]H. J. Ford, *Representative Government* (New York, 1924), p. 3.
[3]G. D. H. Cole, *Social Theory* (New York, 1920), p. 103.

the state, he says, "is no mystic unity but at best and for most purposes a very imperfect and limited harmony of individual wills"[1]—the determination of which, presumably, is up to the representative.

What a representative can represent if that statement is true is not easily determined. Edmund Burke, at least, had no doubts of his function as a member of Parliament; in words which have since become accepted as a classic statement of its kind, Burke once told the electors of Bristol:

Certainly, gentlemen, it ought to be the happiness and glory of a representative to live in the strictest union, the closest correspondence, and the most unreserved communication with his constituents. Their wishes ought to have great weight with him; their opinion, high respect; their business, unremitted attention. It is his duty to sacrifice his repose, his pleasures, his satisfactions, to theirs; and above all, ever, and in all cases, to prefer their interest to his own. But his unbiassed opinion, his mature judgment, his enlightened conscience, he ought not to sacrifice to you, to any man, or to any set of men living. These he does not derive from your pleasure; no, nor from the law and the constitution. They are a trust from Providence, for the abuse of which he is deeply answerable. Your representative owes you, not his industry only, but his judgment; and he betrays, instead of serving you, if he sacrifices it to your opinion. . . . Parliament is not a congress of ambassadors from different and hostile interests; which interests each must maintain . . . but parliament is a deliberating assembly of one nation, with one interest, that of the whole; where, not local purposes, not local prejudices, ought to guide, but the general good, resulting from the general reason of the whole.[2]

This is probably the most widely quoted statement in the English language of the functions of an elected representative, and the theory it sets forth—that what a member ought to represent (or, more accurately, present) is his own enlightened and even inspired view of the national interest—has been repeatedly referred to with approval in the Canadian Parliament. Burke's actual words appear in a section of Beauchesne's *Rules and Forms of the House of Commons of Canada*.

This theory was not original with Burke. In his own time, the general doctrine had been enunciated by Blackstone, and by Arthur Onslow, who was Speaker of the House of Commons from 1727 to 1761.[3] The doctrine was conservative,

[1] R. M. MacIver, *The Modern State* (Oxford, 1926), pp. 203 ff.
[2] E. Burke, *Works* (London, 1900), vol. I, pp. 446-7.
[3] See R. Luce, *Legislative Principles* (Boston and New York, 1930), Chapter XIX.

derived from a concept of Parliament which regarded that institution historically as a collection of representatives from the several communities which composed the realm; the representatives meeting together were presumed to put the common weal ahead of the interests of their own districts, for the realm was simply a greater community to which all the lesser ones belonged.[1] However, Burke's statement differed from this view of representation in one important respect: it was spoken by a professional politician on the occasion of a poll. In its original context, the statement is an even more revealing comment on representation than when quoted by itself. Burke spoke the words in 1774 with specific reference to one opposing candidate who, falling in line with a widespread practice, had indicated his willingness to be bound by the instructions of his constituents. Burke scouted his opponent's view, but it is important to note that he postponed the scouting until after the votes had been counted, with a majority for Burke; his speech, one biographer records, astounded those who heard it. Speaking before the election, he made no reference to the providential and trusteeship aspects of a seat in the House of Commons. As member of Parliament for Bristol after 1774, Burke on two occasions courageously took a stand which he knew to be unpopular with his constituents, and this implementation of his theory was a major factor in his subsequent career, for he never again sat for Bristol. Seeking to be returned for the city in 1780, Burke did not rely on a repetition of his lofty statement of 1774; on the contrary, he cajoled the voters in these words:

I do not very remarkably spare myself in public business; and in the private business of my constituents I have done very nearly as much as those who have nothing else to do. My canvass of you was not on the 'change, nor in the county meetings, nor in the clubs of this city: It was in the House of Commons; it was at the custom-house; it was at the council; it was at the treasury; it was at the admiralty. I canvassed you through your affairs, and not your persons. I was not only your representative

[1]An interesting short discussion of the survival of medieval concepts in contemporary British government is found in the B.B.C.'s publication, *The Listener*, for March 17, 1949, pp. 441-2. See also R. Luce, *op. cit.*, Chapter IX; Luce takes a contrary view of early parliamentary representation, claiming that the early members were agents or delegates, not representatives.

as a body; I was the agent, the solicitor of individuals; I ran about wherever your affairs could call me; and in acting for you, I often appeared rather as a shipbroker, than as a member of parliament.   There was nothing too laborious or too low for me to undertake.[1]

In exercising his trust from Providence, in short, the great Burke often acted very like a politician.   But it availed him not, and after Burke satisfied himself in 1780 that his immediate services to his electors were not going to outweigh his opposition in Parliament to some of their wishes on public matters, he withdrew from the contest.   Thereafter he sat for a pocket borough.

Burke's theory of representation, as it relates to democratic government, has thus one flaw which is nicely illustrated by his own experience: when put into practice, it may prevent a representative from continuing as a representative.   A second objection is that his theory is devoid of real meaning, or, if not that, at least open to so broad an interpretation as to leave members of Parliament free to represent what they like.   A member who regards himself as a trustee for the national interest may be an admirable person, but he is equally free to be a drone, a party hack, or a scoundrel. The Canadian House of Commons, judging from Dr. Beauchesne's monumental *Rules and Forms*, appears to accept officially a secular version of Burke's theory.   The Canadian Parliament has had, as a matter of record, members who took their duties so lightly that their occasional appearance in the legislative chamber called forth speeches of congratulation, thanks, and welcome from their honourable friends.   We have had members whose attitude is summarized in these words by one of them: "I believe I am serving the best interests of my electors, in keeping with the spirit of the mandate entrusted to me, when I enthusiastically express my determination to support the policy of the . . . government."[2]   Another has recently confessed, in the fourth year of his parliamentary career, "I hardly know just why I am

[1]Burke, *op. cit.*, vol. II, p. 132.   In "Thoughts on the Cause of the Present Discontents," Burke wrote: "The virtue, spirit, and essence of a House of Commons consists in its being the express image of the feelings of the nation. It was not instituted to be a control *upon* the people, . . . [but] a control *for* the people."
[2]*Debates* (unrevised edition), March 7, 1949, p. 1235.

on my feet. I am not much of a talker anyway, and I am never exactly sure what I should or should not do since I came to this place."[1] Yet another moved permanently to England while still a member, and came back for a session mainly because he had been unable to get a "pair" for the whole parliamentary year. The people of Canada paid his travelling expenses back and forth across the Atlantic. However, the money was not entirely wasted, since the member had private business of his own on this side of the water.[2]

The theory that members represent the common weal has as a corollary the theory that the freedom of members must be guaranteed. Dr. Beauchesne has written:

> The privileges of Parliament are based on the fact that members of both Houses must be untrammelled in the performance of their legislative duties . . . Members elected and Senators appointed as Dominion legislators have the inherent right to perform with independence all the work required for the supervision of Government activities and the passing of legislation; they possess the power to remove all impediments in the performance of their duties.[3]

This refers specifically to the privileges of members, which include such matters as the right to attend parliamentary sessions unmolested and to speak freely without being held to account outside the chamber; but privileges and immunities of this kind are inseparable from a theory of representation such as Burke's, for they can be justified only on grounds of national interest. The rights granted to members (it is difficult to follow Dr. Beauchesne when he states that these rights are inherent) have never been defended because they were to allow an individual to represent freely the interests of only his local electors. That local affairs were regarded as of secondary importance by Sir John A. Macdonald is suggested by the fact that he not infrequently proposed to disfranchise a constituency by leaving it unrepresented after its member had been unseated for particularly flagrant

[1]*Ibid.*, March 8, 1949, p. 1288.
[2]*Ibid.*, 1890, p. 3197.
[3]A. Beauchesne, *Rules and Forms of the House of Commons of Canada* (Toronto, 1943), pp. xxvii-xxviii. Apart from privileges and immunities, the independence of members is further protected by statutory provisions which make it illegal for a member to sit in Parliament if he holds an office of emolument (excepting members of the ministry) or a government contract.

electoral corruption, apparently basing his argument on the assumption that a constituency so depraved ought to be punished in the national interest.

The extent to which Canadian members regard themselves as representatives of the whole commonwealth is not easy to determine, for parliamentarians are no more than most people given to critical self-examination, and representation as such is not a frequent subject of debate. Two matters in recent decades have forced members of Parliament to think aloud about what they represent, and both matters are worth explaining at some length, since they reveal an extraordinary amount of confusion—which is only to be expected if members are free to act as they think best.

Immediately after the First World War the recall of members of Parliament became an issue in Canada, because of practices which were developing in the West. Even the provincial Conservative party in Alberta favoured the recall device, and other groups were moved to obtain signed but undated resignations from their elected representatives, so that any recalcitrant member could be recalled by simply dating and publishing the document. Now if a member of Parliament is to be a free agent, it appears to follow that he should be free to decide whether or not he should sign an undated resignation; but when the general topic of recalls and signed pledges came up in the House of Commons, a majority of the members were opposed to this particular use of a member's freedom. A statutory disqualification of any member who signed an advance resignation was subsequently inserted in the Dominion Elections Act, where it still remains despite frequent attempts to remove it.[1] The debates on this subject, somewhat obscured because several members seem to have opposed not the recall device but those who were in favour of it, cannot be said to prove anything except that members do not agree about their functions as representatives.

The following will bear out this conclusion:[2] One member from Alberta opposed the recall because it would reduce a representative to the status of a delegate. Mr. Fielding, a

[1]The latest attempt was in 1939.
[2]*Debates*, 1920, pp. 2024 ff.

Nova Scotian, deplored the recall but thought that the various parties should be free to use it if they wished. A second Albertan said:

> I think it is his [a member's] duty first to lay before Parliament the rights and claims and needs of his constituents, just as any counsel would do on behalf of his clients. But that done, it is his duty, in casting his vote, to have regard to the best interests of Canada as a whole; if necessary, to compromise on the interests or needs of his own constituents if that must be done.

A Saskatchewan Progressive said:

> I have a committee of fifteen who are keeping themselves well posted upon public matters in [my constituency], and they are advising me from time to time. They are sending me information and their opinions on public questions, and this helps me materially in my course in this House.

Mr. W. L. Mackenzie King, sitting for the moment in a Prince Edward Island seat, revived a theory which had been dead for several hundred years:

> It is for the people to say whom they wish to send to this Parliament as their representatives, not for this Parliament to tell the people whom they shall or shall not send. If the people desire to choose as a candidate . . . a man who is tied, manacled or bound, whether by physical infirmity, by agreement, or in any other way . . . it seems to me that . . . they have a right to say whether or not that candidate should go to Parliament.

Mr. King then immediately added that if he were faced with an opponent who was tied, manacled, or bound by a recall pledge, he would use the pledge as "a strong reason why such a candidate should not be returned." Perhaps the ideal statement on representation was made by a Liberal-Unionist from Saskatchewan who was able both to please his constituents and act in the national interest because, he asserted, his constituents wanted him "to act . . . in the best interests of the country as a whole." If there are many such fortunate members, they do not seem to be noticeable from the parliamentary press gallery, for a veteran reporter wrote not long ago, "In ninety-nine cases out of one hundred, the member goes to Ottawa to speak for his own constituency and no other. That is what the member thinks he is sent to Ottawa to do; that is what the electors think he is sent to do."[1]

---

[1] A. Cross, *The People's Mouths* (Toronto, 1944), p. 114.

A crisis of some proportions, in which representation was involved, arose in 1942 over the conscription plebiscite. It will be recalled that all major parties fought the election of 1940 on a "no conscription" basis, and by 1942 the Liberal government was ready to admit that the pledge to refrain from conscription was becoming a burden. Showing a praiseworthy (and unprecedented) solicitude for the sanctity of a campaign promise, the government allowed the people of Canada to vote "yes" or "no" on the following question: "Are you in favour of releasing the government from any obligation arising out of any past commitments restricting the methods of raising men for military service?"[1] The government, while emphasizing that the plebiscite was not a vote for or against conscription as such, asked the electorate for an affirmative answer to its question, and by the country as a whole an affirmative answer was given; "no" votes carried most of Quebec, but only half a dozen areas elsewhere. In order that the plebiscite might be taken as rapidly as possible, the Government had had recourse to the ordinary general election machinery, so that the plebiscite was held under the direction of the Chief Electoral Officer of Canada, disguised as the Chief Plebiscite Officer, and the results of the vote were known according to members' constituencies. When in due course the Government sought to implement its view of the electorate's decision by amending the National Resources Mobilization Act to provide for conscription by order-in-council, several members of Parliament were embarrassed to find that they wanted to vote in the House of Commons contrary to the expressed wishes of their constituents.

The plebiscite, in effect, asked only if the Government were to be freed from a voluntary pledge given in 1940, and the legislation subsequently introduced in Parliament was exactly consistent with the results of the vote. At no time was a direct vote on conscription taken either in or out of Parliament. The significance of this to representation arose from the fact that members from all parties, freely using their own judgment, interpreted both the plebiscite and the amendment to the National Resources Mobilization Act in

[1]*Statutes*, 1942-3, c. 1, s. 3.

every conceivable way, and these interpretations both affected, and were affected by, the members' views on representation.[1]

A large group of Quebec members argued that while a "yes" vote on the plebiscite was not necessarily a vote for conscription, a "no" vote was clearly a vote against conscription; and they proceeded to vote against the amendment to the National Resources Mobilization Act because they felt bound to follow the wishes of their constituents. One member argued that since the country as a whole had voted "yes" on the plebiscite, every member of Parliament, as a national representative, ought to vote for the amendment—a statement which, carried to its logical conclusion, might be so interpreted as to eliminate all opposition in Parliament. Conservatives in the House of Commons, though not specifically freed by the plebiscite of any pledges of their own, nevertheless campaigned for an affirmative answer and subsequently voted for the amendment. The Conservative leader, indeed, argued eloquently that the plebiscite was unnecessary, since the parliamentary system meant that the people gave to their representatives the power to make all laws which were necessary and constitutional. This the Prime Minister admitted, but implied that the elected representatives had pledged themselves in 1940 not to use the sovereign powers of Parliament in regard to conscription— i.e. it appears that a majority of the representatives, for this one purpose, were prepared to refrain from representing. A few members actively campaigned for a "no" vote in the plebiscite, and having secured it, proceeded to vote "no" on the amendment in the Commons. A few members campaigned for a "yes" vote on the plebiscite, and having received a "no" vote, voted for the amendment anyway, although aware that they were perhaps endangering their political futures. A few members campaigned for and received a "yes" vote in the plebiscite, and then voted against the amendment on a point of principle. Of the eighteen members of Parliament whose votes on the amend-

[1]See *Debates*, 1942, on "Dominion Plebiscite Act" and "National Resources Mobilization Act."

ment to the National Resources Mobilization Act were contrary to the wishes of their constituents as expressed in the plebiscite, sixteen sought re-election in 1945, and only two were defeated.

The debates of 1920 and 1942 referred to above suggest that one statement concerning what members should and do represent can be made without fear of contradiction: the members of the Canadian House of Commons fall somewhere short of unanimity on the subject. One point seems clear, that they are free to define their own functions as they like. They are free to follow their leaders blindly, free to bolt the party, free to vote as their constituents want them to, or free to consider their constituents mistaken, and on each of these matters the responsibility is entirely their own. Yet this apparent freedom, though strikingly demonstrated in some instances in 1942, becomes illusory when one considers the nature of party organization. The Quebec Liberals, who in 1942 voted against the Government's amendment to the National Resources Mobilization Act, could do so without endangering the Government because other parties in the House of Commons supported the amendment, and the Government could therefore avoid forcing an issue, and allow the enviable luxury of a "free" vote to the Quebec representatives. But the freedom of parliamentary representatives is ordinarily incompatible with the workings of the cabinet system of government, and the theory that a representative is free to use his personal judgment, although paradoxically the tradition both here and in Great Britain, can remain acceptable only so long as the majority of representatives identify the national interest with their party's interest; in effect, they must use their freedom to subjugate themselves. There is one further paradox: where there are only a few major parties in a legislature in which the Cabinet system exists, a member of Parliament, by following without question the dictates of his party leaders, is perhaps not far from the ideal of using his free judgment in the national interest. This is because the party leaders, assuming on their part a modicum of enlightenment, will be doing their best to please the electorate in order to win the next election. (That of course assumes that what pleases the electorate is in the national interest.)

If it be conceded that a member is a true representative of the whole commonwealth when he follows the party line, what does he represent when party discipline is relaxed? A generous sampling of debates on the address in reply to the Speech from the Throne, and of questions asked of the Ministry—two opportunities for members to reveal their dearest interests[1]—suggests that representatives from time to time represent three important things in addition to their party. These can only be indicated here. The first is each member's constituency, and one distinguished parliamentarian can speak for all his brethren on this topic. Mr. Jean-François Pouliot so frequently mentions his constituency that a fellow member has remarked that he fights all the world's battles on the assumption that the county of Témiscouata is in the front line. "I know by name at least 99% of my electors," Mr. Pouliot has advised the House of Commons.[2] This is not without its disadvantages, for Mr. Pouliot has also said, "Most of our indemnity goes back to our electors in the form of contributions of funeral wreaths, masses for the dead, wedding gifts and charity."[3] Contributions such as these are of course a member's own affair, but they are probably not unrelated to his chances of re-election, and are thus an inseparable part of representation. The same is true of the countless favours performed for individual correspondents and visitors to Ottawa, and doubtless occasionally of the indispensable bridge or post office erected in the member's riding.

In second place comes each member's province or geographic region. The Quebec Liberals who voted against the amendments to the National Resources Mobilization Act in 1942, while following the expressed wishes of their own constituencies, did not speak for their own electoral district alone; they spoke, many of them in most explicit terms, for Quebec.

[1]I am indebted to an essay by Miss June Green, a student at the University of Saskatchewan, for suggestions concerning the use of questions asked in the House as a measure of a member's interests.

[2]*Debates*, 1932-3, p. 5348.

[3]*Ibid.*, 1940, p. 2400.

The acute interest in anything connected with wheat displayed at all times by members from the prairies; the concern of British Columbia members in 1948 when flood waters ran riot along part of the Pacific province; the prolonged irritation of members from the Maritimes over the loss by their provinces of seats in the House of Commons when several consecutive censuses made drastic redistributions necessary; and the unanimity with which Manitoba members in 1949 opposed the removal of part of the Trans-Canada Air Lines' staff from Winnipeg to Montreal, are all examples which show that representation in the Commons has a regional aspect which is sometimes more important than party discipline.

Finally, as parts of this book reveal, there are times when members of Parliament cannot honestly be said to represent anybody but members of Parliament. Members of Parliament, within broad limits, are free to lay down the terms of their own employment and, like any other group of people so fortunately situated, they are not hard taskmasters. A later chapter indicates that the statute which governs the payment of the sessional indemnity is a striking example, for it counts every member present for every day on which the House does not meet because it is adjourned. Since adjourned days comprise from one-third to one-half of nearly every session, this means that each member is entitled to a substantial portion of his pay whether he is ever in Ottawa or not. Again, the laws supposed to prevent (or at least punish) electoral corruption protect members to an extraordinary degree. The statute which holds members to account for election expenditures is a farce.[1] There are other examples which might be cited, and all suggest that parliamentarians, whatever they ought to be, are only human.

A Canadian member of Parliament, according to the semi-official *Rules and Forms* written by the Clerk of the House of Commons, is thus presumed to represent the whole country in the manner that Burke described in 1774. As we have seen, there is profound confusion in the minds of members themselves about their functions as representatives. But at least they are free agents, and they use their freedom

[1] See *infra*, Chapters VI, XIV, and XV.

to assume different roles at different times.   The same individual, in a single day, can expound his own enlightened view of the national interest; be the agent or delegate of his party; be a counsel for his chief client, his constituency; be a spokesman for his geographic region, or perhaps his racial group; and be a private citizen riding a hobby-horse of his own.   It would be pedantic to attempt to assess how much of this activity is genuine representation and how much requires the representative to be an agent or delegate, for the excellent reason that a conscientious member is both a representative and a delegate at the same time.

The devices which make it possible for Canadians to become representatives of their compatriots are assessed in the pages which follow.

PART II

THE CONSTITUENCIES

CHAPTER II

REDISTRIBUTION, 1867-1892

REPRESENTATION in the Canadian House of Commons rests
on a geographic basis. The entire country is divided into
areas called constituencies, each of which ordinarily returns
a single member of Parliament.[1] Adjustment of the boundaries of these constituencies, to take account of population
changes, is a decennial task imposed upon the Canadian
Parliament by virtue of a section of the British North America
Acts of 1867 and 1946. The constitutional statutes prescribe
that seats in the House of Commons are to be apportioned
among the provinces after each census according to certain
explicit rules and limitations. Distribution of seats among
the provinces is thus automatic, for Parliament is left
with no discretion in the matter short of a constitutional
amendment. Within any one province, on the other
hand, the settlement of constituency boundaries is entirely
a problem for Parliament, and the major difficulties that
have arisen in Canada over the decennial readjustments
have been concerned primarily with this phase of redistribution, rather than with the fundamental divisions among
provinces.

Few things seem to excite a member of Parliament so
much as a proposal to alter the boundaries of the constituency
which elected him. When a redistribution takes place on a
large scale, the House of Commons frequently rings with what
one member, Mr. C. G. Power, has frankly described as an
"unseemly, undignified and utterly confusing scramble for
personal or political advantage."[2] Of all the aspects of
parliamentary representation examined in this study, indeed,
the debates on redistribution reveal the Commons at its
worst. Happily these peculiar interests and passions are
aroused only every ten years, and the redistribution disputes

[1]There are two two-member constituencies, and there have been as many as
ten. See Norman Ward, "Voting in Canadian Two-Member Constituencies,"
Public Affairs, Sept., 1946, pp. 220 ff.
[2]*Debates*, 1939, p. 1808.

are really misleading as an indication of how the Commons ordinarily pursues its affairs. As one of Sir Alan Herbert's celebrated but fictitious lawyers once remarked in court, "If elderly bishops were seen leaving the Athenaeum with jugs of stout in their hands, the casual observer would form an impression of the character of that institution which would be largely unjust."[1] So with the House of Commons at redistribution time.

The Quebec Resolutions of 1864, which outlined in detail most of the clauses incorporated in the British North America Act of 1867,[2] laid down the essentials of the redistribution scheme subsequently adopted. Quebec was to have a fixed representation of 65, and the other provinces were to be represented in proportion; although a clause was added to protect any province from a loss of representation as long as its population was growing at a pace proportionate to that of the country as a whole. The resolutions also proposed a definite agency (later abandoned) which was to settle constituency boundaries within each province; the provincial legislatures were to perform this function, and they were also empowered to alter boundaries from time to time.

Sir John A. Macdonald, one of the leading architects of Confederation and the first Prime Minister of Canada, explained that Quebec was chosen as the pivotal province because it was "the best suited for the purpose, on account of the comparatively permanent character of its population, and from its having neither the largest nor least number of inhabitants."[3] It had the further advantage that a legislature based on a scheme that gave Quebec sixty-five members would not be a large one, a point which seems to have weighed heavily with some Lower Canada leaders; the larger the legislature, they argued, the larger would be the absolute majority that Upper Canada would have over Lower

[1]A. P. Herbert, *Misleading Cases in the Common Law* (9th ed., London, 1935, p. 41.

[2]The British North America Act, 1867, was the result of several conferences held successively in the Maritimes, Quebec, and London. See e.g., J. Pope, *Confederation Documents* (Toronto, 1895); R. MacG. Dawson, *The Government of Canada* (Toronto, 1947), Chapter II.

[3]*Confederation Debates*, p. 38.

Canada.[1] In any case, the granting of sixty-five seats to Quebec
was a remarkably convenient arrangement, for not only did
it mean that the existing Lower Canada constituencies could
be retained for the new Commons, but it raised no problems
in New Brunswick and Nova Scotia. There, with but a
slight violation of the principle of representation by population, the allocation of seats could be left equal to the number
of counties, with two extra seats because of the cities of Saint
John and Halifax.[2] Even in Ontario, where seventeen new
seats were to be added to the existing sixty-five which Upper
Canada had had in the united legislature of 1841-66, no
trouble was caused, and the adjustment occurred without
friction. "I am now consulting the leading members on the
point," Macdonald wrote to Lord Monck in 1866, "in order
to prevent discussion in the House. I have prepared and
printed a population return, and hope in a few days to perfect
a scheme with the consent of my Reform colleagues."[3] The
new seats allotted to Ontario, it may be noted, were given
entirely to the counties, and only six of the total of eighty-
two seats crossed municipal or county lines.[4]

It is one thing to provide for an initial allocation of seats,
as above, and quite another to lay down the rules for all
future alterations. This latter problem involves two important points: who is to do it, and how it is to be done.
On the first of these, the official documents are singularly
vague. Although for a time it appeared that the provinces
were to be charged with the duty, Sir John subsequently
altered the relevant portion of the Quebec resolutions on
this point, and in the debates of the Canadian Legislative
Assembly in 1865 blandly explained the amendment away

[1]J. E. Cauchon, *L'Union des Provinces de L'Amerique Britannique du Nord*
(Quebec, 1865), p. 79. The author explains here that if Quebec has 65 members,
Ontario will have 82; but if Quebec has more members, Ontario will have a
larger absolute majority with the same relative strength. Both Macdonald and
Galt favoured a larger legislature than the one settled on. See Pope, *Confederation Documents*, p. 66; *Confederation Debates*, p. 39.
[2]See J. H. Gray, *Confederation* (Toronto, 1872), p. 58.
[3]J. Pope, *Memoirs of Sir John Macdonald* (London, 1894), vol. I, p. 301.
From 1841 to 1866, Upper and Lower Canada (later Ontario and Quebec) each
had 65 seats in the colonial assembly.
[4]See British North America Act, 1867, Schedule I; Norman Ward, "The
Basis of Representation in the House of Commons," *Canadian Journal of Economics and Political Science*, November, 1949, p. 477-494.

on the grounds that the resolutions were in error.[1]   He then
stated most emphatically that the new Commons "must
have the full power of arranging and re-arranging the electoral
districts."   However, when the Canadian delegation reached
London in 1866 on the last lap of the Confederation negotiations, the first draft of the British North America bill contained nothing in regard to constituency boundaries except
this significant note: "The readjustment to be made by an
independent authority, as some of the Judges, to be specified
in the Imperial Act."[2]   As if to support this point, the
B.N.A. Act itself did not specifically empower the House of
Commons to execute changes, but stated that representation
"shall be readjusted *by such authority*, in such manner, and
from such time, as the Parliament of Canada from time to
time provides."[3]   Whatever that was intended to mean, Sir
John took it from the first as a grant of power to Parliament,
and with one exception it has never been seriously suggested
that Parliament does not have the power to readjust constituencies.[4]   That Parliament ought not to do so is of course
another argument, which is discussed below.

The manner in which constituencies were to be distributed
among the provinces was set forth with greater clarity than
the description of the agency that was to settle actual boundaries, but the rules laid down were by no means complete.
The fundamental principle was "representation by population," for nothing emerges more emphatically from the
Confederation negotiations than the insistence of Upper
Canada on that point.   "Rep. by pop." (a phrase which had
become a battle-cry in the western division of the colony
of United Canada in the years preceding 1867) applied only

[1]The proposal to leave readjustment of boundaries with the provinces was
declared to be a proposition which did not convey "the true meaning of the
conference," and "an obvious blunder, which must be corrected." See *Confederation Debates*, 1865, pp. 39-40; Pope, *Confederation Documents*, p. 298;
Pope, *Correspondence of Sir John Macdonald* (Toronto, 1921), pp. 14-15; W. M.
Whitelaw, "Reconstructing the Quebec Conference," *Canadian Historical Review*,
1938, pp. 123-37.
[2]Pope, *Confederation Documents*; First Draft of British North America
Bill, s. 25.
[3]British North America Act, 1867, s. 51.   Hereafter this statute is ordinarily
referred to as the B.N.A. Act.
[4]See *infra*, pp. 36-7.

to the apportionment of seats among the provinces: the B.N.A. Act and all the recorded transactions are silent about the principles which were to govern the boundaries of constituencies within any one province. After the first allocation of seats in 1867, which was somewhat arbitrary, the following statutory rules were to divide federal seats among the provinces:

1. Each province was to have as many seats as its population warranted in proportion to Quebec's fixed number of 65.

2. No reduction was to be made in any province's representation unless the ratio of its population to the national total had declined by more than one-twentieth of the same ratio at the previous redistribution. For all practical purposes, this meant the previous census.[1] This guarantee was put in to protect those provinces whose population was increasing the least rapidly. It was originally regarded by many of the Fathers of Confederation as an almost water-tight guarantee to the Maritimes, and it was thought improbable that the protection would ever be needed;[2] as it worked out, the guarantee was useless to the Maritimes but protected Ontario, which needed it least.

3. After a province's quota of seats was determined, any remainder of population greater than one-half of the quotient obtained by dividing Quebec's population by 65 entitled a province to an additional member.

These legal details concerning representation, although complicated, were neither so comprehensive nor so precise as to cover all contingencies. Even the fundamental principle of representation by population (which was, curiously enough, not stated in specific terms in the B.N.A. Act, although the earlier resolutions had embodied it) did not last long, for it was thrown to the winds when Manitoba and British Columbia entered the federation in 1870 and

[1]The Act refers to the "last preceding readjustment of the number of members for the province." Since redistribution usually takes place at least two or three years after the census, it is remarkable that no province ever tried to argue that while its relative population might have declined the required one-twentieth between, say, 1911 and 1921, it did not decline one-twentieth between 1914 (when a redistribution occurred) and 1921. According to the Act, this would appear to be a valid argument. See Appendix A.

[2]Pope, *Confederation Documents*, pp. 66-7.

1871. Manitoba, which had an electorate far too small to entitle it to even one member, was given four; British Columbia, which could muster almost enough citizens to justify a single representative, was given six.[1] Both these provinces exacted this heavy over-representation as part of the agreement by which they entered the federation.

The Liberal opposition objected strongly to this departure from "rep. by pop.," and also questioned the constitutionality of granting representation to new provinces on a basis inconsistent with the terms of the B.N.A. Act. The Government answered the second of these arguments merely by pointing out that as far as new provinces were concerned, the B.N.A. Act was, in effect, altered to the extent that the terms of union varied from it, for the Act did not begin to apply until after a province had entered federation. British Columbia, in any event, came in under an Imperial order-in-council authorized by the B.N.A. Act itself. As for the departure from the fundamental principle of representation, that could be readily justified also. "I suppose," declared a government spokesman in the Senate in 1871, "that almost everyone . . . will agree that the rule of representation by population cannot be fairly applied to a new territory . . . . It must be admitted that, in considering the case of a sparsely settled country, we must provide arbitrarily for the representation. . . . We [have] to consider not merely the existing state of the country, but to look forward to the time, not far distant, when there would be a large and energetic population."[2] In addition, there was a problem in British Columbia which necessitated more than one member, for rivalry between Vancouver Island and the mainland was too strong to allow for the interests of both to be adequately looked after by a single representative.[3] Six seems to have been an unduly large allotment to meet this difficulty.

The first two provinces to enter Confederation after 1867 were thus greeted with extravagant generosity. The liberality accorded them was not diminished by the fact that the

[1]See *Debates*, 1870, pp. 1290 ff.; 1871, pp. 660 ff., 683 ff., 753, and 772 ff. British Columbia originally asked for eight members. See *Sessional Papers*, 1871, no. 18.
[2]*Debates*, 1871, p. 774.
[3]*Ibid.*, p. 693.

initial gift of membership was in each case an irreducible
minimum. This was a temporary guarantee to Manitoba,
but a permanent one to British Columbia.[1] The third new
province, Prince Edward Island, was also given too many
federal seats when it entered the union, but on a scale so
far below British Columbia and Manitoba that this constituted a fruitful source of grievance for years to come. The
Island had originally refused to enter Confederation partly
because it regarded the quota of five representatives it would
have received under the B.N.A. Act as too small. Island
delegates at the early Quebec conference of 1864 had held
out for more seats in the Commons, but the majority of the
Conference adhered to "rep. by pop." and the Island's
interest in Confederation seems to have declined drastically
after its defeat on this point.[2] In 1873 the Island became
the seventh Canadian province, and though entitled to only
five members, received six because the population had increased "by fifteen thousand or upwards since the year 1861."
These six were not protected as were the seats of the two
western provinces, and in due course the operation of the
B.N.A. Act—to the great dismay of the Maritime members—
reduced the Island's six to three.[3]

Within six years of Confederation, representation in the
House of Commons was thus resting on three separate bases.
The four original provinces shared nearly 190 seats appor-

[1]This was specifically guaranteed to British Columbia by the fact that no
arrangement was made for the reduction of its membership in accordance with
the relevant sections of the B.N.A. Act. (*Sessional Papers*, 1871, no. 18, p. 27;
Statutes, 1872, pp. lxxxiv ff.) In the case of Manitoba, four members were
guaranteed until the census of 1881, when the terms of the B.N.A. Act came
into effect. (*Statutes*, 33 Vict., c. 3, s. 4).

[2]Pope, *Confederation Documents*, pp. 66-72.

[3]It is impossible to determine why the P.E.I. quota of seats was not protected. It is of course entirely reasonable that the Island's membership should
have been subject to the same rules as that of the four original provinces, except
that the special treatment accorded British Columbia and Manitoba makes the
Prince Edward Island terms seem somewhat unfair. The two western provinces
were in a much better position than the Island to drive a hard bargain, as is
seen in the excellent financial terms granted them. In addition, there is at
least the possibility that the protection given British Columbia, particularly,
was more or less accidental; the discussions proceeded so completely on the
assumption that the West would have a great boom that it would have been
inconsistent to make any provision for the decrease of the province's representation. Since Manitoba entered with four members in 1870, her representation
would have been wiped out after the census of 1871 had some protection not
been given.

tioned among them approximately according to population; the two western provinces shared a guaranteed ten seats on no basis whatever except expediency; the smallest province was over-represented to the extent of one member, thus straddling the wide gap between principle and convenience. There was also, until 1872, a differentiation in the methods by which constituency boundaries were drawn, for while the ridings of the four original provinces had been agreed upon by a conference of the two major parties, the constituencies of British Columbia and Manitoba were arranged by the Canadian government. That this was performed with an eye to party advantage is suggested by the fact that at least nine of the ten western seats returned Conservative Government supporters in 1872. By one of those coincidences that make politics such a fascinating study, Prince Edward Island—which was treated so much less generously than the two western provinces—returned a Conservative in only one of its six new seats in 1874.

Four members were allotted to the North West Territories in 1886, although on a population basis only two were justified.[1] The enormous size of these new western constituencies necessitated a departure from representation by population, and the entry of the Territories was by no means carried out with the same calculated generosity shown to Manitoba and British Columbia. In 1903, although only six seats were justified, territorial representation was raised to ten in anticipation of a great western boom. The prairie census of 1905 proved the soundness of this optimism, for, with the creation of the provinces of Alberta and Saskatchewan in the same year, seven and ten members respectively were allotted strictly on the basis of population.

All these arrangements to some degree concerned bargains made by individual areas with the federal government under unique circumstances. After the first decennial census and each succeeding census, the Government in power had the

[1]See *Debates*, 1886, pp. 866 ff. and 1205 ff. The government seemed strangely reluctant to grant representation to the N.W.T. and had been evading the question in Parliament since 1883.

opportunity to tamper with constituencies to its own advantage on a comprehensive scale, a procedure known to American politics as gerrymandering.   The tampering was done with some hesitation and pretence of principle in 1872, with a gay abandon in 1882, and with dignity and persistence in 1892.   All three of these redistributions took place under Conservative auspices,[1] and all three were enacted in the same general way: the Government introduced a bill which included a detailed definition of all constituency boundaries; the opposition talked itself hoarse in pointing out alleged unfairness and discrimination; and the bill was then pushed through by the Government majority, ordinarily with no major concessions being made.   All three redistributions were thus marked by great outcries of "Gerrymander" from the opposition, and while this charge was justified,[2] all three followed a strategy which, no doubt unintentionally, seemed to benefit the Liberals as often as the Conservatives.   Indeed, when the Conservatives gave Quebec a thorough overhauling in 1892, they were so carried away by the mathematics of counting ballots that they failed signally to consider the intangible human factors involved; and in the two general elections held on the 1892 readjustment the Conservatives in Quebec were almost annihilated.   Nevertheless, the Liberals could foresee no better than the Conservatives the results of future elections; like the celebrated gentleman who was cremated by mistake and sealed in a small jar, they felt throughout the first redistributions that they were being put to a good deal of unnecessary inconvenience.

The technique of the gerrymander is highly interesting, and it is fortunate that the man who in 1882 helped to plan the greatest of them all, has recorded for posterity how he went about it.   Possibly because he was anxious to have a clear conscience during his declining years, or possibly because his bill for services rendered in 1882 was never paid,

[1]Appendix B gives the dates and results of the twenty-one general elections since Confederation, and shows which party has been in power for each year.

[2]The great gerrymander of 1882 has been exhaustively analysed by Professor Dawson.   See his article, "The Gerrymander of 1882," in the *Canadian Journal of Economics and Political Science*, May, 1935, pp. 197-221.

Mr. John Hague, editor of the *Journal of Commerce*, wrote to the *Montreal Herald* in 1899:

On September 15, 1881, I received a notice from a member of the Senate, who represented the government of Sir John Macdonald in Toronto, asking me to call upon him at a certain hour. I was informed that in compliance with the constitution the government proposed to re-arrange the constituencies of Ontario. I was told that the work of preparing a chart showing the boundaries proposed had been entrusted to the officers of the Department of the Interior . . . but they failed to draft a workable plan. I was asked if I would undertake to construct a chart according to the ideas and suggestions of the speaker. On hearing my assurance that I felt equal to such a task, the Senator proceeded to say that he wished a chart made showing the existing boundaries of the electoral districts, the voting strength of each of them, and the majority at the last election.

. . . After most tedious work, extending over several weeks, for I only devoted my evenings to it, the chart with its mass of pink and blue tickets was finished, and a pretty foolish affair it was, as I had predicted. Ontario, so treated, looked like some fabulous animal, covered with loose scales, blue and pink, which fluttered like so many tiny wings. . .

I was informed that what the government wished to effect was a re-arrangement of the electoral districts so far as possible recognizing a common unit of representation. This, however, was to be made sufficiently elastic to allow the grouping of different sections of the district, so as to detach Conservative voters from places where they were in excess for the needs for a majority, and the attachment of such voters to districts where the new accession would turn the scale at an election in favour of a Conservative candidate where a Liberal one had hitherto been returned. Electoral districts which were hopelessly Liberal were, if possible, to be abolished, or the constituencies so arranged as to put the Liberal voters altogether in one district, especially where they could be drawn away from a district where they menaced the Conservative candidate. . . After making a colossal chart, I took each electoral district and its surroundings in hand, and wrote upon each the number polled for each party at the two previous elections, the total number of electors, with the majority in each case. I coloured each district to show at a glance its political complexion. I then made a thorough study of the official returns of the last two elections, and took out hundreds of statistics for comparison and readjustment. Some of the districts were most difficult to alter so as to secure the results desired. It was said the configuration of some of these represented nothing on earth, in the heavens or the waters under the heavens. Quite true, they simply represented an effort to fix the boundaries of electoral districts according to two rules: first, on the principle of equal representation to equal numbers of voters; second, on the principle that electoral districts should be arranged to serve the interests of the party in power. . . These rules do not work well together, hence the highly eccentric shapes of some of the districts on the chart. . . When nearly complete it was taken down to Ottawa. . .

The gerrymander act, as it was called, was simply the chart I had constructed, expressed in legal language. The changes were estimated to have given an absolute gain to the Conservative party of four seats, and a better fighting chance in a number of others. I remember remarking at the time that all such arrangements proceeded on the very doubtful assumption that future elections would proceed on the same lines as past ones, and that each party in the future would command the same support, no more and no less, than it had previously done. On my saying this to Sir John, he said: 'Quite true, but constituencies are governed a good deal by tradition, and Grits are very conservative in sticking to their party!'[1]

The authenticity of a letter such as this tossed into the political maelstrom is always open to doubt, but Professor Dawson's careful examination of the 1882 gerrymander corroborates both the spirit and the practice embodied in the foregoing quotation. It is clear beyond dispute that the first several redistributions after 1867 were effected on lines totally irrelevant to the real point at issue: the fair representation of the people of Canada in their own House of Commons. Even if allowance is made for the extravagant statements engendered by personal and party bias, the first three adjustments of representation in Canada were marvellously unsatisfactory. Nor were the discontented to be found only in the Liberal party; on the contrary, as a Conservative member stated in 1892 with reference to the great gerrymander of ten years before, "where we expected a very large vote we got a very small one because the men who had been brought in . . . were angry and refused to vote for the Conservative party."[2]

As long as constituencies were regularly adjusted by one party, the growth of genuine principles governing the determination of boundaries was not encouraged. True, since seats were allotted to the provinces on the basis of population, a fundamental aim in drawing boundary lines might seem to be the equalization of constituency populations. But from the beginning the application of this principle was undermined by the strength of local feeling for the preservation of existing county and town lines. This sentiment, however

[1]Toronto *Globe*, July 10, 1899. Reprinted in full in *Senate Debates*, 1900, pp. 331-2.
[2]*Debates*, 1892, p. 3280. A leading Conservative member bolted the party on the Representation Act in 1892. See *ibid.*, pp. 3399 ff.

laudable, all too often clashed with representation by population. The mutual exclusiveness of these two ideas played into the hands of anyone interested in manipulating the boundaries and populations of constituencies for party advantage. Sir John Macdonald made this apparent when introducing the Representation Act of 1872. "While the principle of population was considered to a very great extent," he said, "other considerations were also held to have weight; so that different interests, classes and localities should be represented, that the principle of numbers should not be the only one."[1]

A more convenient pair of rules than this could hardly be found. Thus one could plead the necessity of equalizing the populations of constituencies to justify the complete destruction of local boundaries and the ignoring of local interests, as the Conservatives did in 1882. Contrarily, one could ignore population and adhere to an existing county or town line, however small or large a riding it might produce, as the Liberals proposed to do in 1899. As a result, constituencies in Canada have always varied enormously in size, shape, and population, and always for reasons satisfactory to a majority of the House of Commons. The startling disparity in constituencies is shown in Table I, which classifies constituencies according to population for each readjustment since 1867; obviously, the quota obtained by dividing Quebec's population by 65 has never been more than the very crudest of guides in the determination of electoral districts. This single fact undoubtedly accounts for some of the extraordinary anomalies found in Canadian elections between the proportion of votes secured by any party and its share of seats in the Commons.

Two other principles that have been used as justification for various policies of redistribution emerged before the turn of the century, and are still extant. The first of them was enunciated by Sir John Thompson in discussing the 1892 bill: "We have been guided," he declared, "by the principle almost exclusively . . . that we should only interfere with the representation in those districts where additional representation for increased population had to be provided."[2] This

[1]*Debates*, 1872, p. 926.
[2]*Ibid.*, 1892, p. 3255.

THE POPULATION OF ELECTORAL DISTRICTS IN CANADA, CLASSIFIED ACCORDING TO SIZE, AFTER EACH REDISTRIBUTION, TOGETHER WITH THE QUOTA USED ON EACH OCCASION

	1867	1872	1882	1892	1903	1914	1924	1933	1946
Quota obtained by dividing 65 into P.Q. population		18,331	20,908	22,901	25,368	30,819	36,283	44,186	45,627
Population									
3,000- 5,999	4	2	1	2	1	1	—	—	—
6,000- 8,999	8	6	4	6	5	—	—	—	—
9,000-11,999	17	17	11	16	15	1	1	1	1
12,000-14,999	34	24	22	25	13	13	—	—	—
15,000-17,999	34	33	33	47	37	15	3	1	1
18,000-20,999	48	**46**	**38**	**36**	37	27	13	—	—
21,000-23,999	18	28	37	**35**	32	27	18	3	2
24,000-26,999	6	13	31	9	**26**	27	19	8	5
27,000-29,999	4	4	6	6	12	22	23	17	11
30,000-32,999	—	5	5	7	5	**20**	25	17	15
33,000-35,999	—	1	4	5	5	19	36	25	8
36,000-38,999	1	3	3	2	5	15	**30**	17	19
39,000-41,999	1	—	1	5	8	6	19	19	19
42,000-44,999	—	—	—	1	1	6	9	**29**	28
45,000-47,999	2	1	—	—	1	6	6	25	**27**
48,000-50,999	—	—	2	—	1	5	6	14	23
51,000-53,999	—	1	—	—	1	2	10	9	20
54,000-56,999	—	—	—	—	—	3	5	11	16
57,000-59,999	—	—	—	—	—	2	4	8	11
60,000-62,999	—	—	—	—	—	2	4	11	14
63,000-65,999	—	—	—	—	1	—	3	4	6
66,000-68,999	—	—	2	—	—	—	4	7	7
69,000-71,999	—	—	—	—	—	1	3	5	8
72,000-74,999	—	—	—	1	—	1	3	1	5
75,000-77,999	—	—	—	1	1	—	1	1	3
78,000-80,999	—	—	—	—	—	—	—	3	3
81,000-83,999	—	—	—	—	1	—	—	2	1
over 84,000	—	—	—	—	—	—	2	3	3

NOTE: Shown underlined are the groups which include the quota obtained by dividing 65 into Quebec's population. For 1946, the quota was obtained by dividing the total population of Canada, less Prince Edward Island, by 250. For earlier years, the quota was obtained by dividing the total population of Canada, less Prince Edward Island, by 250. The wide variations in the size of constituencies are to a small degree accounted for by the fact that a few double constituencies still existed for part of the period. There were never more than ten of these, and they were not always the largest constituencies.

very conservative statement unfortunately settled nothing, for it left the readjusting agency to decide where additional representation should be given, and where constituencies should be left untouched for the protection of local interests. As a matter of record, the granting of six additional seats to Ontario in 1872 involved the changing of nineteen constituencies; four additional seats for the same province in 1882 involved the changing of fifty-three constituencies; and no additional seats in 1892 nevertheless involved the changing of nineteen constituencies in Ontario, and twenty-two in Quebec. It is true that alterations in constituencies were necessary in many of these instances; but the principle as it operated still did not prevent sweeping changes after each decennial census, nor did it provide for the choice of constituencies for readjustment on any other basis than that of expediency. Furthermore, even when a riding was left alone on the grounds that there were insufficient population changes to justify an alteration, there was still the suspicion that the failure to do anything meant only that it was convenient to both government and opposition parties to do nothing. A glance at Table I suggests that the "do nothing" rule of readjustment has perhaps contributed as much to the misrepresentation of the Canadian people as to their representation.

The application of the foregoing "principle" partially accounts for the continued existence of so many small constituencies. Very large constituencies, on the other hand, have resulted from the urbanization of population in Canada, coupled with the adoption of a theory that urban divisions should properly have much larger populations than rural. This particular idea, which is now acknowledged by all parties, was early admitted to operate in Canadian politics, but developed into a maxim in Canada by accident, for the process of urbanization automatically produced large city and town constituencies before any theory justifying the fact was accepted in the House of Commons.

This can be illustrated by events in Ontario. The original distribution of 1867 in that province slightly favoured the towns, for the nine town seats then existing comprised 10.9

per cent of the province's quota of seats, but only 8.9 per cent of the population. The seventeen new seats distributed throughout Ontario in 1867 went entirely to the counties, so that the pre-Confederation arrangement of constituencies in the province must have been strongly prejudiced in favour of the towns; this situation was largely corrected at Confederation.[1] The balance between rural and urban areas was preserved in 1872, when the six additional seats earned by the province were divided in half, with three going to Toronto, Hamilton, and Ottawa, and three going to the counties.[2] The purpose then, according to Sir John Macdonald, was to maintain the proper ratio between agricultural and manufacturing interests. At that time the Liberal opposition introduced an argument which has clung to redistribution debates ever since, and is still regarded as a reason for making urban divisions much larger than rural: many rural members, they claimed with statistical support, lived in large towns, so that urban constituencies could be made conveniently larger without danger to the interests of urban residents.[3] The opposition urged, in addition, that since Ontario's six new members had accrued to the province from a growth of population, it was only proper that the new seats should be allocated to the areas in which the greatest population increases had occurred; on this basis, a majority of the new seats would have gone to counties, and different counties from the ones selected by the government for extra representation. A motion embodying this singularly reasonable proposition was lost on division.[4]

During the next twenty years, urban population growth began in most instances to outdistance the growth in rural constituencies; this, with the 1882 gerrymander which was occupied entirely with rural alterations, created by 1891

[1]In Quebec, the reverse was true. There the continued use of the 65 existing ridings produced a strong rural bias, for the two seats for Montreal were by a considerable margin the largest in the province.

[2]*Debates*, 1872, p. 927. This policy was reversed for Nova Scotia, whose two additional members were both given to counties, although Halifax's claim to an extra member was as strong as Hamilton's or Ottawa's.

[3]*Ibid.*, p. 932.

[4]*Ibid.*, pp. 1059-65. The same argument was urged in 1882, but again without success. See *ibid.*, 1882, p. 1361.

very large city and town divisions independently of any
principle or theory of representation. Between 1871 and
1891, to cite a few examples, Toronto East grew from 15,090
to 43,565; Toronto West from 20,355 to 73,826; Montreal
East from 46,291 to 92,063; and Montreal West from 37,031
to 62,510.[1] In none of these divisions had there been
boundary alterations between the redistribution of 1872 and
the census of 1891.

The rural-urban aspect of representation thus did not
become a problem on a national scale until 1892, by which
time members on both sides of the House were so accustomed
to large urban divisions that their existence seems to have
been accepted without question. In that year, the Government proposed to raise Montreal's representation from three
to five members, a change which would still have left the
metropolitan ridings far above the average in size. Wilfrid
Laurier, the Liberal leader, objected to even that degree of
adjustment: "I am not prepared to admit for my part,"
he said, "that Montreal is at all entitled to increased representation. It is admitted generally, it is admitted specifically
in this bill, that there is to be a difference between the
representation of urban populations . . . and rural populations. That object is obvious. Urban populations are
represented generally to a greater degree than are rural
populations, because urban populations generally furnish to
rural populations many of their members . . . [Montreal] is
represented in this House by no less than thirteen of its
citizens."[2] Sir John Thompson, the Conservative leader,
was equally emphatic in denying to cities their proportional
share of representation, not only accepting Laurier's argument *in toto*, but adding "the further reason that the public,
in great centres . . . is more alive to political questions, and
political feeling there is more vigorous and more likely to
receive prompt expression than in rural districts."[3] Another
member gave yet a third reason for large urban divisions:
"In a large city, where the population is concentrated, it is

[1]*Census of Canada*, 1891, vol. I, pp. 368-9.
[2]*Debates*, 1892, p. 3119.
[3]*Ibid.*, p. 3255.

a very easy matter, during an election, for a candidate to meet his constituents, within a couple of hours notice . . . whilst in the rural districts candidates are obliged to travel long distances in order to visit the different localities. . . . In a city like Montreal, the people, being concentrated, have more means to receive education and information, they have easier access to the newspapers and all the other sources of information."[1]

A total of four separate theories, frequently masquerading as principles, have thus appeared in the history of representation in Canada. They are resurrected in one form or another in every decade, and their more recent appearances are referred to in the next chapter. For the immediate purpose, it is sufficient to observe that they developed early in Canadian politics, and that since the beginning they have been used indiscriminately as genuine guiding principles and as excuses to justify perversions of representation.

[1]*Ibid.*, p. 3175.

CHAPTER III

REDISTRIBUTION, 1892-1948

THE Redistribution debate of 1892 marked a turning point in the settlement of constituencies. Although the particular alteration effected then was by a government bill, dissatisfaction with the system, even on the part of one or two Conservatives, was so apparent that a change of government was almost certain to result in a new method of making adjustments. The Liberals, indeed, proposed in 1892 that the Conservative Government appoint a bi-partisan committee to lay down fixed rules for the alteration of boundaries, although the committee was not expected to draw up an actual schedule of electoral districts.[1] The suggestion that redistribution should be left to a commission of judges was also revived. This proposal, however, was sternly denounced by Liberal leaders;[2] a step of some historical interest because just seven years later a Government led by them introduced a bill embodying that very provision.

The ingenuity of the Liberal opposition in 1892 was not exhausted by their stand in favour of readjustment with the aid of a committee and their opposition to the use of judges. Wilfrid Laurier, for example, proposed in all seriousness that redistribution should be so executed as to leave undisturbed "the equilibrium existing now between parties."[3] By this he meant that Liberal constituencies should be so arranged that they remained Liberal, and the same guarantee was to be given to the Conservatives. This proposition is unique in Canadian annals, for neither before nor since has a leader in opposition advocated a principle whose adoption might well have kept his party there in perpetuity. Another suggestion, ludicrous in view of the precedents already established, questioned Parliament's power to readjust

[1] *Debates*, 1892, p. 3129.
[2] E.g. *ibid*., pp. 3126 and 3240.
[3] *Ibid*., p. 3120.

constituencies at all.[1] Be it recorded to the glory of the
Conservatives that they scouted both these absurdities.

A party so full of notions on representation as the Liberal
could be expected to make some interesting changes when it
came into power. At its first national convention in 1893
the Liberal party had gone on record in favour of a return
to county boundaries as the basis of membership in the
House of Commons, and in 1899 the new Government led
by Sir Wilfrid Laurier endeavoured to implement this convention plank. The bill which resulted was remarkable in
establishing three precedents: it was the first attempt to
readjust constituencies apart from the decennial census;[2] it
made the first serious proposal to use an outside agency to
assist in drawing boundaries; and it embodied for the first
time a principle which was applied consistently to the problem of representation. Primarily, the Liberals strove to
repair the damage done to them by the three preceding
gerrymanders in Ontario by returning to constituencies based
on local boundaries. To this end they proposed to restore
twenty counties and alter twenty-three others; and where any
county had to be divided, the operation was to be performed
by a board consisting of Ontario Superior Court Judges.[3]

The theoretical justification for these plans was stated by
one of the more ardent reformers, George Casey: "It had
always been our principle . . . that exact equality of population was not so much a desideratum as the keeping together
for political purposes of those who are naturally associated
for municipal and other purposes—in other words, to limit
constituencies within county boundaries."[4] Since the Liberals

[1]*Ibid.*, pp. 3240 ff. The Liberal argument here was based on section 51
of the B.N.A. Act, which declares that readjustment is to be effected "by such
authority" as Parliament sees fit, but does not specifically empower Parliament
to do it itself.

[2]I.e., the first *general* readjustment apart from a census. A readjustment
affecting one constituency was attempted by the Liberals in 1874, but rejected
by the Senate. Very minor adjustments characteristically follow a year or two
after each decennial representation act, to correct clerical errors, etc. An
adjustment of some significance was attempted in 1930, when it was discovered
that a part of western Ontario had been excluded entirely in drawing constituency
boundaries in 1924, but the Liberal Government withdrew the bill in the face
of opposition.

[3]*Debates*, 1899, pp. 3442 ff.

[4]*Ibid.*, p. 3471. See also Laurier to E. T. Reed, March 25, 1903: "I can
tell you . . . at once that our purpose is absolute to adhere to county frontiers."
(Laurier Papers, vol. 357, no. 2201).

had been out of power when all previous adjustments had been executed, this was as fair a statement as any of the principles they had hitherto advocated, for their lack of responsibility in the past had left them even more free than the Conservatives to advocate whatever rules seemed convenient. To do the Liberals justice, it should be added that for many years after 1867 they had indeed been strong proponents of the rights of local organizations and governments in electoral matters, not merely in regard to constituency boundaries, but also such allied items as the franchise, electoral officers, and voters' lists.[1]

The Conservative opposition was not impressed by the Liberals' concern for local integrity or by their protestations of principle. While Sir Wilfrid Laurier (according to Sir Charles Tupper) sat gloating fiendishly, the Conservatives denounced the scheme as unconstitutional, because it contemplated a redistribution apart from a census; as a gerrymander, because the use of counties as constituencies would probably favour the Liberals;[2] and as a poor thing generally, because they were opposed to it. The Conservatives felt so keenly about the plan, indeed, that they refused either to interfere with the bill in any way or to move amendments, a device which enabled them without committing themselves unduly to fall back on their secondary line of defence in the upper house. The Senate rejected the bill as "inexpedient" and "a violation of the spirit" of the B.N.A. Act,[3] and when the same bill again passed the Commons in 1900, the Senate gave it a six months' hoist.[4]

The reforms of the Liberals were thus compelled to await the usual opportunity furnished by the decennial census.

[1]See Part III.

[2]There was undoubtedly some truth in this, as is shown in the following letter from David Mills to Laurier, May 27, 1899: "Mr. Mulock, in this matter, is considering the interests of some friend whom he desires to run for North Victoria. . . . I am afraid, if our Bill does not become law, we will be put in a very compromising condition before the country in allowing Victoria and Peterboro to remain as they are." (Laurier Papers, vol. 357, no. 2201).

[3]*Senate Debates*, 1899, pp. 824 ff. Conservative lawyers in the Senate were careful not to challenge the legality of the Liberal bill, and their amendment, according to Sir Mackenzie Bowell, was carefully drafted so as not to bring up the question (p. 1050).

[4]*Ibid.*, 1900, pp. 240 and 377. In this year the Conservatives in the Commons endorsed the principle of redistribution by judges (*Debates*, 1900, p. 1586).

Their Representation Act of 1903 was unique on two major counts: it involved the first serious dispute over reductions in the quotas of seats for several provinces; and it introduced, contrary to the Liberal proposals of 1892 and 1899, the readjustment of constituency boundaries by a House of Commons committee on which the government naturally had a majority.

It will be recalled that section 51 of the B.N.A. Act provided that each province was to have as many seats as its population warranted on the basis of Quebec's fixed quota of 65. Until the redistribution of 1892, this provision had caused no trouble, for the majority of the original provinces had gained at least a seat or two in the readjustments of 1872 and 1882, while the new provinces of the West had a guaranteed minimum number of representatives well above the requirements of their populations. In 1892 the three Maritime provinces lost four members among them, a reduction that was effected almost entirely without fretting. But when it appeared that the 1903 redistribution was going to cause a further loss to the Maritimes, the provincial governments concerned began to importune the Liberal cabinet for special consideration.

The three provinces had two separate arguments to put forth, although both of these turned on interpretations of arrangements made when the provinces entered the federation. Nova Scotia and New Brunswick challenged the constitutionality of reducing their quotas of seats by a scheme adopted in the B.N.A. Act of 1867, when since that time both the boundaries and the population of the country had altered in a manner possibly not contemplated when the statute was drafted. Specifically, it was argued that for purposes of determining the provincial quotas of seats, the term "Canada" could refer only to the four original provinces, and thus excluded both the western territories and a new section added to Quebec in 1898. The acceptance of this argument, which received some weight from the fact that the relevant section of the B.N.A. Act particularly referred to "the representation of the four provinces," would have saved the two Maritime provinces several seats in Parliament, for the rapid development of the Canadian West had completely stultified the original protection afforded them by the famous "one-twentieth clause." Though the Maritimes had been growing, the rest of the country had been growing so much faster that the populations of the Maritime provinces were becoming relatively smaller in proportion to the national total with an inevitable loss of membership in the House of Commons.

The strict interpretation of the B.N.A. Act sought by Nova Scotia and New Brunswick would not have helped Prince Edward Island, and the Island rested its case on a claim to a minimum of six members as part of a bargain made when the province entered Confederation.[1] The Island was prepared to admit that it could be deprived of any *additional* seats which it had earned by population growth after 1873; but the original quota of six was demanded as an irreducible minimum.

The Liberal Government, while regretting the loss of membership by any province, was opposed to "torturing the letter of the law" in order to reverse its clearly expressed meaning.[2] It was with some reluctance that two cases, covering Prince Edward Island's claim and disputing the meaning of the word Canada, were referred to the Supreme Court. The Court upheld the federal government in both instances, maintaining that representation in the House of Commons must be based on the total population of Canada, and that no exception could be made for Prince Edward Island.[3] What might have become a knotty legal tangle— the specific mention of "four provinces" in section 51 of the B.N.A. Act—was avoided by the ingenious device of taking

[1] A Prince Edward Island member made this claim in the House of Commons in 1900, only to have it summarily rejected by the Liberals. (*Debates*, 1900, pp. 1565 ff.)

[2] *Ibid.*, 1903, pp. 709-10. The quoted phrase is Laurier's.

[3] *In re Representation of Prince Edward Island in the House of Commons: In re Representation in the House of Commons of certain provinces;* [1903] S.C.R., 475, 594. A curious mixture of personalities occurred during these negotiations over Maritime representation. Sir Louis Davies, an Island member of Parliament who scouted the Island's claim in the Commons in 1900, was by 1903 on the Supreme Court Bench, and duly recorded his judgment against the Island. The Island's leading counsel in the 1903 court case was A. B. Aylesworth, who by 1906 was a Liberal cabinet member, and as such played a leading role in refuting the Island's continued claims for better representation.

"four provinces" to mean as much of Canada as existed, in this case seven provinces and the territories. The Judicial Committee, on appeal by Prince Edward Island and New Brunswick, upheld the Supreme Court *in toto*.[1]

The question of Maritime representation was thus thrown back into the House of Commons, where it has been a constant irritant almost ever since. It was discussed several times shortly after the foregoing judicial decisions were handed down (the Government remained adamant on each occasion,[2]) and was brought up at the Interprovincial Conference of 1913. This latter meeting, after two motions for the protection of Maritime interests had been introduced and withdrawn, declined to take any action.[3] During the redistribution debate of the following year, by which time the operation of the law had reduced Prince Edward Island's membership to three, a motion to secure six seats for the Island was again rejected.[4] In that year, however, a constitutional amendment was proposed whereby every province would be guaranteed a minimum of members equal to the number of its Senators, and this was adopted in 1915.[5] But the Maritime Provinces remained dissatisfied, and provincial Attorneys-General lobbied before the Representation Committee of 1923, although without result.[6] In 1926-7, the Prime Minister was once more importuned for an extra member for Nova Scotia,[7] and that province's submission to the Royal Commission on Maritime Claims in the same year brought the matter up again.[8] Ever since then the Maritime pleas have fallen on increasingly deaf ears, and

[1]*Attorney-General for Prince Edward Island* v. *Attorney-General for Canada, Attorney-General for New Brunswick* v. *Attorney-General for Canada,* [1905] A.C. 37. (App. Cas., 1905, p. 37).

[2]E.g. *Debates,* 1906-7, pp. 2147 ff.; *ibid.,* 1909-10, pp. 644 ff.

[3]*Sessional Papers,* 1914, no. 118, no. 118a, no. 119.

[4]*Debates,* 1914, p. 5299.

[5]*British North America Act,* 1915.   (*Brit. Statutes,* 5-6 Geo. V, c. 45).   See Appendix A.   This amendment was altered in 1914 by the Senate in a manner not acceptable to the Commons, and thus delayed a year.

[6]*Debates,* 1923, p. 4737.

[7]*Ibid.,* 1926-7, p. 1824.

[8]*Nova Scotia: a submission of its claims with respect to Maritime Disabilities within Confederation,* Halifax, 1926, pp. 169-74.   The province claimed that it was deprived of an extra member in 1924 by a technicality, and also reviewed the general case for better Maritime representation.

even the latest provisions for representation (discussed below) gave no additional protection.

The most important feature of the 1903 redistribution was not the battle for Maritime rights, but the introduction of the principle of readjustment by a House of Commons Committee representing the major parties. This device, while it did not make the gerrymander impossible, made unfair manipulation of constituencies more unlikely, for the Opposition, through its membership on the committee, was better able to attack adverse proposals and to influence decisions. Sir Wilfrid Laurier stated its purpose thus:

> If this Bill is accepted by our friends on the opposite side, we intend, after it has been debated and read the second time, to refer it to a special committee composed of seven members, on which the opposition will be represented by three, to be selected by themselves. The object of the committee will be to create the constituencies which will be allowed to elect the members of this House. In other words, we do not present to the House today a scheme cut and dried which has to be swallowed holus bolus by our friends and by the opposition, whether they like it or not; no, we propose to invite our friends now sitting on the opposition benches to meet us in the committee room. . . . We believe that if our friends opposite will meet us in this way, we can prepare a measure which will at all events be fair to all parties.[1]

The last part of this declaration is significant, for it suggests the major weakness of the scheme. The assumption that what is fair to all parties will necessarily produce a system of representation which is fair to the whole Canadian electorate, is not valid.

The Conservatives accepted the principle of readjustment by a House committee without serious question; although, as their leader pointed out, they were well aware that the Government's majority on the committee could mean that the apparent fairness of the proposal "might not in the end be so real as suggested."[2] The bill then went to a committee to which the Liberal Government appointed four

[1]*Debates*, 1903, pp. 713-14. The bill, establishing a procedure followed ever since, embodied merely the changes in provincial quotas made under the terms of the B.N.A. Act; constituency boundaries were undefined, this work being left to the committee which was to fill in a blank schedule attached to the bill.

[2]*Ibid.*, p. 715; also p. 1294, where Borden claimed that the partie should have equal representation on the committee.

members, and the Conservatives three. Neither side took
unnecessary chances in regard to the committee's personnel,
for the four Liberals included two Cabinet Ministers and a
party whip, while the three Conservatives included the party
leader, a former Cabinet Minister, and a prominent provincial
leader. The committee also was geographically significant
for its members represented, respectively, Ontario (3), Quebec
(2), the Maritimes (1), and the West (1). The committees
in subsequent years have not departed radically from this
practice; the parties have shown the same disposition to
choose their heavy artillery for membership, and the
geographical nature of the committee's work has always
been considered. With the increasing number of political
parties, the newer ones being largely regional groups, a
continual enlargement of the committee's personnel has been
necessary.

There is ample evidence that the first Redistribution
Committee took its work seriously, for it sat for well over a
month, and took voluminous evidence. Every member of
the House without exception appeared before it, both to
give information and, no doubt, to keep an eye on proposed
alterations in his own constituency. So far as the two parties'
interests were concerned, the Committee accomplished a great
deal, for it was able to agree on the boundary lines of 165
divisions. But a struggle developed over thirty Ontario
seats which became so bitter that it produced as violent a
discussion as had ever been heard over any of the gerrymander bills. There was indeed ample reason for disagreement, for the whole problem of readjustment had been
dumped on the Committee almost without a word of instruc-
tion concerning the principles to be followed, so that the
wrangling in the Committee was of precisely the same sort
that had disfigured all previous debates. The Conservatives
argued, apparently accurately, that the Government members
of the Committee had come to the meetings with a completed
schedule, just as in 1882 and 1892, and this fact, combined
with the fixed majority on the Committee and the absence
of guiding principles, was so fruitful a source of dispute
that Borden nearly resigned. He declared:

I do not know of one important provision, so far as the province of Ontario is concerned, emanating from the minority which was accepted by the major- ity. . . . It was not a conference, but simply a partisan committee, upon which were four Liberals and three Conservatives. . . . There were certain matters about which there could not possibly be any disagreement, but, when we came to places where there could be a little carving, we soon found out what was the disposition of our hon. friends on the other side.[1]

In view of the Liberals' protestations of fairness in the readjustment, the Conservatives had a genuine grievance. The Committee had not only received no instructions, but the Liberal majority refused to adopt any rules to govern the adjustments, and the boundaries were thus rearranged on purely expedient grounds. A series of principles proposed by Borden, which would have made alterations largely auto- matic depending on the populations contained within existing municipal and county lines, was rejected by the majority of the Committee for the curious reason that it would "tie their hands."[2]

The committee system, while superior to previous methods of effecting redistributions, was thus not satisfactory in itself, nor did it supply the answer to all the problems posed by each decennial census. The first use of the technique in 1903 was by no means exceptional, for apart from that of 1914, subsequent readjustments have been marked by the same acrimony, and for substantially the same reasons. By a coincidence, the two major parties have been in power alternately at redistribution time since 1903, so that while each has been critical in opposition, each has thought suffi- ciently well of the committee system to try it a decade later. On occasion, party leaders have even spoken kindly of the last redistribution conducted under the auspices of their rivals and have advanced it as a justification for using the same system again.[3] In 1914, when a committee of nine

[1]*Debates*, 1903, pp. 11440 ff. For evidence of the seriousness with which the Liberals took the 1903 redistribution, see the detailed memoranda in the Laurier Papers, vol. 357, no. 2201. Laurier wrote to a New Brunswick supporter on August 29, 1903, to reassure him about changes in New Brunswick: "The present Bill, with regard to New Brunswick, has been drafted by Mr. Blair, who gave it his careful attention."

[2]Borden's proposals are given in *Debates*, 1903, pp. 10840-1. The Liberals' explanation of their refusal to adopt them is given at p. 10842.

[3]Thus Borden in 1914, forgetful of the fracas of 1903, thought the 1903 system "did its work fairly well." (*Ibid.*, 1914, p. 617.)

members was employed, a harmonious redistribution was effected—which, it must be remembered, merely means that the parties agreed, and is without relation to the public interest.   In 1923, when the presence of a large Progressive group in the House necessitated a committee of nineteen, the Redistribution Committee dawdled throughout a session without reaching agreement, and its work was carried over into 1924.[1] At this readjustment, the work was broken down into provincial subcommittees for the first time, a device which has been used on each occasion since.

The 1924 debates were more disputatious than those of 1914, but they were a pale shadow compared with those of 1932-3, when redistribution took place under conditions which reached a record low. Twenty members began work as a committee in November of 1932, and although they could hardly be accused of undue haste in approaching their problem,[2] the various party organizations seem to have undertaken considerable work on their behalf. The Prime Minister announced to the House on one occasion that the parties were at work on their schemes, and added, "Yes, schemes is the word I used, and the correct word too."[3] He was not exaggerating, for after weeks of work which included some dramatic episodes such as "maps torn up, threats and invitations to mortal combat,"[4] the Committee (which had rarely met) collected the work of its subcommittees and reported to the House a schedule over which there was still substantial disagreement. The problem was then taken over by an informal committee of "older heads of this house,"[5] the proceedings of which were terminated abruptly by a decision of the Government;[6] final bargains, therefore, were struck on the floor of the Commons. "If," said Mr. Mackenzie King in a statement which reveals much about the conditions governing the 1932-3 readjustment, "the government is prepared to reconsider and to meet us in the few particulars I

[1]*Debates*, 1923, pp. 4510 ff. and 4736 ff.; 1924, pp. 4347 ff.
[2]On March 23, 1933, work on Quebec had not yet been begun. (*Ibid.*, 1932-3, p. 3303.)
[3]*Ibid.*, p. 3354.
[4]*Ibid.*, p. 5240.
[5]*Ibid.*, p. 5146.
[6]*Ibid.*, pp. 5235 ff.

have mentioned, there would be no desire on our part further to discuss the situation in Saskatchewan."[1]   R. B. Bennett, for his side, frankly explained the partisan nature of the redistribution and made it clear that it was only right, proper, and democratic that the government majority should in the final analysis have its own way.[2]   The latest redistribution, executed in 1947 by a committee of twenty-five members, was also marked by some exasperation, although on the whole it was a fairly agreeable arrangement, unmarred by the extraordinary exhibitions seen in 1932-3.[3]

At the risk of repetition, it must be emphasized that harmony in the House Committee guarantees nothing; as Mr. Mackenzie King has observed, in one of the shrewdest remarks of his long career, "anyone reading the Hansard report . . . must realize to how small an extent the redistribution being effected at the moment is based upon the foundational [sic] principle of the division of the various constituencies according to the general interest of the country as a whole."[4]   Although this statement was being applied specifically to the fiasco of 1933, it could be made with equal force concerning even the most peaceful of the eight redistributions which have occurred thus far.

It does not necessarily follow that redistribution by a House Committee is always bad; but it is indisputable that redistribution has so far taken place with reference to none but the vaguest of principles.   At one time or another in this contentious history, as we have seen, no less than four principles have been followed: the use of local boundary lines; the adoption of relatively large urban divisions; the establishment of compact divisions; and the equalization of population.   But one or more of these principles has always been applied in relation to the wishes of a majority of the House of Commons, and when it has been expedient not to

[1]*Ibid.*, p. 5437.
[2]*Ibid.*, pp. 5341 ff.
[3]*Ibid.*, 1947, pp. 5568 ff.; pp. 5641, ff. Mr. Diefenbaker, one of the members whose constituency was most adversely affected by the readjustment, agreed to the dismemberment of his own riding, but only because there was "a gun at my head." (*Ibid.*, p. 5600.)
[4]*Ibid.*, 1932-3, p. 5468. See also p. 5293, where a member of the committee admitted that "personal considerations for members of this House, as well as political considerations, have taken up altogether too much time."

observe a principle, it has been conveniently forgotten. A glance at Table I will show how closely the fourth principle has been followed. A perusal of Professor Dawson's analysis of the gerrymander of 1882 reveals how the fourth has been used as an excuse to ignore the first and third; while a study of the electoral map for any year will show how the first principle has operated to the detriment of the fourth.

Of all these rules, indeed, the only one that has been followed with any consistency is that which upholds large urban divisions as compared with rural, and even here there has been no agreement about how much larger than rural ridings urban divisions should be. In 1947, for example, the city of Toronto had one constituency of 44,000; six constituencies in the 50,000's; two in the 60,000's; one in the 70,000's; and one with over 86,000. The metropolitan area of Montreal, in the same year, had five constituencies in the 40,000's; eight in the 50,000's; six in the 60,000's; and one of 70,000. At the same time, there existed in Ontario the rural riding of Glengarry, with 18,732,[1] and the semi-rural riding of Welland, with 93,836. In Quebec, the constituency of Iles-de-la-Madeleine had 8,940, while Joliette-l'Assomption-Montcalm had 63,462. Even if the justice of large urban ridings is admitted, that will not explain why some of these are nearly twice the size of others; why some rural ridings show an even greater discrepancy; nor why some rural ridings are actually larger than many urban ones That there is nevertheless a sound case for large urban divisions is undoubted, for in addition to the arguments cited above on this score, it is plain that giving the cities anything like proportionate representation would bring into existence many geographic-

[1]The small size of Glengarry, until 1949 held by W. L. Mackenzie King, recalls an extraordinary theory advanced by Mr. King in 1933, that party leaders should have safe seats (*Debates*, 1932-3, p. 5278). This proposition was supported by a leading Conservative member in 1947 (*ibid.*, 1947, p. 701). No doubt it is difficult for a Prime Minister to give much time to his party, but since one of the soundest arguments against proportional representation is that it *does* guarantee safe seats to party leaders, and thus helps convince them of their indispensability while tightening their hold on the party, Mr. King's suggestion ranks as one of the most absurd notions put forth in all the redistribution debates. Fortunately, in neither 1933 nor 1947 did many members seem impressed by its forcefulness.

ally enormous rural ridings which only a superman could cover during an election campaign.[1]

The truth is that the incessant wrangling which occurs at almost every allocation of seats is not the result of any genuine clash of consistent but opposing principles, but rather an opportunistic grasping at special advantages. So lamentable and petty a display suggests that some definite action should be taken either to place redistribution on a more objective basis, or to transfer the responsibility to another body, or, conceivably, to do both.

The first solution might involve the adoption of a set of rules which would make the rearrangement of constituency boundaries by a House Committee as automatic as the apportionment of seats among the provinces under the British North America Act. Borden suggested such a plan in 1903 in regard to Ontario, which was the major source of trouble in that redistribution. Although Borden's proposals have never been applied, so that their practicality cannot be assessed, it is worth reproducing some of them here to indicate one possible method of simplifying the decennial tangle over constituencies:

> The separate representation to be allotted to cities . . . shall be first fixed and determined before proceeding with the representation of the rural constituencies.
>
> The unit of representation for such rural constituencies shall be determined by deducting from the total population [of the province] the combined population of the said cities and by dividing the remainder by the total number of seats to be allotted to rural constituencies.

[1]The absence of any rigid formula in determining the relative size of urban constituencies naturally is a disadvantage to parties which draw a large proportion of their strength from metropolitan areas. Mr. Meighen, for example, raised the point in 1924 (*Debates*, 1924, p. 4533), arguing that the Conservatives were penalized by the hiving of voters in cities. An analysis of the 1930 and 1935 elections, which the Conservatives won and lost respectively, reveals that this point is valid to a degree. While it is true in Ontario, the contrary is true in Quebec, so that if the two major provinces are taken together, neither party has an absolute advantage or disadvantage in the large urban divisions. Thus in 1930, ten of the sixty Liberal victories in Ontario and Quebec were in divisions of over 50,000; and thirteen of the eighty Conservative victories were in constituencies of the same size. In 1935, twenty-eight of 112 Liberal constituencies were over 50,000, as compared with eighteen of thirty-one Conservative constituencies. It appears therefore that the Liberals carried their share of large constituencies, but had an advantage over the Conservatives in the smaller ones. A genuinely urban party like the Labour Progressives, on the other hand, would have a much stronger case against large urban ridings.

Counties having a population below the unit:
(a) Each county having a population of not less than two-thirds of the unit shall be entitled to one member.
(b) Any county not entitled to one member shall be added to that adjoining. . . .
Counties having a population larger than the unit:
(a) Each county or combined county having a population of not less than 50 per cent and not more than 150 per cent above the unit shall be entitled to two members, and each . . . having a population not less than 150 per cent and not more than 250 per cent shall be entitled to three members.[1]

These suggestions still leave considerable discretion to the Commons, for they do not determine any ratio between rural and urban divisions, nor do they provide any rules for the actual division of a county entitled to more than one member.

The ratio between rural and urban constituencies, it may be noted, has been settled, though not without difficulty, in other Dominions.[2] In New Zealand (until an urban-minded Labour Government repealed the law in 1945) a fixed quota of 28 percent was added to the rural population, so that urban constituencies were to that extent larger than rural, but no major discrepancies could occur as in Canada. In the Australian state of Victoria, a ratio of 22-15-10 has been adopted to govern the size of divisions which are very populous urban areas, fairly populous rural ridings, and lightly populated rural ridings respectively.[3] Exactly what the ratio should be for Canada would of course require careful study, and would perhaps have to be varied somewhat among the several regions. But it would be absurd to conclude that no formulae can be found which would not at least eliminate some of the major anomalies in Canadian representation, and prevent much of the unnecessary irritation that follows the decennial census.

[1]*Debates*, 1903, p. 11441. Borden's plan could be applied only east of Manitoba, for the western provinces do not use the county system.
[2]Some of the provinces of Canada have also fixed an urban-rural ratio for the assemblies, but this has been done as a matter of policy at particular readjustments, rather than as a fixed statutory requirement. Thus Manitoba in 1920 adopted a 2-1 ratio, but by 1948 this had grown askew. See "Unfair Representation," in the *Winnipeg Free Press*, May 7, 1948.
[3]A convenient comparison of redistribution techniques in other countries is given in *Reports of Special Committee on Elections and Franchise Acts*, 1936 and 1937. For New Zealand, see *New Zealand Parliamentary Debates*, 1945, *passim*.

The other method of adjustment, which would relieve
Parliament entirely of the duty, is the simple one of having
the work done by an independent commission.   In Australia,
three Distributional Commissioners are employed, consisting
of the Chief Electoral Officer or his equivalent, the Surveyor-
General of the state concerned, and a chairman named by
the Governor-General, who must arrange each constituency
within a range of one-fifth above or below the population
quota.   In New Zealand, seven Commissioners are employed;
three include such public servants as the Surveyor-General
and the Commissioner of Crown Lands, and the other four
are nominated by the House of Representatives.   These four
nominated members may not be either public servants or
members of the Assembly.[1]

In Canada, mention has already been made of a redistribution commission in the Representation Bills of 1899
and 1900, both of which were rejected by the Senate.   A
Government bill was drafted in 1940 which included provision for a tribunal of three commissioners, but it was never
introduced.   Under this bill the chairman was to be a judge
of a superior court, with two assistant commissioners for
each province; the commission was to be instructed to consider the physical features of constituencies, the means of
communication, the existing boundaries both of constituencies and of administrative areas, and "such other pertinent
factors as may occur to it or to which its attention may be
drawn."[2]   As recently as 1947, the Prime Minister indicated
his preference for redistribution by an independent commission, but a Co-operative Commonwealth Federation amendment to achieve that end was defeated by a vote which
divided on non-party lines.[3]

Unlike the redistribution commissions of Australia and
New Zealand, the proposals for a similar Canadian tribunal
have been bedevilled from the start by the strange notion

[1]*Statutes of New Zealand*, 1945, c. 10.
[2]*Debates*, 1947, p. 699.   This bill grew partly out of the Special Committees on Elections and Franchise Acts of 1936 and 1937, and partly from a
discussion in the House in 1939, when Mr. Power moved for a committee to
examine (among other things) redistribution; the committee was to prepare a
draft bill to include provision for a redistribution commission. (*Debates*, 1939,
pp. 1807-41.)
[3]*Ibid.*, pp. 690 ff.; pp. 725 ff.

that, of all the citizens of Canada, only judges can be trusted with the ticklish business of constituency boundaries. Apart from the reflection thus cast on the integrity of all Canadians who do not happen to be judges, this proposal seems to be based on the erroneous assumption that the drawing of boundary lines is a judicial problem. It is, on the contrary, an administrative one, albeit one of the first magnitude, and while the arguments for employing an impartial commission in Canada are overwhelming, it is difficult to understand why the commissioners should be judges. Since almost all Canadians live in houses, it would seem quite as logical to argue that readjustment should therefore be effected by building contractors, plumbers, or possibly social workers.

It is true that some degree of judgment will be required in determining exactly where various boundaries should be drawn. On the other hand, the use of judges in such electoral matters as controverted elections and the preparation of voters' lists has in the past dragged the judiciary more than once into political controversy.[1] Considering that, in fairness to the House of Commons, constituencies reorganized by a judicial commission would still almost certainly have to be reviewed by Parliament before they were enacted into legislation, the proposal to have redistribution effected in this way seems to be highly dangerous to the judiciary itself.[2] There is a much stronger case for adding the readjustment of constituency boundaries to the duties of the Chief Electoral Officer, a development which would probably require an expansion of his administrative staff. An even better plan would be to have a Redistribution Commission of impartial officials as in Australia and New Zealand.

The greatest change since 1867 in the distribution of seats in the Commons occurred in 1946; at that time, an amendment to the B.N.A. Act altered the fundamental scheme whereby a fixed number of seats from Quebec formed the

[1]*Infra*, Chapters VIII-X.
[2]See R. MacG. Dawson, *The Government of Canada* (Toronto, 1947), pp. 486 ff., for comments on the use of the judiciary on Royal Commissions, etc. Members of Parliament have rarely objected to the proposal to use judges on a redistribution tribunal; one of the very rare exceptions occurred in 1947, when Mr. Hackett, a distinguished member of the bar, while endorsing the establishment of a commission, strongly opposed the appointment of judges. (*Debates*, 1947, p. 3652.)

pivot on which provincial representation turned. This alteration was necessitated by circumstances which developed
partly from the war and partly from the breakdown of the
old system. Parliament's preoccupation with the war effort,
together with heavy wartime shifts of population which
profoundly disturbed Western members because of the possible
effect on their representation, led to a constitutional amendment in 1943, which postponed redistribution until the first
session of Parliament after the war.[1] The postponement,
although it contemplated no change in the system of redistribution, paved the way for the alterations of 1946 by
affording members more time to emphasize the degree to
which the old system had broken down.

That the old system had broken down is a proposition
hardly open to dispute, for if redistribution had been executed
after the 1941 census, only four provinces out of nine would
have been allotted seats according to their actual populations. This peculiar fact had resulted from the operation
of the original system, as amended, over a period of eighty
years. The following scheme of representation was in force
in 1941:

1. Quebec had a fixed quota of 65 seats, and the other
provinces had as many seats in proportion to their population
as Quebec's 65 seats bore to its population. The population
of Quebec, for purposes of this calculation, included the
provincial boundary extension of 1898, but not that of 1912.[2]

2. No province was to have its membership in the Commons reduced unless the ratio its population bore to the
total population of the country had declined one-twentieth
of the similar ratio at the previous readjustment of seats.

3. No province was to have its quota of seats in the
Commons reduced below the number of senators which the

---

[1]*Debates*, 1943, pp. 4335-47. Earlier in this session, the Government
apparently intended to proceed with redistribution as usual, for the Speech
from the Throne forecast a Representation Act, and Mr. King confirmed the
intention when the session was several weeks old. (*Ibid.*, p. 2677.)

[2]The boundaries of Quebec were extended by Dominion statute in 1898
and 1912, by a procedure authorized by the British North America Act. (See
Statutes, 61 Vict., c. 3, and 2 Geo. V, c. 45). The Act of 1912 specifically excluded
the area added in that year from calculations made for the redistribution of
seats among the provinces. It also stated that representation of the new territory
was to be determined according to the rules established by the B.N.A. Act for
regulating the representation of provinces *other than Quebec*.

province had in the upper house. This was added to the original scheme in 1915.

The application of this system of representation after the census of 1941 would have produced these results:[1]

Prince Edward Island
would have had 4 seats instead of 2 (1915 amendment)
New Brunswick would have had 10 seats instead of 9 (1915 amendment)
Nova Scotia   would have had 12 seats instead of 11 (1/20 clause)
Alberta   would have had 17 seats instead of 16 (1/20 clause)
Ontario   would have had 82 seats instead of 74 (1/20 clause)
Quebec, Manitoba, Saskatchewan and British Columbia would have had seats in proportion to their population.

In all this confusion, the strangest case of all was that of Ontario, for the one-twentieth clause had saved the province a steady 82 seats since 1914. The operation of this clause was such that unless the population of a province declined the required one-twentieth *within the ten years between each census*, the province suffered no loss of seats. Ontario's population, although on the increase, was nevertheless becoming a progressively smaller fraction of the total for the country. Yet for several decades it remained just within the limit set by the B.N.A. Act, so that Ontario's representation remained unchanged. Strict representation by population would have reduced Ontario's quota of seats to 81 in 1924 and to 78 in 1933. If this trend had continued another few decades, Quebec would have been faced with the interesting but disturbing picture of a population equal to or even greater than Ontario's, but a representation of sixty-five seats, as compared with eighty-two. The demand for fair representation, which had been so familiar a cry in the mouths of Upper Canadian statesmen before Confederation, was logically taken over in 1946 by Quebec. "Quebec," as Professor Dawson has recorded, "not unnaturally, began to demand 'rep. by pop.'; the whirligig of time had indeed brought in its revenges."[2]

A new scheme of representation, involving the repeal of the one-twentieth clause, was therefore adopted by a consti-

[1]*Debates*, 1943, p. 192.
[2]Dawson, *op. cit.*, p. 365.

tutional amendment in 1946.[1] The redistribution of 1947, which carried the new system into effect, was made on the following conditions:[2]

(1) The total number of members in the House was fixed at 255. The entry of Newfoundland in 1949 raised this total to 262.

(2) One seat was assigned to the Yukon Territory together with any part of Canada which might be added by Parliament and which did not form part of a province. This provision has already produced a remarkable constituency in the far north, where the addition of a large part of the Mackenzie District to the Yukon has resulted in a constituency some 700,000 square miles in extent, divided in two by mountain ranges that are virtually impassable except by air.[3]

(3) The total population of all the provinces was divided by 254 to obtain a quota, and this in turn was divided into the population of each province in order to find the number of members each was to receive.

(4) If (as was a virtual certainty) this operation did not fill all 254 seats, the remaining seats were to be given to the provinces with the largest remainders (one to each province) beginning with the one having the largest remainder and continuing down in order of the magnitude of the remainders until the vacancies were all filled.

(5) If, after this had been done, any province had fewer members than senators, it was forthwith given a number of members corresponding to the number of its senators.

(6) The operation then began anew and was repeated as above, the total number of seats to be filled being then 254 minus the seats assigned under paragraph (5) and the total

[1]*Brit. Statutes*, 10 Geo. VI, c. 63. (See Appendix A.) The debates in the Canadian House of Commons on the resolution requesting this amendment paid almost no attention to the details of the proposed change, but raged around the necessity or otherwise of consulting the provinces about it. This the Government refused to do. (*Debates*, 1946, pp. 2227 ff.)

[2]I am here following Professor Dawson's summary of the B.N.A. Act of 1946. Dawson, *op. cit.*, pp. 365-6.

[3]*Debates*, 1947, p. 5655. The platform of the Conservative party, approved at the party convention in 1948, includes a plank for the creation of a separate constituency of Mackenzie.

population used being that of the nine provinces less that
of the province or provinces given special consideration in
paragraph (5).   Remainders were again filled as in paragraph
(4).   In 1947, paragraph (5) was applied to Prince Edward
Island to give four seats instead of the two which the province
would ordinarily have received.   Under the final calculation
only 250 seats were to be filled, and the quota was obtained
by dividing the total population of the existing provinces,
Prince Edward Island excluded, by 250.   With the addition
of Newfoundland, which received seven seats in 1949 independently of the redistribution in force, the fixed membership
of the House of Commons was raised to 262 without altering
the rules by which seats are allotted to the provinces.   Future
adjustments will, therefore, follow the foregoing principles
with the exception that the basis of the calculation will be
262 instead of 255.

The operation for the whole country under this new
scheme of redistribution worked out as follows:

Province	Seats under Quota	Remainder of Population	Seats Allotted by Remainders	Total Seats
Prince Edward Island	4 (gu	aranteed by par	agraph (5)	above) 4
Nova Scotia	12	31,026	1	13
New Brunswick	10	1,621	0	10
Quebec	73	4,688	0	73
Ontario	83	4,681	0	83
Manitoba	16	496	0	16
Saskatchewan	19	30,010	1	20
Alberta	17	21,343	0	17
British Columbia	17	43,035	1	18
Yukon and Mackenzie				1
Newfoundland (1949)				7
	251			262

Thus nine of the ten provinces now have representation by
population, and further changes in representation will be
based on changes over the whole Dominion, and not just

TABLE II

GENERAL AND PARTIAL REDISTRIBUTIONS OF CONSTITUENCIES AMONG THE PROVINCES SINCE 1867

Year	No. of Seats	Ont.	Que.	N.S.	N.B.	Man.	B.C.	P.E.I.	N.W.T.	Sask.	Alta.	Yukon	Nfld.
1867	181	82	65	15	19								
1871*	185	82	65	15	19	4							
1872	200	88	65	21	16	4	6						
1873*	206	88	65	21	16	4	6	6					
1882	211	92	65	21	16	5	6	6					
1887*	215	92	65	21	16	5	6	6	4				
1892	213	92	65	20	14	7	6	5	4				
1903	214	86	65	18	13	10	7	4	10			1	
1907*	221	86	65	18	13	10	7	4		10	7	1	
1914	234	82	65	16	11	15	13	3		16	12	1	
1915*	235	82	65	16	11	15	13	4		16	12	1	
1924	245	82	65	14	11	17	14	4		21	16	1	
1933	245	82	65	12	10	17	16	4		21	17	1	
1947	255	82	65	13	10	16	18	4		20	17	1	
1949*	262	83	73										7

*Partial redistributions occasioned by special circumstances such as the addition of territory, etc.

one province.[1] Table II shows the results of the latest redistribution, compared with all previous changes.

As a long term project, the greatest single advantage of the new system is its abolition of the one-twentieth clause; the unwarranted protection afforded the strongest province under this provision is thus completely removed. The more defensible anomaly which arose from the guarantee given the weakest provinces that they would always have at least as many members as senators, is retained. This provision, considering the varying rates of population change among the several provinces, may be merely a temporary evasion of a fundamental problem in representation in the House of Commons.

If the population trends of the past thirty years continue into the future, Canada must consider the probability that Prince Edward Island will be entitled to but one member, while the guaranteed minimum remains at four; New Brunswick's representation will remain at ten, while probably her proper representation will in thirty years have declined to seven or eight. The ultimate weakness of the present system thus derives from the fact that the number of senators in which a province luxuriates has no relation whatever to its population. Nova Scotia and New Brunswick, for example, have ten senators each, and the four larger western provinces have six. While there is no indication that any western province will soon be falling back on its guaranteed minimum of six seats in the Commons, it would be manifestly absurd for New Brunswick to continue to have ten members while Alberta, with possibly twice the population, may have only thirteen or fourteen. This is no mere theoretical consideration; at the moment, Alberta's population is nearly eight and one half times that of Prince Edward Island, but Alberta's representation is just over four times that of the Island.

A fundamental problem in representation is, therefore, the probable development of a situation which may involve

[1]It was this particular alteration which made necessary a constitutional amendment. Section 52 of the B.N.A. Act, 1867, states that "the number of Members of the House of Commons may be from time to time increased by the Parliament of Canada, provided the proportionate representation of the Provinces prescribed by this Act is not thereby disturbed."

either an open abandonment of the principle of representation by population for provinces (which is only tacitly accepted at present for the exceptional case of Prince Edward Island) or a House of Commons constantly increasing in size to allow the representation of the larger provinces to keep pace with the guaranteed quotas of the smaller.[1] The abandonment of representation by population for the provinces, it is worth emphasizing, is by no means indefensible in a federal state. The various provinces have interests as provinces, quite apart from the relative or absolute size of their populations, and one has only to read a few volumes of Hansard to discover that surprisingly large numbers of members sometimes forget that they belong to a national legislature and give precedence to their duties as representatives of a particular province or region. As long as we have the example of the United States Senate, in which every state has two members regardless of size and population, it would be extremely difficult to argue convincingly that an efficient democratic legislature must be based solely on representation by population.

If, on the other hand, strict representation by population is the desideratum, it would be much easier to grasp this nettle now than twenty or thirty years hence. At the moment, only the smallest province would be directly affected; in the future, it is probable that all four eastern provinces will be concerned, and the problem will then be aggravated by the fact that it will include provinces comprising an entire economic region. But to expect a democratic legislature to anticipate contentious problems that may be many years away is utopian indeed; on its record, the House of Commons has sufficient difficulty in keeping up with representation disputes as they arise.

[1]This was suggested as long ago as 1933, when Mr. J. S. Woodsworth objected to the guarantees given to the Maritimes, and argued that Prince Edward Island should be given an adequate representation, with the other eight provinces in proportion. *Debates*, 1932-3, p. 1592.

PART III

THE MEMBERS OF PARLIAMENT

CHAPTER IV

QUALIFICATIONS AND DISQUALIFICATIONS
OF MEMBERS

WITH the exception of a statute of 1919 which rendered
women eligible to sit in Parliament, the requirements which
members of the House of Commons are obliged to fulfil have
not changed materially since about 1880. The positive
qualifications have always been few, as the things that a
member cannot be have outnumbered from the beginning
the things that he must be. At the moment of writing, any
British subject over twenty-one who is a qualified elector is
eligible for the House of Commons, provided he does not
come within the detailed list of disqualified persons given in
the Dominion Elections Act. He does not have to be a
Canadian citizen.[1]

This simplicity was achieved only after considerable
trouble. The whole question of electoral law was evaded
at the beginning by section 41 of the British North America
Act, which stipulated that existing provincial electoral laws
were to obtain in their entirety until Parliament otherwise
provided.[2] As Sir John A. Macdonald said of the franchise,
in terms that applied with equal force to members' eligibility,
"Insuperable difficulties would have presented themselves if
we had attempted to settle [it] now."[3] In the first Parliament, therefore, there was no uniformity in the qualifications
of members returned from the various provinces. All had
to satisfy a property requirement, but some were allowed to
sit also in the provincial legislature while others were not, and
there was material variation in the disqualifications enforced.

The first few years after 1867 consequently provided
ample opportunity for argument and disagreement about
qualifications; party spirit, sectional jealousies, and anti-

[1]This includes the changes made in 1948.
[2](See Appendix A.) This arrangement was continued temporarily by Acts
in 1871 and 1873, which prolonged the use of election laws *in force in 1867*, even
though several of the provinces had made changes in the meantime.
[3]*Confederation Debates*, 1865, p. 39.

confederation sentiments all played an active part in these battles. More than a decade was required to settle the fundamental principles. At one time or another no less than seven major issues were raised: the property qualification; offices of emolument; government contracts; membership in the provincial legislatures; employment by provincial governments; rejection by the House of Commons; and disqualification for violation of the election laws.

Before these are discussed, it is convenient to dispose of the few positive qualifications that have been required. In addition to the property qualification, which is discussed below, the provincial electoral laws prevailing in 1867 all asserted that candidates must be British subjects, male, and of the full age of twenty-one years. These statutory provisions were actually no more than legal statements of what Bourinot called the common law of politics; observance of these terms was so completely accepted in 1874 that the federal government, enacting its own election law, did not think to include them as part of the statute. The Senate added an amendment to insist that candidates be British subjects by birth or naturalization, so that one of the three qualifications was included. The other two, that candidates should be male and at least twenty-one, were not part of the statute law of Canada after 1874; it was not until 1919, when women were admitted to the House, that a new section of the electoral law specified that candidates should be British subjects (provided they were male or female) and over twenty-one.[1] Except for the addition in 1948 of a clause requiring candidates to be qualified voters, the law in that regard has not since been changed.

The same cannot be said of the other aspects of qualification and disqualification. Some of these have had such chequered careers that they must be presented separately;[2] only those which can be disposed of summarily are treated in this chapter.

[1]*Statutes*, 9-10 Geo. V, c. 48. See W. D. McPherson, *The Law of Elections in Canada* (Toronto, 1905), p. 74: "As to minors being permitted to sit in the House of Commons, there appears to be no express exclusion. Women are clearly ineligible to Parliament." This latter point depended on judicial decision.
[2]See Chapters v and xiv.

THE PROPERTY QUALIFICATION

The provinces which entered Confederation in 1867 were
all accustomed to some form of property qualification for
members of their assemblies.   In Nova Scotia, the qualification dated back to Cornwallis's original instructions in 1749,
and the other colonies usually recognized the principle as
soon as they were granted assemblies.   Without going into
statistical detail, it may be said that a property qualification
was an accepted practice, and entirely in accord with both
Imperial and American precedent.   However, the property
qualification in Great Britain was repealed in 1858, by which
time most of the American states had either abolished it or
were about to do so;[1] in Canada, repeated attempts to
remove it began as early as 1854.[2]   The Canadian ventures
were all failures, with the result that all members of the
first Canadian House of Commons were elected on a property
requirement.   This was lowest in Nova Scotia, where anyone
who had a freehold worth $8.00 annually or who could
qualify as an elector was eligible: electors had to possess
real estate to the value of $150 or a combination of personal
with real estate to the value of $300.   For New Brunswick,
the qualification was £300 clear of all charges, and in the
Canadas the amount was £500.[3]

Nobody seems to have taken the property qualification
very seriously.   Edward Blake, a leading Liberal, said in
the legislature in 1870 that it was "a farce, and it was well
known was frequently evaded.   Candidates did not require
to shew any property qualification the very next day after
an election."[4]   Another Liberal member threw further light
on the situation a fortnight later by observing that, "Some
candidates qualified through lent property, and afterwards
the property reverted to the real proprietors, and in many
cases members sat in that House without qualifying, and . . .

[1]See *Statutes of Great Britain*, 21-2 Vict., c. 26.   Also R. Luce, *Legislative
Assemblies* (Boston and New York, 1924), Chapter XI.   The American Congress
from the first required no property qualification.
[2]*Journals of Canada* (Prov.), 1854-66.
[3]*Statutes of Nova Scotia*, 1863, c. 28; *Statutes of New Brunswick*, 1855, c. 37;
in Ontario and Quebec, the property qualification was established by the Act
of Union, 1840.
[4]*Debates*, 1870, p. 363.

there were members in that House who had not qualified and could not legally qualify.   If there was to be a property qualification it should last for the whole of a Parliament."[1]

That last statement was merely the enunciation of a hypothetical principle; actually the Liberals favoured the abolition of the qualification.   The Conservatives, on the other hand, were strongly in favour of a property requirement. A government election bill drafted in 1869 included a clause compelling candidates for the Commons to possess property worth $2000, and this clause reappeared in a bill in 1870.[2] For various reasons, these Conservative bills were not pressed through, and in 1874 the Liberals seized the opportunity afforded by their accession to power to remove the property qualification; a Conservative amendment to salvage it was lost on a division.[3]

The qualification became an issue in one single instance just before it was abolished.   A Liberal candidate at a by-election in West Peterborough in 1873 failed to supply evicence of his property qualification at the proper time (although he did so subsequently), and despite the fact that he was victorious at the polls, his election was rejected by the returning officer.   The runner-up was returned as the member, and the Committee on Privileges and Elections upheld the returning officer's decision, as much for partisan purposes, one suspects, as for any genuine concern over the Liberal's qualifications.[4]   Significantly enough, a statement made in debate by one member charging that the Liberal had not been qualified at the time of the election, but had obtained his property qualification after he had learned of the result at the polls, was not only not investigated but was not even challenged.

[1]*Ibid.*, p. 704; see also *Parliamentary Debates*, (Scrapbook Hansard) April 7, 1874.   This evasion of the property qualification was by no means unknown in the United States and Great Britain, where some illustrious members were chronically disqualified.   (See Luce, *op. cit.* Chapter xi.)   Evasion of the property qualification was facilitated by the fact that the requirement in some cases was compulsory for *candidates*, but not for members.   An elected member, as Blake pointed out, did not have to qualify as to property.

[2]See Macdonald Papers, vol. 73; *Parliamentary Debates* (Scrapbook Hansard), May 18, 1869.

[3]*Ibid.*, May 20, 1874.

[4]*Report of the Select Standing Committee on Privileges and Elections*, 1873.

The property requirement has been a dead issue since 1872. This is not to say that its re-enactment has not been suggested, for as recently as 1932 a delegate to a convention of the Canadian Manufacturers' Association advocated its re-establishment as an aim to be pursued by that organization.[1] The House of Commons has not for decades exhibited any interest in the return of a property qualification.

MEMBERSHIP IN PROVINCIAL LEGISLATURES, AND EMPLOYMENT BY PROVINCIAL GOVERNMENTS

The problem of dual representation in the provincial and federal legislatures occupied the attention of Canadian statesmen before the first Parliament had assembled. The two Maritime provinces, prompted partly by a natural desire to preserve the independence of their own legislatures, enacted statutes in 1867 to disqualify members of the House of Commons from sitting in the local House; the Nova Scotia law went so far as to disqualify *candidates* for the federal House from the assembly.[2] Ontario and Quebec were unable to take such action, since there were temporarily no provincial assemblies in session to do so; and in any event the Conservative party in Central Canada was not opposed to dual representation. However, the assemblies in both these provinces subsequently took steps to prevent their members holding federal seats.[3]

In the first House of Commons there were about twenty-five members from Ontario and Quebec who also sat in the local House, and in both provinces a majority of the provincial Cabinet held federal seats.[4] The strategic advantage enjoyed by the Conservatives because of this hardly needs to be expounded, and it was natural that the Liberals should oppose the practice. Bills to abolish dual representation were introduced every session after Confederation, with

[1]S. D. Clark, *The Canadian Manufacturers' Association* (Toronto, 1939) p. 39n.
[2]See J. H. Gray, *Confederation, 1864-1871* (Toronto, 1872) p. 393.
[3]The Quebec statute failed to pass the legislative council.
[4]The entry of Manitoba in 1871 brought two more members of a legislative assembly into the Commons. Figures computed from *The Canadian Parliamentary Companion*, 1869.

persuasive arguments being used each time concerning the serious effects of the custom on the independence of members.[1] Some progress towards abolition was made in 1872, when the Conservatives introduced a statute which disqualified members of the provincial assemblies from being candidates for the federal House in provinces where dual representation was not allowed.[2] At first sight, this merely seemed to prevent the practice in areas where it had already been abolished; but the new act did make changes in Ontario and New Brunswick, where until this time a provincial member could be a candidate in a federal election and then fall back on the local assembly if unsuccessful. It was true that the act operated only where the provinces had already taken some action themselves, and consequently it did not affect Quebec, British Columbia, and Manitoba.[3] But in the following year, when the accession to power of a Liberal government in Ontario had somewhat dimmed Conservative interest in dual representation, a Liberal private member successfully sponsored a bill to make the practice illegal.[4] The division on the bill was not on party lines.

Only two members of provincial assemblies were elected to the House of Commons after dual representation was abolished. The first instance occurred in 1874. Mr. S. F. Perry, the Liberal Speaker of the Prince Edward Island Assembly, decided in that year to resign his position to become a candidate for the federal legislature; but he discovered to his embarrassment that although as an ordinary member of the assembly he could do as he wished, there was no law to authorize or regulate his resignation of the Speakership. In good faith, he placed his resignation in the hands of the Lieutenant-Governor and, hoping for the best, was elected

[1]See, for example, Parliamentary Debates (Scrapbook Hansard), November 28, 1867; Debates, 1871, pp. 198 ff. and 1023 ff. The committee on Privileges and Elections examined the formal question of whether dual representation was a breach of the Independence of Parliament Act, and decided in the negative.
[2]Statutes, 35 Vict., c. 15.
[3]It was not until 1881 that Manitoba completely abolished dual representation, and for many years one of the leading members of the provincial assembly was also a federal Senator. In Quebec, legislative councillors may still be Senators. See J. G. Bourinot, Parliamentary Procedure and Practice (Montreal, 1892), pp. 165 ff.
[4]Statutes, 36 Vict., c. 2.

to the House of Commons. There his position was not allowed to pass unchallenged, and a debate arose during which Sir John A. Macdonald, in the friendliest manner, suggested that Perry petition for a committee to consider his case. Perry did so, but the Government promptly took statutory action to relieve him of any penalties attached to his unusual position.[1]

Mr. Perry, strangely enough, was in trouble again in 1887, when he was elected to the federal House at a time when he had just been elected to the Prince Edward Island Assembly. The local legislature had not met since his election to it, and Perry, a cautious man, took two steps to protect his federal seat: he formally resigned from the Assembly, although there was no law to cover the resignation of members before a newly elected legislature had met; and he fled the province before his Conservative opponents could serve a writ on him to deprive him of his federal seat—a shrewd gesture which confused his enemies and greatly enhanced Liberal prestige on the Island.[2]   The case ultimately found its way to the Supreme Court, which found on appeal that Mr. Perry was in the clear again. This was not because he had not been elected to both Houses, which was indisputable, but because, with his penchant for becoming involved in complicated situations, he had disqualified himself for the provincial House by accepting a provincial contract, and was thus rendered ineligible to sit in the assembly by the provincial Independence of Parliament Act.[3]   His federal seat was thus safe, although not, one suspects, through any fault of its occupant.

The other individual guilty of dual representation after 1874 also did so through an ambiguity in the law. Another Prince Edward Islander, Mr. J. E. Robertson, was elected to the Commons in 1883 when he was allegedly a member of the provincial assembly. The provincial assembly, on the

[1]*Statutes*, 37 Vict., c. 11.
[2]See Macdonald Papers, vol. 154. E. Hodgson to Macdonald, April 21, 1887; the same, April 27, 1887.
[3][1888] S.C.R., I, 265. Justice Taschereau dissented, on the grounds that Perry did not have a legal contract with the Crown in Prince Edward Island (which in any case had repudiated it) and had not legally resigned his P.E.I. seat.

other hand, had not recognized his election, and had gone so far as to declare a second candidate elected in his place. The House of Commons Committee on Privileges and Elections nevertheless rejected Robertson as a member by declaring his opponent to be the victor in the election.[1] It is worth noting that Perry and Robertson were both Liberals, that Perry's first election was ratified in a Liberal legislature, while Robertson's was rejected by a Conservative one.

There are at least two other instances of local legislators who were candidates for the federal House. In 1887 a member of the North West Council was an unsuccessful candidate in Assiniboia for the Commons without resigning from the Council; and in 1896 an Ontario member of the legislative assembly contested Nipissing, and on his defeat reclaimed his seat in the provincial legislature because of a technicality concerning his resignation from it.[2] Both these cases were clear violations of the statute, but no great stir was made over either of them; a different result might have been expected had the two candidates not been defeated.

The eligibility for the Commons of provincial officials and employees (as distinguished from assembly members) has come up from time to time, and the issue has been complicated by such irrelevant matters as provincial disqualification of federal employees, and party strategy. Immediately after Confederation a member from Nova Scotia took the bull by the horns and accepted an appointment as provincial Queen's Printer in Halifax. Sir Charles Tupper then presented a petition in the Commons which requested the disqualification of the erring member. Two lawyers who were consulted gave Sir John Macdonald their considered opinion that the member was not merely disqualified from sitting in the Commons, but was ineligible even as a candidate because provincial law, which applied in federal elections, rendered him ineligible as a candidate for the local assembly.[3] Notwithstanding this, and the fact that the member was a Liberal, the federal Government confirmed his eligibility by

[1]*Journals*, 1883, Appendix no. 2.
[2]See *Canadian Parliamentary Guide*, 1901, p. 212, and *Debates*, 1900, pp. 6729-31.
[3]Macdonald Papers, vol. 55, pp. 70-4.

a statutory relief measure which asserted flatly that "he has been and is capable of . . . sitting and voting."[1]

The Liberals, perhaps because they were already at a considerable disadvantage through the operation of dual representation, seem to have viewed this gesture with alarm, and ungratefully continued to favour the disqualification of provincial employees. Edward Blake sought such a law in 1871, basing his argument partly on the reasonable proposition that under the existing electoral law provincial officials managed important parts of the federal electoral machinery.[2] In Nova Scotia, for example, the returning officer in most districts was the sheriff, and the sheriff was appointed annually by the Government.[3]   To have such officials eligible for Parliament, particularly when at least one of the provinces had not merely disqualified but also disfranchised federal employees,[4] was a strange anomaly.   Again in 1878 the Liberals proposed to disqualify provincial employees of all kinds.   But in the face of strong opposition, they yielded part of the bill so that, for example, lawyers acting in an advisory capacity to provincial governments, were not rendered ineligible.[5]   The only officials disqualified, in fact, were sheriffs, clerks of the peace, county crown attorneys, and registrars, all of whom had a hand in the electoral machinery.

No changes have been made in this provision since 1878, and to this day no federal law disqualifies provincial employees for the House of Commons. It appears to be highly improbable that any provincial government would allow an employee to retain his job while contesting a federal election.

REJECTION BY THE HOUSE OF COMMONS

The Canadian House of Commons has from the beginning reserved the right to reject a member, notwithstanding any of the legal qualifications or disqualifications, and however proper the member's election.   Acceptance by the Commons

[1]*Statutes*, 31 Vict., c. 26, s. 2.
[2]*Debates*, 1871, p. 1023.   See *infra*, Chapters VIII-X.
[3]*Ibid.*, pp. 979 ff.
[4]Nova Scotia.   See *ibid.*, pp. 971 ff.
[5]*Ibid.*, 1878, pp. 1226 ff. and 1327 ff.

is thus a test which all members must meet.[1]   For this practice there is ample Canadian and Imperial precedent, and a celebrated British case of 1870 (Mr. O'Donovan Rossa) was a timely reminder, if any were needed, of Parliamentary privileges in this regard.   Expulsions were effected in Canada in 1800, 1829, 1831, and 1858.[2]

Although actual rejection of an elected member by the House is rare, legislators have frequently challenged the right of other members to sit and vote.   The grounds on which representatives have advocated, directly or indirectly, the expulsion or censure of a colleague have varied enormously; members have sometimes been willing to take action against their honourable friends for most trifling reasons, while at other times the House of Commons has shown a broad tolerance for impressively shady transactions.

These facts can be made clear by consideration of a few examples.   Before the celebrated Riel case in 1874, certain members of the House pricked up their ears over the election of the first member from Provencher, Mr. Delorme, who was allegedly a former colleague of Riel's; in that case he was guilty (also allegedly) of treason, murder, or both.[3] Mr. Delorme denied all accusations to such good effect that he was not even investigated by a Select Committee.   This was the first instance of the House inquiring into the position of a fully qualified member.

In 1874 occurred the expulsion, re-election, and re-expulsion of the rebel Louis Riel, a case which hardly needs recapitulation here.[4]   In 1875 another (although very minor) problem arose when a member failed to qualify by taking the required oath of allegiance before taking his seat.   The House did not consider disqualifying or expelling him, since there was no statutory provision providing penalties for such an omission by a member; but it refused to recognize the votes he had cast before the oath was taken, despite his

---

[1]Properly speaking, this concerns the privileges of the House rather than qualifications, but it is convenient to discuss it here.

[2]Bourinot, *op. cit.*, pp. 193 ff.

[3]*Debates*, 1871, pp. 992 ff.

[4]Riel was legally elected, properly presented to the House, sworn, and his name entered on the rolls, but he did not attempt to exercise any of his privileges as a member.

valid election.[1] In the following year, yet another case arose when somebody remembered that Mr. Daoust, the member for Two Mountains, had ten years before been convicted of forgery, although because of some complicated judicial manoeuvring he had neither been cleared of the charge nor had he served a sentence. As it was, he was apparently still open to further judical action. The Commons accepted the explanation given, and he was not disqualified or expelled.[2] In 1880 a serious charge of misappropriation of county funds was laid against a member by petition, but the House refused on a partisan vote to accede to opposition demands for reference of the case to the Committee on Privileges and Elections.[3]

A lull of a decade followed the foregoing cases, but it was the proverbial lull before the storm.[4] In 1891 and 1892, three members were investigated for charges which, if proven, would certainly have resulted in the expulsion of all three, even by a most partisan government. As it was, one member was cleared of all charges; one was expelled; and one was neither cleared nor expelled but was merely subjected to an exhaustive investigation of his affairs. The exonerated member had been accused of getting political appointments for some persons for a consideration, but his accusers were unable to satisfy a committee of the validity of their claims.[5] The expelled member, Thomas McGreevy (by a strange stroke of fate, the contractor who had erected the Parliament Buildings), was involved in an astonishingly complicated and corrupt scheme concerning public works.[6] The third member under fire was Adolphe Caron, who was accused of crimes similar to Mr. McGreevy's and was honoured with investigation by a Royal Commission instead of the usual House of Commons Committee. The Government took no action on

[1]Report of Select Standing Committee on Privileges and Elections, 1875. (See Journals, 1875, p. 176.)
[2]Debates, 1876, pp. 686 ff.
[3]Ibid., 1880, p. 196 and pp. 395 ff.
[4]This is not to say that members were not frequently being accused of misbehaviour. See e.g., the debate on timber limits in Debates, 1890, pp. 1714 ff. and pp. 2050 ff.
[5]See Journals, 1891, Appendix no. 4.
[6]Ibid., Appendix no. 1. At the height of the storm, Mr. McGreevy tried to resign, but his resignation was rejected in view of the charges pending against him.

the Royal Commission's report, however, and a Liberal motion in the House to declare Caron "unfit" was lost on a straight party vote.[1]   In none of these cases are details of the charges of particular relevance; what is of interest is the readiness of the House to disqualify or expel, even though no statute may have been violated—and provided, perhaps, that party lines could stand the strain.[2]   Since McGreevy was the last member to be expelled from the House, this is a convenient place to add that expulsion provided (and still provides) no disqualification for future election to Parliament.   Both Riel and McGreevy were re-elected after expulsion, the latter after having served a term in jail.

Some comic relief from these sordid events was provided in 1911, when a member rose solemnly in his place to accuse a colleague of having his private house painted by government painters, with government paint, on government time. However, the accused was able to clear himself to such good effect that a Select Committee not only exonerated him but criticized his accuser.[3]

A much more involved problem, worth elaboration as an excellent example of Parliamentary manoeuvring, arose shortly thereafter.[4]   On March 10 and March 13, 1913, Mr. Gauthier, member for St. Hyacinthe, gave notice that he intended to present certain charges against Hon. Louis Coderre, Secretary of State, for conniving at personation in his own election; on the first occasion Gauthier postponed his speech when he was advised that Coderre was out of town, and on the second, that Coderre was ill in hospital.   Since an accused member is entitled to be heard in his own defence (which usually in such cases consists of a denial of the charges and withdrawal from the House, inasmuch as a rule provides that members are not to be present during discussion of charges concerning themselves), it was not until March 17 that Gauthier was able to present his facts.   The Government had thus a full week to prepare a defence, and there is

[1]*Debates*, 1893, pp. 2822 ff.   Report of the Caron Commission is no. 27 of the 1893 *Sessional Papers*.
[2]See also the cases mentioned in the discussion of the Independence of Parliament Act, Chapter v.
[3]*Debates*, 1910-11, pp. 4645 ff. and 7873 ff.
[4]See *ibid.*, 1912-13, pp. 6050 ff.

evidence that they deliberately stalled for time for the purpose, since it later appeared in debate that Coderre had not actually been ill in hospital during the period of delay.

The case against Coderre, amply supported by affidavits and other documents, accused him not only of tolerating personation in his own election, but also of rewarding at least one of his accomplices with an appointment to the public service of Canada. After the introduction of a motion to refer the matter to the Select Committee on Privileges and Elections, Coderre denied the charges absolutely, withdrew, and the Government presented its defence—or, more accurately, a counter-offensive. Hon. Charles Doherty, Minister of Justice, opened the Government attack with a double question: is there anything here to be investigated; and if so, to what tribunal should it go? His answer to the first question was in the negative, and was supported by a group of documents which denied the main points of the case against Coderre, and were remarkable in that they bore the same signatures as the affidavits on which the Liberals relied. Surely, Mr. Doherty argued persuasively, the House will not think it necessary to investigate charges based on statements such as these? The Liberals were unconvinced and still pressed for an investigation, even though their case was now based largely on the word of discredited witnesses.

Mr. Doherty then shifted his defence to his second question. He argued that the proper tribunal to hear the case was a court, since the Liberals' agitation was over an election matter, and the Controverted Elections Act had removed election disputes from the House of Commons into the calmer atmosphere of the judicial system.[1] To this the Liberals objected that the time limit required for petitions under the Controverted Elections Act was now almost exhausted, so that it was too late to dispute the election in that way, and that in any event the House had not delegated its authority over elections. There then followed a prolonged battle of quotations and precedents, with each party supporting its argument so far as possible by utterances made in the past

[1]See Chapter XIV.

by leaders of the other. From this the only point that emerged with unmistakable clarity was that the fate of charges against a member—whether dropped, referred to a Select Committee, or examined by a Royal Commission— depended largely on a balance of forces unrelated to the particular point at issue.

Had the charges concerned Coderre merely as a candidate for Parliament, and not as a member, there is no doubt that the election laws would have provided for necessary action. But with the discrediting of their case so far as the election itself was concerned, the Liberals transferred their emphasis to Coderre's action as a member, a matter which was certainly within the purview of the Commons. The Liberals had, indeed, documentary evidence to show that after Coderre learned of the charges to be made against him, he wrote damaging letters in connection with their appointment to the civil service to two of the men concerned in the alleged personation. So that, as more than one Liberal observed smugly, while the government had proven some of the witnesses to be perjurers, liars, and poor creatures generally, it was still necessary to account for their appointment (real or pending) to the public service of Canada under most surprising circumstances. Conservative leaders, despite the Liberal documents, denied the fact of appointment, and still argued that there was nothing to investigate. The Liberals had no opportunity to prove their point (although they asserted vehemently that they could) for the motion to refer the whole matter to a committee was lost on a party division.

That there was nothing to investigate is inadmissible, for even if Coderre's innocence is accepted, there still remains the conduct of those who sought to implicate him in such grave matters. Their actions certainly constituted a serious breach of the privileges of the House. But these extraordinary circumstances were never examined at all; in the eyes of the Government at least, Mr. Coderre's reputation suffered no ill, for he was appointed to one of the next vacancies on the Quebec bench.

The Coderre case of 1912-13 was the last great "scandal" which involved a single member of Parliament. The authority of the House of Commons to reject a fully qualified and duly elected member nonetheless remains undimmed by time or disuse, and the fact that the House rarely questions the qualifications of its members is no indication that an elected candidate does not have to meet the test of acceptability to his colleagues. The latest edition of Beauchesne records that a member may be expelled for such offenses as open rebellion, forgery, perjury, fraud, and breach of trust, misappropriation of public money, conspiracy to defraud, corruption in the administration of justice or in public office, and violation of the oath of allegiance.[1] As the instances which have been cited suggest, members have been challenged on these and less grave matters, and their ultimate fate has usually depended on forces irrelevant to any principle involved.

OTHER QUALIFICATIONS AND DISQUALIFICATIONS

There are a number of other points of varying importance which concern the qualifications of candidates and members of the Commons.

1. Senators are disqualified by section 39 of the British North America Act. No violation of this has occurred. A Senator is, of course, free to resign from the upper House to become a candidate for the Commons, and several have done so. At least one such Senator, who resigned shortly after a dissolution of Parliament, was defeated for the Commons, and was once again snugly ensconced in the Senate before the new Parliament met.[2]

2. When for any reason a member is incapable of discharging his trust as a legislator, the House may declare his seat vacant; this is a different matter from disqualifying or expelling a competent member. If a member were to become insane, it is probable that his seat would be vacated, although it is in accord with Imperial precedent that every consideration for the member be shown before taking such a serious step. In 1884, for example, a member of the

---

[1]A. Beauchesne, *Parliamentary Rules and Forms* (Toronto, 1943), p. 42. See *Debates*, 1949, (1st session), pp. 13-14, for an instance of a member being threatened with expulsion for referring to his colleagues in the House of Commons as a "bunch of crooks."

[2]*Ibid.*, 1891, p. 1577.

Ontario legislature announced a plan to re-organize the world with Toronto as the centre of a grand and beautiful universe. He was subsequently adjudged on petition to be a lunatic by the Chancery division of the High Court of Justice, and his seat was declared vacant after electors had formally requested that a new writ be issued to fill the seat. The Committee on Privileges and Elections, in recommending this action, reported that, "In similar cases Parliaments appear uniformly to have inquired into the nature of the alleged malady, and to have granted or refused a new writ according as there seemed to be a permanent or temporary incapacity in the member."[1] No case like this has occurred in the Canadian House of Commons, but it may be presumed that the legislature would follow the precedents suggested above.

Another instance where a similar right was exercised by the Commons, although for a different reason, occurred in 1947 after Mr. Fred Rose had been found guilty in the espionage trials of 1946. Rose was neither disqualified nor expelled, although the latter step was certainly a possible way of vacating his seat. The Prime Minister merely introduced a motion to the effect that, "having been adjudged guilty of an indictable offence and sentenced to six years and not having served the punishment . . . [he] has become and continues incapable of sitting and voting in this house."[2]

In all such matters, the final word rests with the House of Commons, and it is therefore impossible, in the absence of precedents covering every conceivable phenomenon in regard to members' qualifications, to lay down any precise rules under which the House might find a member incapable of sitting. Lunacy and treason are obvious reasons; there could be many others less apparent, in which the discretion of the majority of the House would decide the issue.[3]

3. Persons found guilty of corrupt practices at elections are disqualified for Parliament for a period of seven years; illegal practices disqualify for five years. Since the incidence of controverted election trials has declined almost to zero,

[1] *Journals of Legislative Assembly of Ontario*, 1884, Appendix no. 1.
[2] *Debates*, 1947, pp. 1-2.
[3] The Imperial Parliament has refused to accept members guilty of mere misdemeanours. McPherson, *op. cit.*, p. 65.

this is no longer an important consideration. For several decades after Confederation, however, large numbers of elections were voided for bribery, treating, and analogous offences, and in each case presumably one or more persons were rendered ineligible for Parliament by their complicity.[1] On rare occasions, the member whose election was voided was disqualified for having played a personal part in the corrupt practices.[2]   If any person disqualified for corruption was elected to the Commons during the period of his ineligibility, no trace of it has been left in official records.

4. Canadian legislators have never been required to fulfil a residence requirement in their own constituency or province.[3]   Until 1948, when candidates became obliged to qualify as electors, candidates and members did not even have to be residents of Canada.   In 1890, an elected member moved to England without resigning his seat in the Commons.[4]   The recent provision that candidates for the Commons must be qualified as voters involves a twelve-month residence in Canada immediately preceding election day; once elected, however, there is no statutory residence qualification for members.

Practical politics impose in actual fact a residence qualification which, while in no sense as binding as a legal requirement would be, is nevertheless widely observed. Reference to the *Canadian Parliamentary Guide* reveals that the overwhelming majority of members reside in their constituencies; in the older parts of Canada there is a further strong tendency for them to have been born and brought up there.[5]   In many more instances, a metropolitan member not actually resident in his constituency nevertheless lives in the metropolitan area, and possibly maintains a business address in the constituency itself.   It may fairly

[1]See Chapter xiv.
[2]See e.g. *The Week*, May 13, 1892.   The same paper observed on September 20, 1889, that candidates for Parliament were rarely implicated personally in corrupt practices.
[3]An extremely modified form of residence qualification did exist for a time in Nova Scotia, when after 1758 the law required that a member's property qualification must exist in the district for which he was elected.   Senators from Quebec still are required to have either their residence or their property qualification in the senatorial district for which they are appointed.
[4]*Debates*, 1890, p. 3197.
[5]See Chapter vii.

be said, in short, that members normally do have some connection with their district. But non-residents are none-theless common. Porritt records that there were thirty in the Parliament elected in 1911, and this is roughly the figure to be found in any House.[1]

The nomads of politics are the party leaders. Since a successful party leader frequently finds living in Ottawa a necessity, and the number of seats in and near the capital is small, leaders are often obliged to hold seats apart from their main place of residence. Many of course have seats in their home districts, where, perhaps, they are still partners in a law firm or have a business. But a defeat in the home seat of a member whose services are required in the House of Commons will force him to seek another constituency, and it is here that the absence of a legal residence rule is most useful in parliamentary government. Thus Sir John Mac-donald with a home seat in Ontario sat for Manitoba and British Columbia districts; Mr. W. L. M. King represented seats as far apart as Saskatchewan and Prince Edward Island.

Party leaders have also roamed in order to throw their prestige into the winning of a doubtful seat. "Unless you again contest the constituency," a supporter from Lennox wrote to Sir John Macdonald in 1883, "we lose it." The lukewarm Liberals, another warned the great Conservative at the same time, would vote "their party's choice with any other candidate in the field than yourself."[2]   Edward Blake captured Bruce South from the Conservatives in 1872, although his federal seat until then had been West Durham; Dalton McCarthy in 1896 won the new constituency of Brandon as an Independent, and also took Simcoe North from the Liberals; Sir Wilfrid Laurier in 1911 won Soulanges from the Conservatives, although his customary seat was Quebec East.

Party strategy often dictates the "placing" of party leaders for campaign purposes. Thus Mr. King continued to run in a Saskatchewan seat after it would doubtless have

---

[1]E. Porritt, *Evolution of the Dominion of Canada* (Yonkers-on-Hudson, 1918), p. 330. For other Parliaments, see the *Canadian Parliamentary Guide* for any year.

[2]J. S. McCuaig to Macdonald, October 12, 1883; E. W. Rathbone to Mac-donald, October 12, 1883. (Macdonald Papers, vol. 65.)

been more convenient to seek a riding closer to his Ottawa office. The finding of safe, convenient, or merely vacant seats also leads to a Minister's straying far from home. In 1935, for example, Charles Dunning went from Saskatchewan to be elected in Prince Edward Island; in 1940, Angus L. Macdonald left his provincial premiership in Nova Scotia to fill a vacancy in an Ontario constituency.

Instances such as these are exceptions to the general rule that members are normally connected in some way with their constituencies. The prevalence of the general rule in no way detracts from the great value of the exceptions to it.

5. No religious qualification has been required of members since 1867, nor have clergymen of any denomination been disqualified from sitting.[1] The oath of allegiance which members are required to take before being seated in the Commons perhaps implies a religious faith; but members who cannot reconcile the oath with their religious beliefs may make a solemn declaration which is as acceptable as the oath. Canada has had no avowed atheists who have refused the oath on general principles, so that the question of whether atheism disqualifies for the House of Commons remains unsettled. The Communist member who was elected in 1943, Mr. Rose, was presumably an atheist who found the oath of allegiance did not interfere with his conscience; but as Mr. Rose was subsequently convicted in the spy trials of 1946, it would be difficult to say whether his acceptance of the oath of allegiance established a precedent of any significance. It is certain that a member who refused to take the oath or make the solemn declaration would have no seat in the House, nor could he draw his sessional indemnity.[2]

6. A member is disqualified if he signs any pledge or undated resignation that will restrict his freedom of action as a member.[3]

[1]Religious qualifications were not unknown in the colonies. Nova Scotia before 1820 required its members to take an oath renouncing the Roman Catholic religion; the Constitutional Act of 1791 disqualified clergymen for the assemblies of Upper and Lower Canada. See Shortt and Doughty, *Canada and Its Provinces*, vol. 14, pp. 452, 485; A. Todd, *The Practice and Privileges of the Two Houses of Parliament* (Toronto, 1840), p. 82n.

[2]Beauchesne, *op. cit.*, pp. 10-11.

[3]*Statutes*, 2 Geo. VI, c. 46, s. 106. See Chapter I.

7. A member is qualified to sit for only one seat at a time and if he already holds a seat is automatically ineligible for any vacancy. At a general election all seats are vacant and for over fifty years after Confederation a member was free to be a candidate in any number of constituencies; if successful in more than one of them, he was required by a House of Commons rule to choose the one for which he would sit when Parliament met.[1] On the other hand, a member cannot resign a seat which is being contested under the Controverted Elections Act,[2] so that it was possible for a member to hold two seats long after the election if, as was common, either one or both was not clearly his. A seat could always be vacated by the acceptance of an office of emolument. There is on record one interesting case of a member who was unseated for corrupt practices but who appealed the decision; before the appeal was heard he accepted an office of emolument, and thus vacated his seat regardless of the outcome of the appeal; then he resigned from his office of emolument and ran again for the same seat in the Commons. He was defeated.[3]

Sir John Macdonald had two constituencies for over a year after the 1882 election, being unable to resign from one of them because of an election petition. Mr. Lemieux performed a similar feat for two years after the 1904 election and for four years after 1917; while Laurier set a record in this regard by having two seats from 1911 to 1917.[4] Laurier at least had the excuse of a controverted election in this last instance, but Sir Rodolphe Forget during the same period sat for two seats not only with neither of them in dispute but with nobody in the House raising an eyebrow over it—a clear indication that the rule forbidding the practice was not taken seriously.[5]

A private member's bill to enact the rule as a statute was passed in 1919. Members elected in two districts then had to choose one of them or be penalized for it, unless it

[1]Bourinot, *Parliamentary Procedure and Practice* (1892), p. 160.
[2]*Ibid.*, p. 161n.
[3]*Ibid.*, p. 184n.
[4]See *Journals* for appropriate years.
[5]See Bourinot, *loc cit.* No penalty was provided for violation of the rule.

could be established that one of the candidatures was without their knowledge; however, the act was not to take effect until the next Parliament.[1]   Mr. Lemieux, who was elected as a Liberal for Gaspé and Maisonneuve in 1917, was still legally holding these two seats in 1921; a petition challenging his rights to Maisonneuve had been lying idle for nearly three years, and several members became restless about the situation.   During the debate which ensued the Conservatives introduced evidence to suggest that Lemieux was himself a party to the delay in settling the court case,[2] and the House spent the better part of a day in arguing about the propriety of his position.   The matter was finally referred to the Committee on Privileges and Elections, which exonerated the member; he in return assured the Committee that he would resign one of the seats as soon as the controverted election was settled.   This worthwhile goal was never reached because the election of 1921 came too soon.   Oddly enough in view of the stir made over Lemieux's position, the legislature never considered the Committee's report.

Undoubtedly it was at times most expedient for party leaders, to whom the practice was always confined, to seek two seats.   It was never a widespread phenomenon even among leaders, but it seems to have been a convention of the constitution after 1874 that the Prime Minister seek two seats, for Macdonald and Laurier both did so throughout their careers as Cabinet heads.   The usefulness of the practice is indicated by some examples.   In 1878, Macdonald was defeated in Kingston, Ontario (previously Liberal) on September 17, but elected by acclamation in Marquette, Manitoba, two days later.   He vacated this seat at once on acceptance of office, and was elected to the safe seat of Victoria, British Columbia, on October 21.   All these elections took place in the general election of 1878, since at that time polling was not held on the same day across the Dominion;[3] they provide the only instance in which one candidate has sought three seats in the same election.   In 1896, Laurier

[1]*Statutes*, 10 Geo. V, c. 18.   See *Debates*, 1919 (2nd session), pp. 241, 439 ff., 524 ff., and 1375 ff.
[2]*Ibid.*, 1921, pp. 2310 ff.
[3]See *infra*, Chapter VIII.

won his own safe seat in Quebec East, and also captured
Saskatchewan, N.W.T. from the opposition. Borden performed the same operation in 1908 by winning the safe
constituency of Carleton, and the doubtful one of Halifax.
He relinquished Carleton, thus saving two seats where his
party normally might only have had one.

Of fourteen instances of this phenomenon, twelve provided
a relatively safe seat for a party leader, and in ten of them a
seat was also captured from the Opposition. In one notable
instance, Lemieux in 1917 took Maisonneuve from a labour
group and recaptured Gaspé from the Conservatives and,
as shown above, proceeded to retain both.

Although a convenience for party leaders, dual-sitting was
not unobjectionable. It meant that normally one constituency was disfranchised for a time, for in only six of the
fourteen instances above did the member resign one seat
immediately. The country was put to the expense of an
extra by-election. Since there was no obligation on a government to hold a by-election in any case, one seat might easily
remain vacant in a party's interest for many months. This
was most probable when a party leader had taken a seat
from the Opposition, to whom it was likely to return in a
by-election between two ordinary candidates. When one
man held two seats for a time, his party lost a vote in the
House of Commons, for a member could only vote as a
member, no matter how many seats he held. (Where a
member's interest would lie when his two constituencies were
in direct conflict on an issue is an interesting question.)
The practice not only put a premium on those able to win
two constituencies, but it also placed a peculiar burden on
them. As Lemieux observed when under fire in 1921, holding
two seats is no sinecure. Unfortunately for political science,
no member will have an opportunity to test his strength in
this way again.

CHAPTER V

THE INDEPENDENCE OF PARLIAMENT

IT is an ideal of democratic government that representatives should be independent of undesirable forces that might bias their judgment on public matters. In particular they should be free of the executive, at least insofar as direct pecuniary benefit is concerned. For that reason the Imperial Parliament has for many decades jealously guarded its independence, refusing to accept members who were in a position of reliance on the Crown for any part of their income. The sole exceptions to this practice are members of the Ministry,[1] and, under certain circumstances, members of the armed forces.

In Canada, the independence of Parliament has had a relatively short history, for at various times before Confederation many public officials, including judges, sat in the assemblies beside members of the executive. Bourinot has written:

In the old legislatures of Canada judges and other public officers were allowed to sit for many years in both houses, until at last the imperial government yielded to the strong remonstrances of the great majority of the representatives in the assemblies, and expressed their readiness to assent to such legislation as might be necessary to render the legislatures independent of official influence. Several statutes were passed ... in Upper and Lower Canada, prohibiting judges from sitting in the legislative assemblies; but all attempts to prevent them from sitting in the legislative council were rendered nugatory by the opposition given in that house to all measures in that direction.[2]

The independence of the assembly was a strategic issue in the prolonged struggle for responsible government in Canada, and progress was slow indeed. In the colonies that later became Ontario and Quebec, for example, legislative councillors were disqualified from the assembly in 1791, but it

[1] A modification of this rule for special purposes was enacted during the Second World War. See *Parliamentary Debates of Great Britain* (5th series), 1940-41: debates on House of Commons Disqualification (Temporary Provisions) bill.

[2] Bourinot, *Parliamentary Procedure and Practice* (1892), pp. 170-1.

was not until 1811 (in Upper Canada) and 1837 (in Lower Canada) that judges were disqualified.[1] During the same period legislation was passed in each colony to require a member to vacate his seat on the acceptance of certain offices of emolument, although he was immediately eligible for re-election;[2] these were the first Canadian precedents for the practice which obliged Ministers to seek re-election on the acceptance of office.

Upper and Lower Canada were united in 1841 to form a single province, and in 1843 the newly constituted assembly enacted a stringent act which is of great historical interest because it contained all the principles now accepted as necessary to parliamentary independence.[3] Judges, contractors, and public officers generally were rendered ineligible for the legislature, while executive councillors were obliged to seek re-election on acceptance of office. The principles here embodied were restated in 1857 in the clearest terms possible; all persons "accepting or holding any office, commission or employment, permanent or temporary, at the nomination of the Crown, to which an annual salary, or any fee, allowance, emolument, or profit of any kind or amount whatever from the Crown," were disqualified. In New Brunswick and Nova Scotia, similar laws for the protection of the assemblies also existed before Confederation.[4]

The most effective of these several statutes was that in force in the province of Canada. So comprehensive were its terms that it is not easy to understand why the first federal Parliament thought it advisable to enact a law for the purposes of the new Dominion which involved a retreat from the ideal position which had obtained (on paper at least) before 1867. The federal Act of 1868, so far as office-holders were concerned, disqualified merely persons who held "any office, commission, or employment in the service of the

---

[1] *Upper Canada Statutes*, 7 Will. IV, c. 114: *Lower Canada Statutes*, 51 Geo. III, c. 4.

[2] *Upper Canada Statutes, ibid.*: *Lower Canada Statutes*, 4 Will. IV, c. 32. See Bourinot, *op. cit.*, pp. 170 ff.

[3] *Statutes of Canada* (Prov.) 7 Vict., c. 65: amended by 16 Vict., c. 154 and 18 Vict., c. 86.

[4] *Statutes of Canada* (Prov.) 20 Vict., c. 22; *Revised Statutes of Nova Scotia*, 1864, c. ii; *Consolidated Statutes of New Brunswick*, 1877, c. iv.

Government of Canada, at the nomination of the Crown, to which an annual salary, or any fee, allowance, or emolument, in lieu of an annual salary" was attached.[1] This, it will be noted, omitted the phrase "permanent or temporary;" even more significantly, it said nothing whatever about members working for the Crown on a weekly, monthly, or any other basis than an annual one.

The natural result was that advantage was immediately taken of these loopholes. In the year the statute was passed, a New Brunswick member began to draw in addition to his sessional indemnity the sum of $300 monthly for work in the Department of Justice, as well as an additional fee of $5500 for his arbitration of a dispute at the Crown's request: a total emolument substantially more than was received by any cabinet member.[2] The enviable situation of this member was of more concern to the Opposition than to the Government, and repeated bills to tighten up the law were introduced energetically but unsuccessfully by the Liberals. The Act was amended in 1871 by the insertion of the words "permanent or temporary."[3] But a new loophole was soon created; in 1873 a statute brought within the gift of the Crown a number of inspectorships in certain ports; so that any such inspectors who were also members of Parliament were holding offices of emolument. (These inspectors were not paid by the government but in fees from the parties whose goods were inspected.[4]) A minor ciisis arose over a Liberal member who was a flour inspector at Montreal, since the Government not unnaturally coveted either his inspectorate or his place in the Commons. The anxiety of the Conservatives to obtain at least one of these two prizes resulted in a battle of some proportions, in which any concern over the breach of the independence of Parliament was

[1]*Statutes*, 31 Vict., c. 25. Bourinot claims (1884 ed., p. 128) that the 1868 statute was a re-enactment of the 1857 one, but this is obviously an error. During the debates on the federal bill, Blake moved for the disqualification of temporary government employees also, but the motion was lost.
[2]See *Debates*, 1871, pp. 151 ff. That this violation of the principle of the independence of Parliament was not inadvertent is indicated by the fact that in 1869 and 1870 Liberal motions to prevent the payment to members of money granted in Supply were lost on party divisions. See also *Debates*, 1870, pp. 32 ff.
[3]*Statutes*, 34 Vict., c. 19.
[4]*Ibid.*, 36 Vict., c. 49.

clearly subordinate to the possibilities of exploitation for partisan purposes.[1]

Members who held offices of emolument were thus not unknown to the first Canadian Parliaments, although instances were rare. Government contractors, on the other hand, sat in the House in large numbers during the first decade after Confederation. These lapses were unmistakable violations of the Independence of Parliament Act. The act read:

> No person whosoever holding or enjoying, undertaking or executing, directly or indirectly, alone or with any other, by himself or by the interposition of any trustee or third party, any contract or agreement with Her Majesty, or with any Public Officer or Department, with respect to the public service of Canada, or under which any public money of Canada is to be paid for any service or work, shall be eligible as a Member of the House of Commons, nor shall he sit or vote in same.

Though the prohibition could hardly have been more precisely stated, so many contractors were sitting in the House after 1867 that the situation ultimately became critical. It was discovered in 1877 that the Speaker, Mr. Anglin, was the proprietor of a newspaper press which supplied post office forms to the government, and an action was started against him. The statute levied an extraordinary daily penalty of $2000 on disqualified persons who sat in the legislature, which was recoverable *by anybody who chose to sue.*[2] Either because of the ready source of income thus offered to virtuous citizens, or because there was a particularly virulent outbreak of party spirit, in no time at all several members of the House were served with writs claiming from one-half to one million dollars;[3] members and even Ministers became busily engaged in suing their honourable friends.[4] In the whole unhappy affair, the only trace of silver lining was provided by a lone member who, with a fine regard for the niceties of parliamentary etiquette,

[1]The incident, which included such dramatic episodes as an intercepted letter, is recounted in full in Tuttle's *Popular History of the Dominion of Canada,* vol. II, p. 424. A somewhat analogous case also occurred in 1873, when a member was elected at a time when he was allegedly an employee of the Intercolonial Railway. See *Parliamentary Debates* (Scrapbook Hansard), May 5, 1873.

[2]*Statutes*, 31 Vict., c. 25.

[3]*Debates*, 1877, p. 1854.

[4]*Ibid.*, p. 1809 and pp. 1851 ff.

refrained from mentioning an impending suit against Sir John A. Macdonald because of all the members in the House he alone had never been introduced to the great party leader. He had another Liberal bring up the case against Sir John.[1]

The untidy situation which existed in 1877 was unique in that the thirty or forty members who were government contractors had all violated parliamentary independence unknowingly. As one member pointed out, possibly with tongue in cheek, the Independence of Parliament Act omitted the operative phrase, "knowingly and wilfully." A relief bill was subsequently passed to save the guilty but innocent members from the statutory penalties, and at the same time several individual cases were referred to the Committee on Privileges and Elections.[2] The Committee had time to consider only the case of the Speaker, and while a clear violation of the Act on his part was established, so also were several important precedents to support the practice of which he was accused. The Speaker, arguing that he did not know he had broken the law, and in any case having ample evidence to prove how notorious were such transgressions, had additional confirmation of his position in the findings of an 1864 Committee on Privileges and Elections which had taken a very narrow view of what constituted a contract. However, the Committee of 1877 bravely declared all practice and precedent erroneous, and the Speaker, of all people, was consequently disqualified.

The Committee also recommended revision of the Act. This was accomplished in 1878 by a statute whose original clauses were considerably more sweeping than those which finally passed. The government bill at first proposed not only to tighten up the existing disqualifications, but also to extend the Act to cover pensioners of the Crown,[3] provincial government employees, and Senators who were government contractors or office-holders. The first two of these three extensions were yielded in the Commons, and the upper House struck out the clause disqualifying Senators holding

[1] *Debates,* 1877, p. 1861.
[2] The Committee's report is Appendix no. 8 of the 1877 *Journals.*
[3] The reason for this proposal was that the *Superannuation Act* of 1871 stipulated that pensioners might be called back into public service.

offices of emolument,[1] so that the final act disqualified fewer people than the Government wished.[2] In addition to the usual provisions affecting office-holders and contractors, the act disqualified those provincial officers who were concerned with federal voters' lists and other parts of the electoral machinery,[3] and permitted certain important exceptions. Thus shareholders in companies holding contracts with the government, unless for public works or the Canadian Pacific Railway, were not disqualified; although, as more than one member observed, any member could circumvent the independence of Parliament by the simple feat of incorporating himself with some other person. Militia officers and men, unless on full pay, were specifically declared eligible. Nor were persons contracting to lend money or securities ineligible except under certain circumstances; this provision had a humorous echo half a century later when a sharp-eyed Senator discovered that its terms did not protect the Upper House, so that any Senator who owned a government bond was a contractor within the meaning of the Act.[4] It is a disturbing reflection that large numbers of invaluable Senators between 1878 and 1933 should have been legally disqualified from the Upper House.

The Acts of 1877 and 1878 established the principles of the independence of Parliament with sufficient clarity that they remain substantially unchanged today. An additional point arose in 1884, however, when Sir Charles Tupper, while a member, was appointed High Commissioner in England without accepting an emolument. The Government was sufficiently uncertain of its position to introduce a special bill to allow members to work without payment; it also proposed to relieve Tupper from any real or imagined violation of the Independence of Parliament Act. Tupper, in the meantime, sat in the House on occasion but refrained from voting.[5]

[1]A similar provision had been lost in second reading in the Commons in 1871 and 1872. See *Debates*, 1872, pp. 773 ff.
[2]See *ibid.*, 1878, pp. 369, 1226, 1327, and 2038 ff.
[3]This particular provision was, again, merely a reenactment of a pre-Confederation provision. See *Statutes of Canada* (Prov.), 1858, c. 22, s. 2.
[4]*Senate Debates*, 1933, p. 478. The Act was promptly amended, by 23-24 Geo. V, c. 48.
[5]*The Week*, March 6, 1884.

The Liberals took up the challenge immediately. They argued variously that an appointment to an office of emolument disqualified a member whether the emolument was taken or not; that Tupper's appointment was invalid, since the High Commissioner's office carried a statutory salary which he had refused to take; that Tupper actually was being indemnified indirectly as High Commissioner, since he was neglecting his parliamentary duties yet drawing his indemnity and ministerial salary therefor; and that he was being paid directly anyway, since the accounts showed expenses of $5500 paid for him by the Government.[1] These cogent if inconsistent arguments were without avail and the Government's bill passed unscathed. Thus was established the right of members to work for the Crown without pay, and a convincing precedent for paying the expenses of members while engaged on such work.

The independence of Parliament was for years inextricably mixed with problems which arose from government policies for the disposition of Canada's natural resources. There is, for example, evidence of busy trafficking by members in such matters as timber limits during the seventies and eighties, which involved a clear violation of the spirit, if not the literal terms, of the Independence of Parliament Act.[2] The leasing of Crown lands to friends of the Government at low rates would clearly interfere with the independence of any member involved, but it was not illegal. "It is obvious," Alpheus Todd wrote to Sir John Macdonald in 1872, "that no public money is paid on behalf of a lease from Crown property; the reverse is the case, the lessee pays his own money in return for the use of the property. Whether or not it might be possible for a government to use corrupt influence in dealing with property of this description is not the question."[3]

----

[1]*Debates*, 1884, pp. 624-5 and 861 ff. A similar point arose in the British Parliament in 1941, when it was discovered that a member accepting a High Commissionership to a Dominion was ineligible for the Commons, although an ambassador to a foreign country was not. A special Act was passed to circumvent this anomalous situation. See *Parliamentary Debates of Great Britain* (5th series), vol. 369, 1940-41, pp. 655 ff., 795 ff., and 853 ff.

[2]*Debates*, 1886, pp. 1574 ff.; 1890, pp. 1714 ff., pp. 2050 ff.

[3]A. Todd to Macdonald, September 18, 1872 (Macdonald Papers, vol. 55).

It was Todd's opinion that the leasing of land from the Crown did not disqualify a man for Parliament, and members were not slow to take advantage of this authoritative interpretation of the law. In 1882, to cite a conspicuous example, one Rykert, M.P., was accused of using his influence to obtain a valuable timber limit for a friend, for which his wife received $70,000. Though questionable, Rykert's behaviour was not proved illegal. Nevertheless the Committee on Privileges and Elections found his conduct "discreditable, corrupt and scandalous," and Rykert, even before the Committee had reported its conclusions to the legislature, resigned his seat in profound indignation. In 1886, according to calculations by one legislator, 3,550 square miles of timber land were granted to members and ex-members.[1] Another weakness of the law was revealed in 1892, when Sir. A. P. Caron, as a shareholder in several companies dealing with the Government, was accused of using his position to get special favours for the businesses in which he was interested, and had to submit to an exhaustive examination of his affairs by a Royal Commission.[2] Nevertheless, whatever Caron did or did not do, he did not violate the Independence of Parliament Act, for he was protected by the clause relating to shareholders. In a broader sense, however, such members of Parliament could scarcely be regarded as independent.

The truth is that the Canadian statutes have not been drastic enough to accomplish their avowed purpose. Apart from the frequent violation of the law, members have been permitted voluntarily or otherwise to put themselves (or to be put) in a position of dependence on the executive. "My chances of re-election," one member, who wanted some government buildings erected in his riding, told a Prime Minister, "depend upon this grant to a great extent." If Berlin were to obtain certain public buildings while Galt did not, wrote another, there is "no chance of myself or any other Conservative getting elected in South Waterloo."[3]

[1]*Debates*, 1890, p. 1766. See also *Sessional Papers*, 1882, no. 30; 1883, no. 118; 1885, no. 52: Macdonald Papers, vol. 67.
[2]The report of the Commission is No. 27 of the 1893 *Sessional Papers*. See also debates for 1892 and 1893, *passim*, and *supra*, pp. 71-2.
[3]H. Kranz to Macdonald, March 17, 1882; (?) to Macdonald, March 25, 1882 (Macdonald Papers, vol. 226).

Such appeals to the Cabinet are sympathetically received and often heeded. Add to these importunities the scores of applications for personal preferment found in the private papers of party leaders like Macdonald and Laurier, and it will be understood why the mere anticipation of some favour from the Government could destroy a member's independence perhaps to a greater extent than the actual holding of a contract or lucrative position. An appreciation of this situation was shown in 1895 by a member who sought to disqualify any of his colleagues who received *promises* of offices of emolument.[1]   He failed.

The disqualification of contractors and office-holders by the Independence of Parliament Act has thus been only a partial protection to the House of Commons.   Moreover, the incomplete safeguard thus afforded has declined in importance as the incorporated company has replaced the partnership and the family firm as the fundamental unit of organization in the national economy.   The implications of this first emerged in the House of Commons during the war of 1914-18 when it became clear, as R. B. Bennett observed, that "there are in this House, and have been ever since 1867, many men who are directors of companies having contracts with the Government."[2]   Because of the brisk trade in war contracts, many of which were let without tenders being sought, a member moved a sweeping resolution to disqualify any director:

During the time he is a director of or holds, either directly or indirectly, a controlling interest in any incorporated company having a contract or agreement, expressed or implied, or any unsatisfied claim arising therefrom, with or for or against the Government of Canada on behalf of the Crown, or with or for or against any of the officers of the Government of Canada, for which any public money of Canada is to be paid.[3]

Though an admirable ideal, this proposal had the serious disadvantage that it would have taken a heavy toll of the Parliament then in session.   It would also have disqualified for the future leading representatives of some of the major

[1]*Debates*, 1895, pp. 2257 ff.   See the *Canadian Monthly*, October, 1873, for a report of a member who was allegedly induced to resign his seat by the offer of a Senatorship.
[2]*Debates*, 1915, p. 2140.
[3]*Loc. cit.*

groups which habitually comprise the bulk of the Commons' personnel. "The question would be," declared the Prime Minister, "whether or not it is desirable in the public interest that all persons of that type and possessing that interest . . . should be excluded from representing the people in this house."[1] The House thought not, and rejected the proposal. No change has been made in the law since then, so that while Government purchases from incorporated companies have increased at an accelerating rate in the past few decades, directors and even controlling shareholders of such companies have continued to be eligible to sit as members of Parliament.[2]

The conspicuous exception to all the disqualifications of the Independence of Parliament Act so far as offices of emolument are concerned is the Ministry, which has been so exempted since there has been a responsible Ministry.[3] Until 1931 there existed a single requirement: the Minister had to be elected while holding his office. On three major occasions in Canadian politics this particular aspect of cabinet government has been called into question, and each of them involved a situation ambiguous enough to be termed "unconstitutional" by the opposition.

The first of these, the celebrated "double-shuffle" of the Macdonald Ministry in 1858, turned on a provision of the Independence Act which contained a large loophole: namely, members of the Executive Council were allowed to resign a portfolio and accept another within a month without having to seek re-election. This ordinarily inoffensive section led to a shrewd manœuvre by Sir John A. Macdonald in 1858, when he took advantage of it to avoid by-elections following the resignation, replacement, and quick re-establishment of his administration, within the month allowed by law. By taking different posts from those held before the resignation,

---

[1]*Ibid.*, p. 2143.

[2]Over thirty members in the twentieth Parliament listed themselves as directors of companies in the *Canadian Parliamentary Guide*. Recent changes in the Act have included such routine amendments as the clarification of the position of soldier-M.P.'s. (*Debates*, 1941, pp. 3207 ff.; 1943, pp. 162-3; 1944, p. 4773; 1945 (2nd session), pp. 131-2.) The former Independence of Parliament Act is now a section of the Senate and House of Commons Act. (*R.S. Can.*, 1927, c. 147.)

[3]Other exceptions, which have never been challenged, include the Speaker of the House, and the Leader of the Opposition.

and then reverting to their original offices the following day, the ministers kept within the law yet accepted offices of emolument under conditions at variance with the intention of the Independence of Parliament Act. Opposition motions denouncing the trick as unconstitutional naturally fell by the wayside, for, apart from the partisan aspect of the case, Macdonald's position was entirely legal and was subsequently sustained by the courts.[1] The ambiguity in the Act of which Macdonald took advantage in 1858 was not clarified until 1878.[2]

The second occasion on which the position of the Ministry was called in question occurred immediately after Confederation. The first Dominion Cabinet was formed before the first general election, and its members went to the country holding their various portfolios.[3] As soon as the election was over, however, the position of the Cabinet was in some doubt, for there was no enactment which authorized the Ministers to sit in the new Parliament while holding their offices of emolument. Although provincial electoral law was to apply in national affairs until Parliament provided otherwise, none of the colonial statutes which protected the local assemblies could apply to the federal Cabinet, as the portfolios were newly created and of course not specifically mentioned in existing laws.

The dangers of this unforeseen exigency appear to have been realized first by Alpheus Todd. Todd wrote to Macdonald in confidence in November, 1867, to point out the uncertainty of his Cabinet's status and adjure him to maintain a total silence about it; already, Todd added, he had reason to believe that an opposition member had grasped the secret.[4] Todd's suspicions were confirmed a week later when Edward Blake rose in the House to challenge the

[1]See *Journals of Legislative Assembly of Canada,* (*Prov.*) 1858, pp. 842, 935, 946-7, 972, 973-6, 1001; Bourinot, *op. cit.* p. 177n.

[2]See *Debates,* 1878, p. 1227; *Statutes,* 41 Vict., c. 5, section 1(b) 3, declares that a member cannot accept a new office within one month if there has been a change of administration in the meantime. In 1926 Mr. King, perhaps forgetful of this 1878 Act, was prepared for a manœuvre not unlike a "shuffle," in that he was ready to resume office after having once resigned as Prime Minister. See *Debates,* 1926, p. 5253.

[3]This was in accord with section 11 of the B.N.A. Act.

[4]A. Todd to Macdonald, November 18 and 19, 1867 (Macdonald Papers, vol. 55).

Cabinet,[1] singling out Sir George Cartier as a test case. Blake's argument was a straightforward one: Cartier's office was one of profit, although Parliament had as yet attached no emolument to it; therefore it disqualified him for Parliament because his particular portfolio was not specifically excepted from the operation of the provincial Independence of Parliament Acts. Blake moved for a Select Committee to examine the problem, but after considerable discussion was sufficiently convinced by Conservative arguments to withdraw his motion.

To clear up all doubts, a specific act of indemnity was passed which set forth in a single sentence (albeit one over two pages long) the reasons for the act,[2] and established the eligibility of the first executive to sit in Parliament; while the Independence of Parliament Act of the same year provided for future Cabinets. Strictly speaking, as the preamble of the clarifying law itself suggests, Blake's point was well taken, and the statutory remedy was necessary. Since the statute involved the disbursement of public funds, and since such a proposal could emanate only from the Cabinet, there was an excellent opportunity for somebody to question the legality of an expenditure requested by a Cabinet whose members were not clearly eligible to sit in the legislature at all. Unfortunately nobody raised the point.

The Meighen Ministry of 1926 provided the final instance of a Cabinet whose position resurrected the question of offices of emolument. It must be recorded at once that the most careful scholar of the 1926 crisis, Dr. Forsey, has declared unequivocally that Mr. Meighen's colleagues, who were unpaid, did not accept offices of emolument.[3] There was at the time at least sufficient doubt in the minds of members to facilitate the defeat of the Ministry and to make a recapitulation of the relevant facts important here.

On June 28, 1926, Mr. Mackenzie King resigned the Prime Ministership of Canada (for reasons irrelevant to this study)

[1]*Parliamentary Debates* (Scrapbook Hansard), November 27, 1867.
[2]*Statutes*, 31 Vict., c. 26.
[3]E. A. Forsey, *The Royal Power of Dissolution of Parliament in the British Commonwealth* (Toronto, 1943), Chapters v and vi. This book gives a most painstaking analysis of the 1926 crisis.

and the Governor-General sent for Mr. Meighen, leader of the Conservatives, to form a government. Mr. Meighen's majority in the House of Commons was so slim that the formation of a Cabinet in the ordinary way would have imperilled his position, since at that time the Ministers would have had to vacate their seats at once and seek re-election. Mr. Meighen then sought to avoid the dangers thrust upon him by the Independence of Parliament Act by the establishment of "a temporary Ministry . . . of seven members, who would be sworn in without portfolio, and . . . would have responsibility as acting Ministers of the several departments."[1] The question at once arose whether Mr. Meighen's stratagem was legal and constitutional.

The argument that the Meighen Ministers had accepted offices of emolument[2] was presented by the Liberal Opposition in a variety of forms (some of them mutually exclusive) but only one developed by Mr. Lapointe seems worthy of attention.[3] Mr. Lapointe based his case on parts of several statutes, the first of which were the usual acts which provided for the payment of Ministers and their election to the Commons after acceptance of offices of emolument. The former Liberal Minister then went on to quote the Interpretation Act in a persuasive attempt to establish that acting Ministers were, for the purpose under consideration, in exactly the same position as Ministers—i.e., of having accepted offices of emolument which therefore rendered them ineligible to sit in the Commons without re-election while holding the offices. That they had accepted no emolument, Mr. Lapointe proceeded, did not free them from the effects of the statutes, for the 1884 law which governed the acceptance by a member of an office of emolument without emolument required that the commission or other instrument of appointment "declared or provided that he shall hold such office, commission, or employment without any salary, fees, wages, allowances, emolument or other profit of any kind, attached thereto." Since the orders-in-council appointing the various

[1]*Debates*, 1926, pp. 5097-8.
[2]In which case, as Dr. Forsey points out, much of the rest of the Liberal case against the Meighen Cabinet was invalid, since it was based on a contrary assumption.
[3]See *Debates*, 1926, pp. 5237 ff.

acting Ministers did not mention that they were unpaid, they were subject to the law as stated.

As a narrow technical argument, Mr. Lapointe's case might have had merit had not the Conservatives had an overwhelming defence.[1] In the first place, it was certainly a good point for purposes of debate that the term *"acting Minister"* was a sufficient declaration to comply with the law requiring a statement that no emolument accompanied the office, for the word "acting" usually implied that no pay accompanied the temporary assumption of a portfolio. Secondly, the Ministry had a tremendous weight of precedent behind it to show that acting Ministers had for decades been appointed without any mention of emolument in the appointing instruments, and their position had never been challenged.[2] It was clearly established that so far as acting Ministers were concerned custom had long overlaid the 1884 statute, whether or not acting Ministers were technically the possessors of offices of emolument. It can therefore be concluded that while Mr. Meighen's acting Ministers, on a literal reading of statutes, *may* have accepted offices of emolument and not sought re-election (a point that could be settled finally only by the courts, to which the Liberals did not take the issue) their constitutional position was clear enough in that they did not, for any practical purpose, do so. Such small comfort as may accrue to Mr. Meighen and his colleagues on this score is undeniably theirs. It is perhaps too late to point out that, if instead of becoming acting Ministers in the ordinary way, they had accepted positions as full Ministers without emolument, appointed by *orders-in-council so stating*, the legality of their position could never have been questioned.[3]

One of the contributory causes of the 1926 crisis was removed in 1931 when the law which required Ministers to

---

[1]Dr. Forsey thinks so poorly of the Lapointe argument that he does not bother to dispose of it.

[2]The 1926 situation was unique in that *all* the acting Ministers were Ministers without portfolio, whereas ordinarily acting Ministers are Ministers with portfolio. Many precedents for the appointment as acting Ministers of Ministers without portfolio nevertheless exist. See Forsey, *op. cit.*, pp. 219 ff.

[3]Forsey, *op. cit.*, p. 225.

seek re-election on appointment was repealed.[1] The proposal began as a private member's bill, and was accepted by the Government after it had survived second reading; it passed finally with Conservative and some Liberal support.[2] Liberal leaders opposed the bill, basing their argument in part on the obvious usefulness of by-elections for the testing of the popularity of government policy. For this purpose they proposed that new Ministers should be relieved of the necessity of re-election only for a period of nine months after a general election; any appointments made more than nine months after an election would still have to be endorsed by the electorate as in the past.[3] An amendment to establish this limitation was lost.

Ministers of the Crown are thus absolute exceptions to the general rule that an office of emolument disqualifies for the House of Commons; in a less secure manner, parliamentary assistants are similarly privileged.[4] The independence of private members of Parliament, on paper at least, seems admirably protected by a general prohibition on offices of emolument and government contracts. But in fact, as this chapter shows, the law has been circumvented in the past in a variety of ways, some of them beyond the reach of statutory enactment. The destruction of a member's independence by the mere hope of obtaining some favour from the executive can hardly be prevented by law. The ban on government contractors can be so easily evaded by a simple act of incorporation that it is of limited use. It is clear that in the final analysis the independence of Parliament cannot depend on law, but is based on the integrity of members.

[1]*Statutes*, 21-22 Geo. V., c. 52.
[2]Mr. S. W. Jacobs introduced the bill, as he had done several times before without success. See *Debates*, 1931, pp. 1407 ff. and 4082 ff.
[3]This had been the law in Great Britain from 1919 to 1926.
[4]Ministers are exempted by a general clause in the Dominion Elections Act (repeated in the Senate and House of Commons Act), while parliamentary assistants are provided for annually by money granted "notwithstanding...anything contained in the Senate and House of Commons Act respecting the independence of parliament."

CHAPTER VI

THE PAYMENT OF MEMBERS

THE payment of members of Parliament is closely related to representation in the House of Commons, for the presence or absence of adequate remuneration will naturally affect the attraction which public life has for individuals belonging to various groups in the community. The absolute size of the indemnity offered, its relative size as compared with the payment given members of provincial assemblies, and the ease or difficulty with which the indemnity can be earned, are all factors which bear on representation in the federal legislature.

Before this aspect of the problem can be discussed, it is necessary to establish the factual basis of the sessional indemnity. Three of the colonies which became provinces in 1867 had had some previous experience in the paying of their legislative members. New Brunswick in 1786, Upper Canada in 1793, and Lower Canada in 1831 enacted statutes which paid members a per diem "wage" for attendance at sittings of the House.[1] In all three of these colonies the intention was merely to indemnify members for time taken up by assembly affairs. That a member should be paid a salary large enough to live on apparently occurred to nobody; his living was his own affair. The Upper Canada provisions were particularly interesting in that they put the onus of paying members on the various constituencies, each district being required to submit to a special assessment for the purpose.[2] This was a revival of the old English practice for indemnifying members established in pre-Elizabethan days,[3] and the colonial statute began with a preamble referring specifically to the expediency of reviving the ancient custom.

[1]See C. R. Tuttle, *Popular History of the Dominion of Canada*, vol. I (Montreal, 1877), pp. 371, 386, and 463, for references to the payment of members of an assembly before Confederation.
[2]*Upper Canada Statutes*, 33 Geo. III, c. 3; 43 Geo. III, c. 11.
[3]See A. Todd, *The Practices and Privileges of the two Houses of Parliament* (Toronto, 1840), p. 91. One of the last English members of Parliament so paid was Andrew Marvell, who died in 1678. Some of Marvell's contemporaries had to sue boroughs for their pay.

This statute was amended at various times before the union of the two Canadas in 1840, and in 1841 the assembly of United Canada voted itself a stipend which by 1859 had taken on the essential characteristics of the system later adopted for federal purposes: a flat sum payable when the session exceeded a certain minimum ($600 for a thirty-day session); deductions for non-attendance; and a milage allowance for travelling. All charges were to be made on the Consolidated Revenue Fund.[1] The first session of the first Parliament of Canada enacted an indemnity bill almost identical with the pre-Confederation law of United Canada,[2] and at no time since then have Canadian members of either the Commons or Senate been unremunerated.

The payment of legislative members in the Canadian colonies was contrary both to British practice and to influential British opinion. The Colonial Secretary described as "derogatory to the dignity of the House"[3] the New Brunswick statute of 1786, for example, and further opposition came from the provincial Legislative Council. In Great Britain, the payment of members was a goal sought unsuccessfully in working class struggles of the middle nineteenth century.[4] John Stuart Mill discussed the topic in his essay on representative government, and opposed the whole notion for the same reasons that he opposed expenditures for election purposes by candidates. "The business of a member of Parliament," he wrote, assuming that the member was to be paid, "would therefore become an occupation in itself, carried on, like other professions, with a view chiefly to its pecuniary returns, and under the demoralizing influences of an occupation essentially precarious." A good but impecunious candidate, he suggested, could be supported by public subscription or by his constituents; or, if payment of members was genuinely necessary as in some of the colonies, it should be merely an indemnity, not a salary. That his notions had widespread support is indicated by the rejection

[1] *Statutes of Canada (Prov.)* 4 & 5 Vict., c. 55.
[2] *Statutes*, 31 Vict., c. 3.
[3] Quoted in Tuttle, *op. cit.*, vol. I, p. 463.
[4] See M. Beer, *A History of British Socialism*, 2 vols. (London, 1919).

by the British House of Commons in 1870 of an indemnity proposal by a vote of 211 to 224.

The theory that members should be paid merely an indemnity to compensate them for time spent in Ottawa was completely accepted in Canada. The statute of 1867 gave members $600 for a session exceeding 30 days, and in 1873 the indemnity was raised to $1000;[1] these sums were not poor pay for a few weeks in Ottawa, but were hardly enough to live on without additional sources of income. With occasional minor amendments which did not alter the total remuneration the indemnity remained until 1901 as it was established in 1873.

Several significant developments occurred before the turn of the century which worked substantial changes in the nature of the indemnity. Parliament voted itself an additional $500 in 1885 and 1891, thus establishing the precedent that in special circumstances (in these two cases a prolonged session) the indemnity was flexible. Beginning in 1892, annual amendments were passed which prevented deductions from a member's indemnity for absenteeism until he had been away for a period which varied from six to fifteen days; this further relaxed the moderate "penalties" for non-attendance.[2] In addition to these statutory changes, certain conventions grew up around the indemnity, all of them tending to loosen the restrictions surrounding it. A debate in the House in 1889 revealed clearly that it was tacitly accepted on both sides that when a prorogation was near members could leave two days early and be paid as if they were present up to the last. The same practice involved a peculiar use of "pairing"; in 1897 the Speaker, not for the first time,

---

[1]On both these occasions, Liberal leaders opposed the indemnity bill, not because they objected to the payment of members, but because they favoured a straight *per diem* allowance instead of a flat sum payable for a session lasting beyond a fixed minimum, e.g., *Parliamentary Debates* (Scrapbook Hansard), November 19, 1867; May 8, 1873. From the beginning, the indemnity has been a sessional remuneration so that two sessions in one year mean two indemnities for members. There is on record one case of a member who received two indemnities in a single session: he was unseated and re-elected during the session, but served a sufficient time before and after his unseating to qualify for two indemnities. The Auditor-General ruled that he must be treated as two members. (Mackenzie Bowell Correspondence, vol. 3.)

[2]See *infra*.

found himself considerably embarassed because he had authorized the payment of paired members leaving early but no other.[1] George Foster then observed in a revealing comment, "I think it would be well for this House to come to the conclusion at once to obey the law."[2]

The fact that such a statement could be made unchallenged indicates that a fairly tolerant view was taken of the indemnity provisions. No matter how poor a member's attendance, it was genuinely difficult for him not to draw all or most of his allowance. In 1902, to take a random example from the Auditor-General's annual reports, the House was in session for ninety-two days, and actually sitting for only sixty-five of them; for purposes of the indemnity the days when the House stood adjourned were counted as days of attendance. A member was allowed by law fifteen days' absence before any deductions for non-attendance were made, at the rate of $8.00 daily, with the startling result that Sir Charles H. Tupper was able to be away for thirty-six days beyond the fifteen-day limit (i.e., a total of fifty-one days of a session that included only sixty-five sitting days) and still draw over $1200 of his $1500 indemnity as well as $557.20 in milage allowance. Since the milage allowance was well above actual travelling expenses, he was on the whole better remunerated than any Ontario and Quebec members who attended the whole session and received their total indemnity.[3] Obviously a scheme that allowed a member to draw almost a full indemnity while he was absent from over three-quarters of the sittings was one that cried out for criticism.

The members of both the Commons and the Senate have, however, always shown an understandable diffidence in discussing and repairing the indemnity law, and amendments in 1901 and 1905 made few fundamental changes. In 1901 the maximum indemnity was raised to $1500, and in 1905 a further increase to $2500 was accepted by the legislators.[4]

[1]*Debates*, 1897, p. 5159 and pp. 1710 ff. "Pairing" is a convenient device whereby two members of opposing parties agree not to vote in a division for a specified time; absence of one or both members from the legislature will thus not affect the relative voting strength of the parties.
[2]*Loc. cit.*
[3]See *Report of Auditor-General*, 1901-2, section O, pp. 11 ff.
[4]*Statutes*, 1 Edw. VII, c. 14; 4-5 Edw. VII, c. 43.

Between these alterations, an indirect grant to members was made in 1903 when they were accorded free transportation on the nation's railways yet permitted to retain their milage allowance for travelling.[1]   This change merely legalized a practice about which complaints had been heard for years from independent newspapers and even members of Parliament.[2]   Since successive governments after 1867 had extensive dealings with railways and railway promoters, the granting of passes to members by interested companies had been a form of undue influence—or, to use a more modern term, a matter of good public relations policy.   The abolition of the practice came, somewhat inappropriately, well after the period of greatest need had passed.

The milage allowance to members was revoked in 1905, a step which could hardly be regarded as unreasonable since they were in any case receiving their actual travelling expenses.   Yet this change worked particular hardship on the western and eastern members, who had come to regard the milage allowance as a form of compensation for their prolonged absences from home and private business, as compared with their Ontario and Quebec colleagues who were as frequently to be found at home as in Ottawa.[3]   Some slight recognition of this fact was offered in 1906, when all members living more than 400 miles from Ottawa were granted, instead of expenses, an optional daily travelling allowance of $15.00. In recent years, as sessions have lengthened, the practice has arisen of paying members' travelling expenses to their homes and back for prolonged adjournments as at Christmas and Easter.   On occasion, apparently as a concession to members who lived too far from Ottawa to get home for the adjournment, these extra travelling expenses have been paid to members even if they remained in Ottawa.[4]

All these changes did little to amend the fundamental weaknesses of the indemnity law.   The House of Commons

[1]*Debates*, 1906, p. 1794;   *Senate Debates*, 1901, p. 534.
[2]E.g., *The Week*, May 8, 1891, and May 10, 1895.
[3]See, for example, *Debates*, 1906, p. 1787.   A member estimated that the abolition of the milage allowance cost the members, on the average, $150.
[4]E.g., *Public Accounts*, 1943-4, part II, section I, p. 7.   Each member is here granted "an amount equal *to what would have been his travelling expenses....*" (Italics mine.)

even went out of its way in 1906 to ensure that one abuse would be perpetuated, for it provided that absent members were not to be penalized for days on which the legislature did not sit. This rule seems reasonable until one realizes that it comes close to meaning that absent members were, for purposes of the indemnity, to be counted as present on days when the House stood adjourned. This amiable idiocy still exists.

The general beneficence of the indemnity provisions flourished unchecked until 1920. In addition to the fact that the House of Commons treated the words "present" and "absent" as if they were almost synonymous, a number of other interesting practices prevailed. The illness of members, for instance, has been accorded a sympathetic treatment which must have greatly cheered the patients, although hardly in such a way as to hasten their recovery. The Indemnity Act of 1867, and all subsequent amendments, contained the statement that a member ill at the place in which the session was held was entitled to his full indemnity, and that he was at the place where the session was held whenever he was within ten miles of such place—a provision which may throw some hitherto unsuspected light on the annual complaints in the legislature regarding the inaudibility of debate. Those who had the misfortune to be stricken eleven or more miles from the place, on the other hand, received no emolument under the Act.

It is hardly surprising that frequent attempts to remove this singular clause have been made,[1] but both Liberal and Conservative Governments have retained it, no doubt with an eye to keeping a few reserve troops within at least ten miles of Ottawa. At the same time, successive governments have had no difficulty in enacting annual votes to provide for members losing time because of "illness, public business, and death," notwithstanding anything in the Senate and House of Commons Act. The origin of this practice is uncertain, but in 1898 the Minister of Finance moved for such an appropriation, and then withdrew part of the proposal when opposition arose. "I placed the items in the

[1] The earliest I could find was on March 30, 1885.

Estimates with the idea that there were precedents for it and that it was the usual practice," he said. . . . "It is stated that this practice is an exception and not the rule."[1] But the practice did exist,[2] and a member speaking after the Minister referred to it as if it were not uncommon.   In any case, it was well established soon after the turn of the century, and by 1917 a member could say, unchallenged, "For a number of years the custom has grown up by which members are allowed a certain amount of leeway on account of illness. I have known of men receiving some benefit from that provision in recent years that I thought was very shady indeed. . . ." Sir Wilfrid Laurier interrupted to remark "Parliamentary illness."[3]   A further point of significance is that these special appropriations were arranged by agreement between the whips.[4]   The grants are still made annually.

Nor have members' emoluments been confined merely to sessional indemnities and sick benefits.   From time to time trips *en masse* were taken, the legislators going both West and East to observe such diversified phenomena as the first official raising of the lift-lock at Peterborough, and the last official lowering of Sir Charles Tupper at Halifax, on the occasion of his funeral.[5]   Possibly for this reason, members were for years presented with pieces of luggage as an additional perquisite.   One observer wrote:

We have gone a long way from those spacious days when at the opening of every Parliament a generous tax-paying public presented each member and each senator with a large, handsome and expensive leather trunk, the same delicate courtesy being extended to members of the Press Gallery, probably as a judicious precaution against untimely and ill-advised publicity, the taxpayer being for the most part unaware of his own liberality.   The beneficiaries were always too modest to mention it.   And at the commencement of every session the same deserving servants of the people each received a small wooden trunk stuffed to the lid with every known variety of choice stationery. . . .   Also, more often than not, there was something extra by way of good measure, a fitted leather case or a valise or, as on one occasion,

[1]*Debates*, 1898, p. 7782.
[2]The 1884 edition of Bourinot mentions the practice.
[3]*Debates*, 1917, p. 5790.
[4]*Loc. cit.*
[5]See P. Bilkey, *Persons, Papers, and Things* (Toronto, 1940), pp. 108-9, for a description of these excursions.

a particularly attractive lady's work-basket. All of which largesse was received in a becoming spirit of gratitude but was fiercely opposed and resented by non-recipients on moral grounds.[1]

All in all, the opportunities for members to draw their indemnities and other emoluments without too much wearisome attendance in Parliament have been remarkable, and there is no doubt that many have taken full advantage of these opportunities. More than once complaints have been made in the House of the delays occasioned by the prolonged week-ends of Ontario and Quebec members,[2] and it cannot be doubted that the very slight penalties for non-attendance have been a factor in this neglect of duty. It is hardly surprising that proposals for indemnity increases have never met with serious opposition. On almost all occasions when the indemnity has been raised, Opposition leaders have united with the Government in supporting the move, and the leaders have always put forth serious and sincere arguments to justify the increases.[3] It is obvious, however, that the unanimity with which private members have usually refrained from opposing the proposals is not necessarily convincing evidence that they were all motivated by the same feelings as their leaders. *Grip* remarked as long ago as 1879:

> Yes, 'tis pleasant to think as I sit in the gallery,
> They agree upon one thing, and that is their salary.[4]

Nonetheless, there are not lacking instances where private members have pointed out abuses of the indemnity system. These have been referred to in general terms in the Senate,[5] and from time to time in the House of Commons. In 1898, for example, a mild complaint was lodged against members who were "paid for the whole session, though not present."[6] Henri Bourassa recorded in 1906 a few extraordinary facts

[1]*Ibid.*, pp. 96-7. Members have not received these gifts for years.
[2]E.g., *Debates*, 1917, p. 6047; 1944, pp. 676-91. See also Norman Ward, "Best Commons Attenders Live Farthest Away," *Saturday Night*, June 14, 1949.
[3]E.g., *Debates*, 1900, pp. 9667 ff.; 1901, pp. 5600 ff.; 1906, pp. 7121 ff.; 1920, pp. 4427 ff.; 1945, pp. 3411 ff.
[4]*Grip*, February 15, 1879.
[5]See e.g., *Senate Debates*, 1901, pp. 532 ff.
[6]*Debates*, 1898, p. 7783.

taken from the Auditor-General's report to prove that a member could absent himself more frequently than he attended and still draw considerably more than half his indemnity. A member in that year could legally draw $1,240 for a single day at Ottawa.[1] As other members were quick to point out, a representative's value was not measured by his attendance at dull debates; but it hardly followed that members proved their worth by continual absences.

Members have suggested that the indemnity should be reduced or repealed altogether. Both these drastic amendments were proposed in 1868, and the gentlemanly character of the first Parliament was indicated by the fact that the resolution to stop the indemnity received 47 votes.[2] Between the two wars, a small group led by Mr. Harry Leader frequently suggested reductions as part of a general retrenchment programme, and at least two members felt so keenly on the subject that they once voluntarily returned part of their pay to the Treasury.[3] These activities roused the interest of the House of Commons, but not its support; it was not until 1932 that the indemnity was diminished 10 per cent, along with a general reduction for all federal employees. The reduction was abolished in 1937.

The first and only serious attempt to tighten up the attendance regulations was made in 1920.[4] At that time, the maximum allowance was raised to $4000 for a session of more than fifty days, and a member was entitled to the full indemnity only if he attended three-quarters of the actual sittings of the House. Otherwise he received a mere $25 daily, and the same emolument was paid for sessions lasting less than fifty days. (Oddly enough, no provision whatever was made for sessions lasting exactly fifty days, and members could not have been paid at all if such an event had occurred.) The daily penalty for absences extending beyond fifteen days was set at $25. A member was still to be counted present on adjourned days provided he was present the *day before*

[1] *Ibid.*, 1906, pp. 7125 ff.
[2] *Parliamentary Debates* (Scrapbook Hansard), April 22 and 27, 1868.
[3] Miss A. Macphail and Mr. Roch Lanctot.
[4] *Statutes*, 10-11 Geo. V, c. 69.

the adjournment began [1]—a clause which undoubtedly helped members make up their attendance quota to the three-quarters required. On the other hand, members were to be penalized for absences during the last two weeks of any session, a provision which is eloquent evidence of the abuses that must have existed in regard to attendance towards the day of prorogation.

The 1920 statute was revolutionary, and its effects most salutary.[2] Nobody could complain of its provisions but members of Parliament. The ink was barely dry on the Act before a movement began to revert to the good old days, and in 1923, a Joint Committee of both Houses produced a series of recommendations that took all the teeth out of the new indemnity law.[3] The Committee recommended:

. . . that legislation be introduced by the Government during the present session of Parliament to amend the Senate and House of Commons Act, R.S.C., 1906, chap. 10, and to provide that the sessional allowance of members of the Senate and House of Commons be paid to every member of either House who attends a session of Parliament extending over a period of fifty days or more; that a member shall not be entitled to the sessional allowance for less than fifty days' attendance but that his allowance for any less number of days shall be twenty-five dollars per day; that the said allowance may be paid on the last day of each month to the extent of twenty dollars for each days' attendance; that a deduction at the rate of twenty-five dollars per day shall be made from such sessional allowance for every day beyond fifteen on which the member does not attend the sitting of the House, if the House sits on that day; that each day during the session on which there has been no sitting of such House in consequence of its having adjourned over such day, shall be reckoned as a day of attendance at such session for the purpose of indemnity. . . .

With the single exception that the minimum session was set at sixty-five days instead of fifty, this regrettable report was accepted *in toto*. All restrictions on counting members present when they were absent were removed, so that once

[1] This meant, among other things, that a member taking a Thursday to Monday weekend was penalized more than one taking Friday to Tuesday The attendance of members has never been officially recorded; each member is on his honour to report his absences.

[2] "Under the more stringent regulations now in force the attendance has been excellent." Mr. Fowler in *Senate Debates*, 1923, p. 1252.

[3] The initiative for this committee came into the open in the Senate, where the motion was introduced by the Government leader there. Six of the ten committee members, it is worth noting, came from Ontario and Quebec.

again members were counted in attendance when the House was adjourned; and once again members were completely free to leave before the end of a session. Since sessions of the House were then lasting up to five and six months, the sixty-five day minimum was a useless provision except in years when two sessions of Parliament were held; and with adjourned days counting as days of attendance, a member would have to be unusually ingenious to fail to score fifty days' attendance and thus qualify for the full stipend.[1]

Recent changes in the payment of members have unfortunately taken no cognizance of the fantastic practices that surround the indemnity. Two important and related issues have been settled during the past decade, though in an unsatisfactory manner. Members began in 1935 to exhibit concern because their indemnity was taxed in full as if it were wages paid for work performed, which meant that expenses incurred in earning it could not be deducted.[2] This situation became serious under the pressure of wartime income taxes, and the House of Commons gravely discussed it in 1940 and again in 1944-5.[3] Prolonged evidence concerning members' expenses and the validity of regarding the indemnity as a salary (in which case members were employees of the Crown, which the Independence of Parliament Act forbids) was offered in debate.

The liability of the indemnity to taxation became an increasingly acute problem as sessions lengthened and duties increased, and the wartime debates on the payment of members proceeded, for the first time, largely on the assumption that the indemnity should be sufficient for a member to live on without additional income of his own. With all parties agreeing that an increase was desirable, the dual problem of the taxation and inadequacy of the indemnity was solved in 1945 by the evasive device of giving members an annual tax-free allowance of $2000, payable at the end

[1]A glance at the "Legislation" section of the Auditor-General's report for any year confirms this observation.
[2]*Debates*, 1935, p. 3332. Mr. Ralston here proposed a tax-free expense allowance.
[3]*Ibid.*, 1940, pp. 1820, 2400; 1944, pp. 2011 ff., 4754 ff., 4773 ff.; 1945, pp. 807-8.

of the calendar year. For Cabinet Ministers and Senators, the same allowance was granted but subject to taxation.

A modern member of Parliament thus receives two payments: a sessional indemnity of $4000, which he can draw monthly during the session at a rate of $20 *per diem*, with any unexpended balance being paid after prorogation; and an annual tax-free allowance of $2000. Together, these two payments are now roughly equal to a total *taxable* income of $7000.

The money is dispensed to members in accordance with a set of rules which are unique among large scale enterprises in Canada; this can be demonstrated by the practice followed in the 1947-8 session. Parliament met on December 5, 1947, and prorogued June 30, 1948; a period of 209 days. Since the full indemnity is payable for a session of 65 days or more, every member was thus entitled to the full amount, less any deductions for absenteeism at the rate of $25 daily from the indemnity, and $12.50 daily from the expense allowance. Because the indemnity of $4000 is payable to members at the rate of $20 daily, and adjourned days legally count as days of attendance, the indemnity ran out after 200 days, on June 21, so that Parliament appears to have sat for nine days without remuneration. Needless to say, this contributed to a natural desire for prorogation to be hastened.

Parliament actually sat, however, for just over half the total session of 209 days, as the following table shows:

Length of session 1947-8		209 days
Christmas adjournment, Dec. 20 to Jan. 26	37 days	
Easter adjournment, March 25 to April 4	11 days	
Weekends	42 days	
Total adjourned days		90 days
Parliament actually sitting		119 days

Of these 119 days, a member could be penalized for only 104 (assuming he was absent from them all), as members are allowed fifteen days' absence free of penalty.

To qualify for his full indemnity, a member must have fifty days' attendance. Since adjourned days count as days of attendance, every member in 1947-8 was credited with a minimum of 90 days' attendance, whether he was ever in Ottawa or not. The result of this provision can be demonstrated by assuming that a member did attend one single day during the session:

Length of session		209 days
Adjourned days	90	
Fifteen days before deductions made	15	
Actual days of attendance	1	106 days
Number of days for which deductions made		103 days
Total sessional indemnity		$4,000.00
Penalty for non-attendance (103 × $25.00)		2,575.00
Pay for one day's attendance		$1,425.00
Total expense allowance		$2,000.00
Penalty for non-attendance (103 × $12.50)		1,287.50
Allowance for one day's attendance		$ 712.50

The total remuneration for a single day's attendance in the 1947-8 session was thus $2,137.50, of which $712.50 was exempt from taxation. On the other hand, a member who conscientiously attended every sitting of the House received a mere $6000: for one hundred times the effort, he was paid less than three times the remuneration of the laziest member conceivable.

A private business which paid its employees on such a basis could be expected to go bankrupt; but except for a slight lapse to grace in 1920-23, Parliament has paid itself in this manner for eighty years. Furthermore, the larger the indemnity becomes, the greater is the premium on poor attendance in the Commons; and the longer and more arduous the sessions, the greater is the temptation to members to take advantage of the lax indemnity laws. So poor was the attendance among Conservative members during the long session of 1947-8, for instance, that several groups supporting the party outside of Parliament proposed at a party convention to condemn absenteeism in the legislature.[1]

This is not to be interpreted as an argument that members of Parliament are overpaid. On the contrary, as anyone who has spent much time around the House of Commons can testify, a conscientious member works long hours at affairs which are frequently less than stimulating, and the total remuneration offered is certainly not more than adequate. But because of the peculiar rules which govern the payment of members, indifferent attendance is not adequately penalized, while absence is actually paid for. The sessional indemnity is thus both too small and too large at the same time, its application to any member depending on his own integrity, industry, and no doubt the proximity of his home to Ottawa.

An inadequate indemnity for membership in the Commons may subject the country to the double risk of not attracting able men into politics, and of attracting men who need other sources of income, either from their own endeavours or from subsidization by outside interests. Subsidized members are not unknown in Canada,[2] but far more common are members who earn money from sources other than public life; naturally, members who can get home readily to further their private ends will do so, to the neglect of their parliamentary duties. A member who is obliged to do this is no more independent than one who is subsidized by an interested individual or organization.

That so many members depend on additional earned income has important implications for representation in the Commons. There are only a few professions and occupations which allow a man to be in and out of Ottawa for several months of each year,[3] so that the bare adequacy of the indemnity, coupled with the comparative insecurity of public life as a career and the fact that members receive no pensions, helps confine parliamentary life to a few occupational groups

[1]L. M. McKechnie, "Young Tories Seek Discipline Absentees Among Own M.P.'s," Toronto *Telegram*, April 20, 1948.
[2]*Debates*, 1929, p. 3599.
[3]See Chapter VII.

in the population. On the other hand, the lax regulations which surround the indemnity at least permit a wider representation in the Commons than would more rigid rules; for the number of groups in the community which could afford parliamentary membership would inevitably be diminished if members were compelled to attend every sitting of the legislature.

The peculiar system by which legislators are paid has, therefore, some points in its favour. But it is doubtful if the advantage of somewhat wider representation is not outweighed by the attendant disadvantages. Apart from the apparent extravagance of the bonuses paid for poor attendance, the indemnity laws have undoubtedly facilitated the accumulation of power in the hands of the executive in recent decades. The turnover of members from day to day is considerable, as they are continually coming and going; but the guiding hand of the executive is always present. So easy is absence for ordinary members, indeed, that it is customary to have no important divisions in the Commons on Mondays and Fridays, in order not to interfere with members' long week-ends. The possibility that the Government may threaten to settle matters of particular interest to members on those favoured days cannot fail to help secure co-operation for the executive's plans on the remaining days of the week.

The use of the indemnity system as an instrument in the Government's hands was clearly demonstrated in 1948, when the Prime Minister announced on February 20 that unless Parliament had finished its business by the end of June, the Government would adjourn the session until the autumn.[1] Since the full indemnity of $4000, at $20 daily, had been drawn by members by June 21, Parliament was thus faced with two alternatives: it could finish its business by the end of June, no matter how hurriedly; or it could hold a fall sitting without remuneration. Parliament prorogued on June 30.

Another major disadvantage of the present indemnity system is that it is very unfair to western and eastern mem-

[1]*Debates*, 1948, p. 1428.

bers. Members from Ontario and Quebec, within a relatively short distance of the capital, can maintain close connections with their homes and private businesses; for this useful circumstance, the indemnity law gives every possible opportunity.[1] Members from more distant provinces, on the other hand, cannot hope to get back and forth to their homes so quickly, and the benefits of the law therefore affect them much more casually than their more fortunate colleagues. This suggests that there is a strong argument for abolishing the flat indemnity, and replacing it with one that rewards members in accordance with the work they do and the sacrifices they must make to go to Ottawa. It has been seriously suggested in Parliament that different "zones of indemnity" should be established, to take account of the extraordinary advantages held by Ontario and Quebec members,[2] and a survey of the indemnity provision supports rather than condemns such a notion.

The mere fact that western and eastern members can take the risk of neglecting their homes and businesses to enter public life is a strong indication that there is no fundamental obstacle in the way of enforcing more rigid indemnity rules. To tighten up attendance requirements, and at the same time impose heavier penalties for absenteeism, are not utopian proposals. The events of the 1947-8 session, however, suggest that more fundamental problems are awaiting solution. The consumption of the entire indemnity of $4000 before Parliament had completed its work, which naturally contributed substantially to the haste to prorogue, indicated the necessity of amending the law to take cognizance of the fact that prolonged sessions exist. The statute as it stands was not passed in contemplation of long sessions, for it assumes that a remainder of the indemnity will have to be paid after prorogation.[3]

Since long sessions have become the rule rather than the exception, a fundamental problem to be faced is whether membership in the House of Commons is to be regarded as a part-time or a full-time occupation. If, as hitherto,

[1]See *supra*, p. 105.
[2]*Debates*, 1920, p. 4447.
[3]*R.S. Can.*, 1927, c. 147, s. 35.

politics is to be regarded as a part-time job for which members need only be indemnified for time lost from their own affairs, there is at least no reason why the law should not be amended so that they will not be paid for time they have not lost.   But if membership is to become a full-time occupation, it is high time that the sessional indemnity be frankly regarded as an annual salary for work performed.   There would then be an argument for raising the amount, preferably in such a way as to take account of the enormous advantages enjoyed by members from the central regions.   There is also an argument for altering the basis on which the indemnity is paid, so that a member would not be credited with a full day's pay for a five-minute appearance in the legislative chamber.   Finally, the payment of a recognized salary for work performed would provide a conclusive argument for ensuring that no part of the salary be paid unless it has been earned.   A Parliament which has been able to develop the remarkable contemporary rules for the payment of members should find a more reasonable indemnity system comparatively easy to devise.

CHAPTER VII

THE PERSONNEL OF PARLIAMENT*

THE measurement of representation in the House of Commons, if one attempts to give a general picture of the successful candidates, can be achieved only in impersonal statistical terms. The result is unsatisfactory on a number of counts. A member of Parliament is not merely a repository of qualifications which can be measured statistically, relating to his age, education, and experience, but a human being with aspirations, feelings, and fears. It must be admitted at the outset that these personal qualities cannot be taken into consideration here. This study must concentrate on those aspects which are possibly the least important, and it cannot be emphasized too strongly that statistics may be highly misleading as criteria by which to measure representation. This fundamental weakness in method, combined with the nature of the data, means that the inventory of members which follows must be regarded as a very incomplete picture of representation, and the "facts" given in any particular table must be interpreted with exceptional care. Nevertheless, while the statistics reveal little that is startling, the general tendencies shown are sufficiently clear to suggest that the House of Commons falls short of being truly representative of the Canadian people.

THE TURNOVER OF MEMBERS

The turnover of members, as measured by newcomers to the Commons returned both at general and by-elections, has always been high, rarely falling below 40 per cent of the total seats available. On five occasions, as is shown in Table III, it exceeded half the House. Three of these five occasions (1896, 1921, and 1935) represented a return to power of the Liberals after a term in opposition. Conserva-

*See Appendix C for a description of the material on which this chapter is based.

tive victories after a Liberal regime, oddly enough, have never been marked by any unusually large influx of new members.

TABLE III

TURNOVER OF MEMBERS IN THE CANADIAN HOUSE OF
COMMONS, BY PARLIAMENTS, EXPRESSED IN
PERCENTAGES OF THE TOTAL MEMBERSHIP

Election Year	Turn-over	Election Year	Turn-over	Election Year	Turn-over
1872	48.5	1900	47.5	1926	20.8
1874	43.2	1904	53.9	1930	35.5
1878	48.3	1908	38.4	1935	59.1
1882	47.8	1911	40.7	1940	36.8
1887	48.8	1917	52.3	1945	38.8
1891	46.5	1921	58.7		
1896	54.4	1925	44.5		

In addition to the remarkably high turnover of members, the table reveals a tendency for the entry of newcomers to the Commons in recent years to be rather slower than in earlier decades.   This trend is particularly odd in view of the rise of third parties, which inevitably bring new blood into the legislature.   While the decline in turnover will undoubtedly contribute to the efficiency of the House in some respects, it also means that the opportunities for ambitious politicians to enter federal politics are smaller than formerly.   In part at least, this decrease in opportunity reflects a parallel decline in corrupt electoral practices, for the first several Parliaments sometimes saw scores of seats vacated during a Parliament by the unseating of elected members.[1] Furthermore, the practice of bunching patronage appointments from the House in the last few months before a general election, is a modern development which obviates the need for many by-elections; in earlier days more seats

[1]See Chapter XIV.

were opened up by elevations to the Senate, Bench, and public service. Today, the deaths and resignations of members, together with the occasional deliberate vacating of a seat to make way for a new Minister or party leader, produce approximately thirty by-elections during a Parliament. The third Parliament, by comparison, saw ninety by-elections, and the seventh Parliament over seventy. This phenomenal activity in the electoral machinery increased the opportunities for new members in the past; on the other hand, members unseated for corrupt practices were frequently re-elected, for no stigma whatever seems to have been attached to such misdemeanour nor, for that matter, to actual expulsion from the House.[1]

It may be concluded, therefore, that there are fewer opportunities to enter the Commons today than formerly. When it is considered that the total population of Canada has increased several hundred per cent since 1867, while the number of seats in the House has increased barely 40 per cent and the turnover of members has declined, it will be seen that the present opportunities for any Canadian to become a member of Parliament are substantially smaller than they were during the first Parliaments. But even today it is important to note that although the variations do not follow regular patterns, opportunities vary noticeably among the provinces, assuming that the actual number of new members is a measure of opportunity. If the massive turnover of 1935 be ignored, a new member from Prince Edward Island has had since the election of 1921 one chance in every three elections of entering the House; from Nova Scotia slightly better than one in three; New Brunswick one in two; Quebec slightly less than one in three; Ontario four in ten; Manitoba, Alberta, and British Columbia better than four in ten; and Saskatchewan better than one in two. These figures ignore such relevant factors as party differences and safe seats, and must therefore not be taken as precise statements of new members' opportunities. (Thus a Conservative in Quebec or Saskatchewan has not one chance in three, or one in two, of getting elected.) It is clear,

[1]See *supra*, p. 72.

however, that disregarding party, a man's chances of getting into Parliament are not the same in all provinces.

The explanation of this may be that a federal seat, considered in relation to the nature of seats in the various provincial legislatures, has a different appeal in different provinces. The typical provincial legislature meets for a few weeks in late winter, and the members receive indemnities varying from a few hundred to several thousand dollars. It may often be more advantageous for an ambitious business or professional man to seek election to a provincial assembly, than to the full-time occupation of the House of Commons; his choice will depend to a material degree on his own interests and the nature of the provincial legislature.

Finally, it remains to be noted that the turnover of members in the House, in terms of newcomers, is no exact measure of the turnover of seats, if every time a seat is vacated and filled counts as one turnover. If a member is elected, unseated, and re-elected (this has happened to more than one reputable man in the past) he will be counted only once in Table III, whereas actually two elections for the seat have been held. And if account is taken of the way in which a single seat, in the course of one Parliament, could be held by two or three individuals, none of whom might be new members, it will be seen that, high as is the turnover of members, the turnover of seats is still higher.

AGES AT WHICH MEMBERS ENTER THE COMMONS

The ages at which members enter Parliament, shown in Table IV, can vary in three respects—among provinces, among parties, and over time—and all three of these variations are revealed by a statistical analysis of the subject.

In general, while most members have entered Parliament between the ages of 35 and 50, there has been great irregularity as among provinces (and within provinces, between parties) and there has also been a general tendency for the average entry-age to rise since around the turn of the century.

TABLE IV

Showing Ages at which New Members have Entered Each Parliament Since 1867*

Age Group	1867	1872	1874	1878	1882	1887	1891	1896	1900	1904	1908	1911	1917	1921	1925	1926	1930	1935	1940	1945
20-24	1	3				1	1		2							1				1
25-29	3	2	5	5	3	3	8	6	3	4	1	2	2		2	3	2	6	3	3
30-34	21	14	9	15	13	7	10	6	8	11	10	4	4	8	4	6	4	11	10	9
35-39	24	21	17	20	23	21	15	17	7	22	14	19	19	19	7	7	13	12	8	12
40-44	42	13	15	16	22	20	19	15	18	12	18	22	26	15	6	6	11	25	15	19
45-49	34	20	9	9	14	16	12	18	18	19	12	23	25	21	6	7	16	33	19	12
50-54	35	9	14	10	11	23	14	24	15	20	14	19	17	20	7	3	17	24	9	15
55-59	13	6	5	7	4	4	3	12	7	11	5	15	16	14	3	5	15	22	10	10
60-64	7	2	1	4	4	1	2	2	8	8	4	10	6	14	5	6	3	9	9	8
65-69	2		2	2		3		2	3	3	1		4	5	6	1	3	3	1	2
70-74				1	2		1		2					1	1			1	1	1
75-79				1																1

*Note that several of the age distributions shown in this table, instead of being normal statistical curves, are "M" shaped, as in 1872, 1904, and 1911.

Quebec and Prince Edward Island furnish the most conspicuous variations in members' ages: Quebec returns an
unusually large number of young members and fewer elderly
ones, while Prince Edward Island provides an example of
the exact opposite.

Except for Quebec, where the entry-age of members shows
a remarkable stability over time, the general tendency has
been for all the provinces to elect fewer and fewer young
men to the Commons, and more men who are over forty.
In part at least, this trend may derive from the underlying
fact that the Canadian population has undeniably aged since
1867.[1]   This does not account for the decrease in the number
of members who enter the Commons in their twenties and
thirties, and one must look elsewhere for reasons to account
for this development.   Certainly until 1930, at least, it was
becoming increasingly harder for young men to get federal
seats, either for financial reasons or because they had to
have longer periods of previous political experience.   The
statistics disprove the latter hypothesis.   One's impression
(and it must be admitted that it is nothing more than a
subjective impression) is that the earlier Parliaments contained larger numbers of "gentlemen" who could possibly
afford to enter politics at a younger age than their successors.
They held commissions in the local militia, and were probably
either closely related to active politicians or were their junior
law partners; in any case the path into federal politics was
made smooth for them in ways which do not seem to operate
now.   J. F. S. Ross gives a somewhat parallel explanation
for the large groups of young members in the Conservative

[1]A summary of trends in the age distribution of the total male population
of Canada is as follows:

	1871	1891	1911	1931*	1941*
			Per cent		
Under 20	52.7	46.9	40.8	41.7	37.6
20 to 39	27.6	30.3	35.0	29.8	31.4
40 to 59	13.8	15.5	17.2	20.1	21.0
Over 60	5.9	7.3	7.0	8.4	10.0

*Figures for 1931 and 1941 include female population, because of the ex
tension of the franchise to women after 1917. See, for example, *Census of Canada*
1931, vol. I, tables beginning p. 397.

party in Great Britain,[1] and it probably has some validity when applied to Canada.

As for the variations in entry ages between provinces, again part (although a smaller part) of the explanation appears to lie in the age composition of the various provincial populations, a point which will not be verified statistically here.[2] The variation in provincial age compositions, however, is not marked enough to account satisfactorily for the variation in the ages at which members enter Parliament, and again one must seek the answer elsewhere. The answer seems to be that the way into Parliament lies through different channels in different provinces, a point concerning which some evidence is offered below.

At no time have the groups of new members corresponded even roughly with the age composition of the total adult population. The new members (and indeed the whole House of Commons) do not represent adequately the younger age-groups; they grossly over-represent the middle age-groups; and approximately represent only the older ones.

THE PRE-PARLIAMENTARY EXPERIENCE OF MEMBERS

There are at least two measurable ways in which a Canadian member of Parliament can obtain political experience before entering the House of Commons; i.e., in municipal or county politics, and in the provincial legislatures. There are related fields of importance, such as party organization work, but information on them is not easily found. Ascertaining the facts in regard to actual holding of political positions is possible and worth-while, as it will provide information on how much practical experience new members have actually had and also to what extent local and provincial politics are helpful in a federal career.

The general picture of members' previous experience is given in Table V. It will be noted at once that the number

---

[1]J. F. S. Ross, *Parliamentary Representation* (Yale, 1944), pp. 17 ff. This impression is supported by comparing the brief biographies of members appearing in the early *Parliamentary Companion* with those in the modern *Canadian Parliamentary Guide*.

[2]See *Census of Canada*, 1931, vol. I, table 10; 1941, vol. II, p. 232.

TABLE V*

PRE-PARLIAMENTARY EXPERIENCE OF NEW MEMBERS, BY PARLIAMENTS, EXPRESSED IN PERCENTAGES

	1867	1872	1874	1878	1882	1887	1891	1896	1900	1904
Municipal politics only	17	33	39	38	44	46	37	42	45	37
M. L. A.**	58	24	25	23	25	20	22	26	21	19
Provincial Cabinet Minister	15	12	7	5	8	2	8	5	6	2
No known experience	25	43	36	39	31	34	41	32	34	44

	1908	1911	1917	1921	1925	1926	1930	1935	1940	1945
Municipal politics only	39	30	31	30	32	32	37	29	24	32
M. L. A.**	23	29	15	14	23	12	15	17	15	9
Provincial Cabinet Minister	4	6	3	7	6	4	5	5	5	4
No known experience	38	41	54	56	45	56	48	54	61	59

*Does not include the very few members whose party affiliation is not known.
**Includes provincial Cabinet Ministers.

of members who go directly from local into federal politics, although fluctuating considerably, remains fairly large. Of all the new members entering the federal House, one-third proceeded there directly from local politics, and there is no sign of a decreasing trend. It is true that since the election of 1908 the percentage of local politicians entering Parliament is generally lower than for all the preceding Parliaments; but the figure still remains high, and it appears justifiable to conclude that somewhat less than one-third of the new members entering Parliament have had only local experience.

The situation is different in regard to provincial experience. Not only is the average for all the new members lower than for those having municipal experience only, but there is unmistakable evidence of a continuing decline, which suggests that the provincial legislatures are providing fewer and fewer candidates for the federal House. This may mean merely that members of provincial legislatures are becoming increasingly satisfied with their particular advantages of short sessions and proximity to their homes and private businesses; or it may mark an increasing divergence between provincial and federal politics, based not merely on different interests but on increasingly different personnel.

It appears further, even when the statistics are interpreted with all due caution, that the number of members without any previous political experience whatever has increased substantially, and was actually lowest for the first Parliament. The first Parliament is of course an exceptional case, and its great superiority over subsequent Parliaments, from the point of view of experience, is not so great as the table seems to suggest. *All* the individuals returned in 1867 were new members, as there was no previous Commons to which they could have belonged. Only when the parliamentary experience of re-elected members is added to the previous experience of new members can subsequent Parliaments be compared with the first.

This general picture obscures a number of important points, and further analysis reveals a wide variation in the pre-parliamentary experience of new members as between provinces and parties. At one extreme is Prince Edward

Island, which has no real equivalent to county and municipal government, and the great majority of whose federal members are former provincial legislators. At the other is Ontario, less than one-fifth of whose members are former M.L.A.'s; less than one-twentieth of them have had Cabinet experience, and almost half of them have had only local experience. The Maritime Provinces generally return more than the average percentage of former M.L.A.'s and provincial Cabinet Members, with the three extreme Western provinces next in line, followed by Manitoba, Quebec and Ontario. The Conservative party in Quebec has returned a high number of former M.L.A.'s, but that is largely explained by the fact that that party's hold on Quebec was at its greatest during the days when all provinces were electing more former provincial legislators than they do now. The members of new parties appear to reach Ottawa largely innocent of previous political activity.

Previous political experience, therefore, as an assistance to membership in the federal House, seems to vary widely among provinces but has generally declined. Insofar as the provincial legislatures are concerned, in most parts of Canada the provincial capital has provided experience for no more than one-quarter of the federal members, although experience in municipal politics has been more common. Indeed, if members who have had local experience only were categorized with those who have had *both* local and legislative experience, it could probably be shown that more than half the federal members have started out in local politics, particularly in central Canada. The tendency to return former M.L.A.'s appears to be strongest in the Maritimes, somewhat less strong for the older parties in the western provinces, and weakest in Ontario and Quebec.

BIRTHPLACES OF MEMBERS

It is to be expected that parliamentary representation in a country which has not only been populated by immigrants, but has also experienced heavy internal shifts of population, will reflect these movements. But representation in Canada has sometimes lagged so far behind population changes that

TABLE VI

COMPARING REPRESENTATION IN THE HOUSE OF COMMONS, CLASSIFIED BY BIRTHPLACE, WITH
BIRTHPLACES OF POPULATION AT LARGE, FOR SELECTED PERIODS*

Percentages

Birthplace	1871		1891		1911		1931		1941	
	Parlia-ment	Popu-lation	Parlia-ment	Popu-lation	Parlia-ment	Popu-lation	Parlia-ment	Popu-lation	Parlia-ment	Popu-lation
Canada..........	66.4	83.2	84.6	86.7	92.4	78.0	87.2	77.9	85.4	82.5
British Isles......	22.6	13.8	11.6	9.7	3.8	11.2	7.0	11.0	6.3	8.3
United States......	3.3	1.8	.8	1.8	2.1	4.2	2.7	3.2	5.1	2.7
Other.............	2.4	1.2	.8	1.8	.8	6.6	1.2	7.9	2.0	6.5

*The Parliament used in each case is the one elected nearest to the census year.

it can fairly be asserted that the House of Commons has in this regard been extraordinarily insensitive.

The bare outline of this situation, given in Table VI, shows that native-born Canadians were heavily under-represented in 1871, while immigrants from the British Isles were to a much greater degree over-represented. This condition had levelled out by 1891, when there was a close connection between the composition of the House and the country; but since that time the tendency has been for native Canadians to be substantially over-represented, while immigrants from both Great Britain and the United States have been continually under-represented. The largest divergence, however, is between the percentage of immigrants born in other than these two English-speaking countries and their representation in the House. Obviously, the preference in Canadian politics is now given to native Canadians first, and other English-speaking immigrants second.

A more detailed description of the relations between members' birthplaces and the composition of Parliament is shown in Table VII. It will be observed that the western provinces, including the two which have been within Confederation almost since the beginning, were remarkably slow to return local products to Ottawa, although the trend is now clearly in the opposite direction. In the case of Alberta and Saskatchewan, the failure to return natives of the province is not surprising, since the native-born population grew very slowly; but this is not so with Manitoba and British Columbia where the number of people born in the province has since Confederation been a large proportion of the total provincial population.[1] The provinces east of Manitoba, on the other hand, have each had since the beginning a share in the House of Commons roughly proportionate to the provincial quota of seats. Until about 1890 Ontario returned many members born in the British Isles; but for the last ten Parliaments Ontario has had more than its share of natives, at one period supplying not only most of its own members but also a majority of the members for all the provinces west of it.

[1] See *Census of Canada*, 1931, vol. I, table 75.

TABLE VII

Compositions of Parliaments According to Birthplaces of Members

Birthplace	1867	1872	1874	1878	1882	1887	1891	1896	1900	1904	1908	1911	1917	1921	1925	1926	1930	1935	1940	1945
B.C.											1	1	1	2	2	2	1	1	1	4
Alberta												1	1	1	4	6	6	3	3	5
Saskatchewan														1	1	1	1	3	3	6
Manitoba	1													4	4	6	6	8	11	11
Ontario	39	42	52	52	65	76	92	79	91	105	105	106	104	105	101	106	113	111	99	83
Quebec	58	62	72	78	83	77	78	83	77	78	69	73	69	74	63	67	67	73	67	63
N.B.	10	14	14	13	20	16	19	11	12	16	15	18	16	15	12	13	13	13	10	10
Nova Scotia	17	18	22	13	20	27	24	24	23	18	15	20	20	19	17	18	18	16	16	14
P.E.I.	5	6	5	8	7	6	6	8	7	5	5	5	9	7	7	7	9	6	6	7
England	18	11	13	9	6	7	5	8	7	5	5	7	7	9	9	8	8	11	7	11
Scotland	18	23	29	20	13	17	15	14	8	7	2	2	2	5	7	7	6	11	6	8
Ireland	24	14	17	16	12	11	9	8	8	5	1	2	3	3	5	4	4	4	3	4
Wales		1	1	1	1	1							3	1	1	1				
U.S.A.	6	7	6	9	5	5	2	3	5	3	3	5	2	3	4	7	7	6	13	8
Other	6	5	2	2	2	5	2	3	7	8	2	2	2	1	2	1	3	7	5	3
Not known	19	11	13	7	2	5	8	7	8	4	2	2	9	7	2	5	5	4	3	8

The provinces east of Ontario have since 1867 been represented almost entirely by native sons. A generous sprinkling of members born in the British Isles occurred in the first few Parliaments (but almost never after 1908), and it is now a genuine rarity for a Quebec or Maritime seat to be held by an "outsider." When it does occur, as in the exceptions found for Prince Edward Island, it is often the result of a minister seeking a safe or temporary seat. Although Canada puts no constitutional limitations on where a member may sit, in actual fact this makes little difference; for all of Canada east of Manitoba an overwhelming number of members are not merely residents but natives of the province that elects them.

In summary, it can be said that across Canada the preference undoubtedly is given now to native Canadians, with the single exception of the third parties in the West, which draw an unusual proportion of their strength from immigrants. Although in the period immediately following Confederation immigrants played a disproportionately large part in Canadian politics, native Canadians have dominated the House of Commons since the turn of the century for all the provinces east of Manitoba. Immigrants have thus been consistently under-represented for the nation as a whole, and markedly so in the case of those from countries other than the United States and Great Britain. Native Canadians provide a clear majority of members for the western provinces (except for British Columbia) but they are Canadians born east of the province they represent; native Westerners have so far played a remarkably small part in federal politics. This trend is clearly declining, so that all of Canada may be expected in time to return members born in the provinces they represent. There are no signs yet that the migration of Canadians to central Canada has produced appreciable numbers of central Canadian members born east and west of Ontario and Quebec.

THE AGE COMPOSITION OF THE COMMONS

The age composition of every House of Commons since Confederation is given in Table VIII, the bottom line of which shows the median age in each instance. The most

TABLE VIII

Age Composition of Parliaments Since 1867

Ages	1867	1872	1874	1878	1882	1887	1891	1896	1900	1904	1908	1911	1917	1921	1925	1926	1930	1935	1940	1945
20-24	1	3	1	2	4	4	1		2	1						1				1
25-29	3	3	8	9	4	4	9	6	3	5	3	2	2		2	4	2	6	4	3
30-34	21	17	19	19	21	13	12	13	14	14	13	15	4	10	5	10	11	12	13	13
35-39	24	34	37	36	36	34	28	27	13	34	28	28	26	22	16	22	20	16	15	23
40-44	42	31	38	38	45	45	45	25	34	27	39	43	37	41	32	34	30	38	29	29
45-49	34	44	29	29	44	45	45	41	44	41	37	32	42	46	41	38	36	52	51	35
50-54	35	27	36	41	34	42	43	50	32	50	38	44	42	41	49	55	48	40	43	50
55-59	13	22	24	26	27	21	29	38	38	32	27	36	38	37	36	26	53	40	39	30
60-64	7	6	8	12	14	17	11	17	25	24	21	23	20	25	30	35	25	29	34	24
65-69	2	2	2	3	5	11	12	4	12	13	15	7	16	14	19	18	17	13	16	21
70-74		1	1	1	3	6	6	6	5	2	3	8	4	6	3	4	10	6	5	10
75-79							2	1	2	1	1	1	2		1	1		4	1	3
80-84																	1			
Median Age*	44.9	45.8	44.9	45.7	46.2	47.6	48.9	50.2	50.3	49.9	49.0	49.9	50.7	50.2	52.1	51.4	52.9	50.5	51.5	51.7

*Because of the nature of the data, and the nature of the median, it must be emphasized that the figures in this row are merely indicators. They are not arithmetical averages.

striking fact revealed is the general tendency for the median age to increase, apparently in irregular cycles. From 1867 to 1900 there is a steady rise from roughly 45 to 50, followed by a slight drop and then a further rise to nearly 51 in 1917, another slight drop and a rise to nearly 53 in 1930. Since that time the median has declined and begun to increase again. The result is that present federal legislatures are about five years older than the first ones, the greatest increase having occurred before 1900. Since that time, the median seems to have settled around the 51 mark, although it may still be tending to rise, since the last six elections have included the five oldest Parliaments in the sequence. This trend is quite independent of party turnovers. The victories of 1896, 1911, 1921, and 1930, in which parties formerly in opposition were returned, did not upset it, and the only possible exception is the election of 1935.

The number of young members (under 35) reached its lowest point in the years from 1917 to 1925. The first five legislatures contained an average of twenty-six members under 35 and thirteen over 60; the last five have averaged sixteen young members, and fifty-five elderly ones. Even apart from these variations at the two extremes, however, there have also been changes within the 35-60 group, which has always provided the great majority of members. As the table shows, there has been a general tendency for the age-groups above 45 to increase at the expense of those below it.

These age variations do not affect all the provinces and parties similarly. The Liberal party in Prince Edward Island and the Conservative in New Brunswick, for example, have aged over fifteen years, while the Liberal party in Quebec has aged barely four years, and the Conservative in Ontario just six. In general, age increases have been least in central Canada, and greatest in the Maritimes, British Columbia, and Manitoba; although it is to be noted that, with one or two minor exceptions, all parties and provinces have experienced the increases in some degree. There are no consistently marked differences between the two major parties in the several provinces, and it is impossible to say that the Liberals are younger than the Conservatives, or vice versa.

As among the provinces, however, it may be said that the youngest members come from Quebec and the various third parties, while the oldest groups are now usually from the Maritimes. While the members of the various third parties do not *enter* Parliament at ages appreciably lower than the new Liberals and Conservatives, the latter two are, with few exceptions, distinctly older as parliamentary groups, perhaps because they are older parties.

Unquestionably, the House of Commons has aged, and there are no signs that the process has yet reached its peak. It is true that the number of young members seems to have become stable since roughly 1926, but a fair proportion of these belong to the new third parties, and if these third parties go through the same cycle of development as the Liberals and Conservatives, their tendency to return comparatively young members may be expected to decline and their returns of older members increase. Again, all parties to some degree exploited the political advantages of nominating returned servicemen in the 1945 election and the effects of this, in terms of members' ages, may be expected to wear off in a few years. Finally, it must be emphasized that there are appreciable differences in the ages of members returned from the various sections of Canada. Here again, as in most of the aspects of representation being examined, there is evidence to suggest that the main differences in the groups of members returned at each election are not between parties, but regions.

THE OCCUPATIONS AND ECONOMIC INTERESTS OF MEMBERS

The general composition of each House of Commons, classified according to all the known interests of members (i.e. a member with three interests will be counted three times), is shown in Table IX. At first glance, Parliament seems to have changed remarkably little since 1867, for the same groups tend to dominate throughout the table. Closer inspection, however, reveals that the relative position of most of these major groups has changed considerably; the one conspicuous exception is law, which usually accounts for

TABLE IX

The Composition of Each Parliament Classified According to the Main Economic and Occupational Interests of Members

	1867	1872	1874	1878	1882	1887	1891	1896	1900	1904	1908	1911	1917	1921	1925	1926	1930	1935	1940	1945
Accountants	—	—	—	—	2	2	1	1	1	—	1	1	2	1	2	3	2	2	1	2
Agriculture	10	13	20	25	35	39	39	46	40	40	31	35	46	83	54	59	49	50	48	51
Clergy	—	—	—	—	—	—	—	1	1	—	—	—	1	6	1	3	3	4	6	6
Druggists	—	—	—	—	—	—	—	1	3	2	2	2	2	1	6	3	4	1	1	1
Engineering	7	3	4	3	2	3	—	1	1	1	1	1	—	1	1	1	2	4	5	6
Finance and Insurance	34	41	43	30	39	35	31	23	21	17	19	35	30	21	30	32	22	25	20	17
Labour	—	—	—	—	—	—	—	1	1	3	2	1	1	1	1	2	5	9	7	4
Law	66	71	76	72	83	77	85	74	76	89	86	93	83	80	67	73	81	87	82	81
Manufacturing	15	17	26	24	24	28	30	35	38	47	45	45	44	27	36	33	33	33	26	22
Medicine and Dentistry	14	16	17	20	23	27	22	23	20	22	23	17	22	21	31	31	36	20	18	8
Merchants	39	48	57	44	53	50	54	45	57	45	46	40	32	34	36	35	30	29	27	24
Mining	1	3	4	4	7	7	5	6	4	4	3	3	2	6	6	8	5	4	6	5
Public Service	10	9	9	9	6	6	2	3	2	4	7	5	5	5	4	6	5	8	4	5
Publishing and Journalism	15	18	18	20	19	18	16	21	17	19	14	13	17	15	11	11	13	10	8	10
Real Estate	—	—	—	—	—	—	2	—	—	2	1	3	3	3	3	3	4	3	2	1
Service Industries	7	5	8	11	12	17	9	6	4	4	8	9	12	9	9	6	6	9	6	6
Teaching	5	6	5	2	6	7	8	9	9	7	5	6	5	8	8	8	8	14	14	17
Transportation	31	34	34	32	35	35	28	18	7	9	9	10	5	4	2	12	2	2	2	—
Other	1	1	—	—	—	2	4	4	4	3	3	3	7	1	2	1	1	8	6	9
Not known	27	15	17	20	10	4	10	10	9	5	4	4	6	4	1	5	5	12	10	16

approximately one-third of the total membership of the House. There are two important interests, agriculture and teaching, which reveal an increase in representation over time. The agricultural interest, in fact, shows a greater increase than any other and is now second only to law; on one occasion (1921) it even surpassed law as the largest single group.[1] Teaching also started out a very minor group. Its relative position is now greatly improved, partly because of the decline of some other major groups, and its absolute representation has more than doubled since 1867. The table does not reveal a further important fact: the teachers who sat in the early Parliaments were generally professors of law from central Canada, whereas the teachers now in the House of Commons are more often from primary and secondary schools in the West.

The rest of the major groups in the table—finance and insurance, manufacturing, merchandising, publishing and journalism, and transportation—now have substantially less representation in Parliament than formerly. The most spectacular decline is that of transportation, which has dwindled from a leading position to almost nothing, with the greatest decline occurring before 1900.[2] Manufacturers in the House were greatest numerically between 1900 and 1917, while merchants were at their peak between 1874 and 1900.

Various groups such as labour, clergy, real estate dealers, etc., which had no representation whatever in the first few Parliaments, are now finding occasional seats, some of them in increasing numbers. In addition, the slow and fluctuating increase of representation in the "other" column of the table seems to show a very slight tendency for parliamentary representation to become increasingly diverse as Canada's technological society increases in complexity. Yet there has been a decline of such groups as finance and insurance,

[1] It must be understood that the word "group" in this connection refers only to the rough classification in the tables. It is not meant to imply, for example, that the representatives of agriculture in the House form a "bloc" that is recognizable as the "agricultural group." On the contrary, an agriculturist from the prairies and one from Ontario may have conflicting interests.

[2] The term "transportation" is used in a wide sense. In early days, many members were directors of small railway lines, and the decline in transportation in the Commons reflects, to a large degree, the integration of railways in Canada into two great companies.

manufacturing, and merchants, while the actual importance of these interests in the Canadian economy has unquestionably increased. It follows that the Commons has become seriously unrepresentative of some major interests, but that these same interests, by using other means than direct representation, may be (and in many cases undoubtedly are) influencing the general course of government through techniques beyond the reach of the legislature.[1]

These various trends in representation are apparently quite independent of party turnovers. At first sight, party turnovers do appear to be accompanied by occasional changes in trends of representation (agriculture in 1896 and 1921, for example) but it would be impossible to prove that such variations resulted from the change of government. The Liberal period from 1896 to 1911 seems to include a noticeably smaller representation from finance and insurance than the Conservative reigns that preceded and followed it, but the representation of this group increased again during the period of the Liberal government in the twenties. On the whole, the weight of evidence indicates that these trends in representation are substantially independent of changes of government. The provincial distribution of party support is important, and this is considered below.

At no time has the House of Commons come even close to reflecting in fair proportion all the various occupations and interests of the population at large. Lawyers are obviously grossly over-represented, while what might be called the "working classes" are even more grossly under-represented, since, as pointed out above, the general economic interests listed in the table refer to the managerial and proprietary aspects of the businesses concerned. By way of emphasizing how unequal is the representation of occupations and interests in the House, Table X compares the legislature elected in 1930 with the number of gainfully occupied citizens in major categories in the total population as shown in the 1931 census.[2]

---

[1]See, for example, S. D. Clark, *The Canadian Manufacturers' Association*, pp. 34 ff.

[2]The 1931 rather than the 1941 census is used in order to avoid any disturbances in the "normal" occupational structure that might have resulted from the war. It should be emphasized that the comparison shown in Table X is not completely valid, since the census definitions of occupations and interests are much more rigid than those used here. Table X, like Table IX, is merely a guide, and nothing more.

TABLE X

COMPARING CERTAIN ASPECTS OF OCCUPATIONAL REPRESENTATION IN THE
SEVENTEENTH PARLIAMENT WITH THE POPULATION AT LARGE IN 1931

	Percentage of Seats in Parliament Held by Various Groups	Percentage of Gainfully* Occupied in Similar Categories
Agriculture.................	20.0	28.8
Finance and Insurance......	9.0	.2
Labour.....................	2.4	21.5
Law.......................	33.1	.2
Manufacturing.............	13.5	.7
Medicine and Dentistry.....	14.7	.4
Merchants.................	12.2	2.9
Mining....................	2.4	.03
Public Service.............	2.4	.3
Publishing and Journalism...	5.3	.2
Teaching..................	6.5	2.2
Transportation............	.8	.07

*The figures in this column are not exactly as they appear in the 1931 census.
In a number of places, to make the census figures more comparable with those
for Parliament, the census figures have been re-grouped.

Consideration of the various trends in representation since
1867 indicates that great anomalies have always existed,
with the same two large groups—agriculture and labour—
being least adequately represented throughout. This is not
to be misunderstood as an argument that the occupational
structure in Parliament *should* be the same as in the total
population; it is merely a statement of fact that Parliament
is, and has always been, recruited from particular groups in
the country to the detriment of other groups. Theoretically,
there is of course no reason why a lawyer could not adequately
represent an agricultural or labour constituency.

Further analysis of the occupational statistics reveals
once more that provincial differences in members of Parliament are greater than party differences. Occasional variations of importance between Liberals and Conservatives
occurred in the first few decades after 1867, but in no single
province has there been a serious and continuing difference

of occupational structure between the major groups composing each party in the legislature. Within the limits set by admittedly weak data, it is a justifiable conclusion that similarities between the two major parties' representation far outweigh differences in all the provinces except British Columbia, where it is impossible to find any kind of pattern whatever. Turning to differences between the provinces, however, it is not difficult to show some clear variations. Quebec, for instance, has relied heavily on lawyers, and Prince Edward Island on merchants. Merchants are generally of greater importance in the provinces east of Ontario than in Ontario itself and the West. In Ontario, merchants were among the top three groups up to 1925, but have since disappeared from the dominant groups. In the western provinces, agriculture seems to have played approximately the same role as merchants in the east. While law maintains its dominant position almost all across Canada, there is, therefore, a regional differentiation reflected in the relative importance of the other groups. As might be expected, manufacturing interests are of relatively greater importance to Ontario than to any other province. The bulk of Alberta's agricultural representation in recent years, it should be noted, has come from third parties rather than from the Liberals and Conservatives.

Even when allowances for the limitations of the data are made, it is clear that even in the predominantly agricultural provinces the representation of law and the other professions is disproportionately large, which means that the representation of other important interests is disproportionately small. The groups most favoured, furthermore—the professions, industry, commerce—are characteristically urban in their interests and connections, rather than rural. The new third parties, it is true, tend to give greater representation to occupations and interests that find a smaller place in the older parties, but, apart from the agricultural interest, the third parties are very often just as unrepresentative as the Liberals and Conservatives; they merely return in unduly large proportion different groups such as clergymen and teachers.

THE PARLIAMENTARY EXPERIENCE OF MEMBERS

A general analysis of the parliamentary experience of members in the House of Commons raises two important questions: what is the composition of each legislature in terms of members' experience; and how long does the "average" member, as an individual, remain in Parliament? The answers in both cases are a little disturbing, for they show that most members of Parliament, far from being legislators who enact laws with the competence born of experience, are mere transients.

The high turnover of new members already described has not unnaturally been associated with a short tenure for the great majority of those elected to the Commons. In most Parliaments, as Table XI shows, approximately three-quarters of the members have had either no previous experience in the Commons whatever, or but a single term of four or five years. At the opposite end of the scale, no Parliament has ever met with over one-fifth of the members having had ten years, or more previous experience. In general terms, each Parliament meets with roughly the following composition:

No previous experience	35 to 55 per cent
One to five years' experience	20 to 35 per cent
Five to ten years' experience	10 to 20 per cent
Over ten years' experience	8 to 10 per cent

There is in the statistics no convincing evidence that the passage of time tends to increase the number of experienced members in the House of Commons. The first seven Parliaments, a period of almost unbroken Conservative rule, give indications of a drift towards increasing percentages of more experienced members, but this probably indicates nothing more than that it took some time to build up a reservoir of experienced members between 1867 and 1896. No other period of prolonged rule by one party gives really conclusive proof of a tendency for the "experience-composition" of Parliament to spread out towards the veteran groups of members, and in the absence of convincing evidence it is unwise to seek confirmation of such a trend, however reasonable may be the supposition that it exists. It is true, how-

TABLE XI

The Composition of Parliaments Classified According to the Years of Members' Service at the End of Each Parliament, in Percentages

Parliament:

Years	2	3	4	5	6	7	8	9	10
0- 5	55.7	42.3	45.0	41.8	42.7	38.1	48.7	46.4	49.9
6-10	44.3	38.4	33.2	27.4	25.8	26.5	20.3	27.5	23.7
11-15		19.3	21.8	17.9	16.4	16.0	11.8	13.9	14.2
Over 15				12.9	15.1	19.4	19.2	12.2	12.2

Parliament:

Years	11	12	13	14	15	16	17	18	19
0- 5	43.8	8.8	49.5	57.0	75.0	52.1	34.0	54.0	35.6
6-10	28.8	52.0	19.2	23.1	12.5	29.4	37.1	17.7	37.5
11-15	19.9	21.6	16.2	5.0	4.1	11.0	18.8	14.3	12.7
Over 15	7.5	17.6	15.1	14.9	8.4	7.5	10.1	14.0	14.2

ever, that in some prolonged periods of single-party rule, as from 1896 to 1917, and 1921 to 1945 (making allowance for the Conservative victory of 1930) there appears to be a tendency for the groups of members with between five and fifteen years' experience to increase.

The number who spend only one or two terms in Ottawa nevertheless remains a clear majority of all elected members. Undoubtedly this must simplify the management of a party in the House by its leaders. Since one of the qualifications for leadership is long service in the party interest, the inexperience and general ignorance of House affairs of so many members must greatly facilitate their acquiescence in the leadership of their seniors. This is not to say that new members are always amenable to the discipline of the parliamentary caucus, for the contrary is often true. But the techniques of managing the party group both in the caucus and in Parliament can be learned only by experience, so that the comparatively few experienced members have a great tactical advantage over their more transient colleagues.

Finally, on the subject of members' experience, it is interesting that when the Liberals have been returned to power after a period of Conservative rule (8th, 14th and 18th Parliaments) there has been a marked increase of inexperienced members in the House; but when the Conservatives have taken over from the Liberals (12th and 17th Parliaments) there has been no such change. The obvious explanation for this is that the Conservatives have relied more than the Liberals on experienced members; they have used more often the members they had available. This conclusion must be treated with caution, however, for it takes no account of the several variables that must be considered in relation to the composition of the party groups in the Commons. In 1896, for example, both parties seemed to be replacing their veteran members and there was a heavy turnover of *both* Liberals and Conservatives, which accounts for the increase of inexperienced members in Parliament. In 1911, on the other hand, both parties had a much smaller turnover of members, and in 1930 the Ontario Conservatives and the Quebec Liberals—two of the largest groups in the

House—both returned many more experienced members than novices. As a result, although the total for the whole House on both occasions seems to suggest that the Conservative victories depended on the return of experienced Conservatives, the Liberals also returned many veterans.

The regional aspect of Parliamentary experience, shown in Table XII, is of great importance, for there are marked differences between the various provinces and parties. In general, the largest proportions of experienced representation come from the regions where the parties are themselves largest and most firmly established for long periods. Thus the Conservatives in Ontario and the Liberals in Quebec produce the largest numbers of veteran members, and the Liberals in British Columbia and the Conservatives in Saskatchewan the smallest, while the other provinces and parties vary between these two extremes. Both the older parties, taken together, show more experienced representation from central and eastern Canada than from the West, although where one of them has been firmly established in the West, as have the Conservatives in British Columbia and the Liberals in the three prairie provinces, the proportion of veteran representation compares favourably with that in eastern Canada. Obviously there is adequate justification for the statement that the number of experienced members a party produces in a particular province varies directly with the strength with which it has established itself.

This being so, a satisfactory explanation is provided for the absence, noted above, of any convincing evidence of a trend towards increasing proportions of veteran members when one party remains in power for several consecutive Parliaments. The statistics showing the Parliamentary experience for the total House of Commons obscure the various tendencies in the provinces. Since it is possible for a party to win an election on the strength of its returns from a few provinces, and be defeated in the remainder, it is hardly surprising that figures for the legislature as a whole show no conclusive proof of a trend in the House to improve itself in regard to experience merely because one party is in power. This very fact suggests the interesting hypothesis

TABLE XII

The Composition of Parliaments from 1872 to 1944, by Provinces and Parties, Classified According to the Years of Members' Service at the End of Each Parliament*

Years	B.C. L	C	Other	Alta. L	C	Other	Sask. L	C	Other	Manitoba L	C	Other	Ontario L	C	Other
0- 5	65.8	45.8	66.7	52.4	65.4	59.7	52.7	78.2	80.0	51.8	50.0	72.4	47.3	40.5	79.2
6-10	26.0	31.8	16.7	27.5	19.2	28.4	29.8	17.4	14.3	28.3	34.2	17.2	29.4	30.5	14.7
11-15	8.2	15.0	16.6	17.5	7.7	10.3	12.3	4.4	5.7	14.1	13.2	3.5	13.2	14.3	3.1
Over 15		7.4		2.6	7.7	1.6	5.2			5.8	2.6	6.9	10.1	14.7	3.0

Years	Quebec L	C	N.B. L	C	N.S. L	C	P.E.I. L	C
0- 5	40.5	42.1	41.5	48.3	42.0	51.2	48.3	55.6
6-10	26.5	30.4	27.5	30.6	30.4	33.2	28.4	30.5
11-15	16.4	17.2	19.0	16.7	15.4	8.4	15.0	5.6
Over 15	16.6	10.3	12.0	4.4	12.2	7.2	8.3	8.3

*The term "other" here means parties other than Liberals and Conservatives. It does not include independents.

that no matter how long one party remained in power, the House of Commons could not be expected to become a very experienced body unless the party's strength was great in all the provinces. The regional nature of representation, that is, combined with the fact that one party's strength can now vary ten ways in the country as a whole so far as its provincial bases are concerned, accentuates the high turnover of members. Furthermore, the areas where the party's strength remains most nearly constant (the Conservatives in Ontario, say, or the Liberals in Quebec) are thus in a position to continue returning the same members, with the result that certain parts of Canada habitually return most of the senior members of the House.

This conclusion is confirmed by a more detailed analysis. During the first eight Parliaments the great majority of the members who lasted for four or more Parliaments, and virtually all of those who had five or more terms, came from Ontario and Quebec. For the next five Parliaments, larger proportions of western and Maritime veterans appear, and this trend is further marked in the period 1921-40. But for most of the western and eastern parties, a single member may represent as much as 10 or 15 per cent of the total group, so that the absolute numbers of western and Maritime veteran members have not become large even though they have increased proportionately. Between 1921 and 1940, for example, Prince Edward Island Liberals showed that 12.5 per cent of their total membership had spent five Parliaments in the House, whereas the Ontario Conservatives had 11.1 per cent of their number in the same classification. In absolute numbers, the Island figure represents a single person, whereas the smaller Ontario figure represents nine. While the West and East of Canada are sharing in the trend towards longer parliamentary careers, therefore, the great majority of the senior members come from Ontario and Quebec; this, no doubt, adds more weight to the influence of central Canada in national party councils of both the Liberals and Conservatives. In the Quebec Liberal party since 1921, the proportion of senior members is, in fact, so great as to indicate that not only do the majority of all senior members come from central Canada, but a disproportionately large group of them are Quebec Liberals; this cannot help but influence the policies of the Liberal party. At the opposite extreme stands the Conservative party in Saskatchewan and Alberta, which has rarely had a member go beyond his second term, with the result that the voices of western Conservatives in the caucus, with occasional exceptions, have almost certainly been both stiller and smaller than those of robust veterans from other provinces.

The overwhelming weight of advantage, insofar as seniority is concerned, undoubtedly lies with central Canada. But the turnover of members there is nevertheless high even where one party is firmly established. While much of this may be accounted for by patronage appointments, the figures suggest that an abundance of safe seats for a party does not necessarily mean that the seats are safe for particular persons. The opportunities for a man to make a career out of membership in the House of Commons are consequently very limited in most parts of Canada.

THE POST-PARLIAMENTARY CAREERS OF MEMBERS

The fate of members after they have left the House of Commons has a direct and powerful bearing on the nature of representation in the House, in that it sheds light on the security or insecurity of a political career, and consequently will affect the attraction which politics will have for various types of people. There are at least four ways in which a parliamentary career may be ended, and a member has a degree of choice as to which he will take. He may accept some federal patronage, as a seat on the Bench, a Senatorship, a Lieutenant-Governorship, or a post in the public service; he may go into or return to provincial politics; he may retire, voluntarily or after a defeat; or he may die while still a member. The statistics for some of these matters can be obtained readily from official sources, and can consequently be computed accurately; for the others, the nature of the data makes accuracy impossible.

The general composition of each legislature from 1867 to 1930, classified according to the careers of members after departing, is given in Table XIII. This table does nothing

TABLE XIII

Composition of Each Parliament According to Careers of Members after Leaving House of Commons

	1867	1872	1874	1878	1882	1887	1891	1896	1900	1904	1908	1911	1917	1921	1925	1926	1950
Patronage:																	
Bench.........	20	19	20	19	24	20	25	26	25	31	24	20	18	20	10	14	11
Senate.........	30	30	35	33	32	34	35	38	36	37	40	48	39	35	27	30	25
Lieut.-Gov....	16	19	15	17	14	14	15	9	7	6	5	4	1	3	2	2	2
Public service...	25	17	27	29	27	24	31	28	24	27	24	24	12	13	12	13	12
Provincial politics.	18	25	17	8	11	8	10	13	11	15	14	16	17	12	9	14	10
Died while M.P...	33	25	25	35	37	40	32	37	41	36	27	34	36	42	35	38	32
Apparently retired	95	96	123	108	107	110	119	110	107	104	97	102	130	126	138	131	136
Still sitting.......	—	—	—	—	—	—	—	—	—	—	1	—	2	9	11	17	28

more than indicate what proportion of the House's membership in each case ended up in each of the several categories given. There is a very small amount of overlapping in the table, in that when the same member held more than one patronage post (as happened occasionally) both or all are counted in the table.

TABLE XIV

SHOWING IN PERCENTAGES THE POST-PARLIAMENTARY CAREERS OF MEMBERS WHO LEFT THE HOUSE OF COMMONS DURING THE PERIODS SHOWN

	Parliaments 1-7 incl.	Parliaments 8-11 incl.	Parliaments 12-17 incl.
Patronage:			
Bench	8.9	10.4	5.9
Senate	8.4	9.6	11.9
Lieut.-Gov.	4.4	3.5	1.0
Public service	10.2	9.4	5.1
Provincial politics	7.2	5.4	6.2
Died while M.P.	9.3	10.8	10.3
Defeated and retired	22.3	24.7	30.7
Retired undefeated	26.3	25.2	28.7
Retired after election voided	3.0	.9	.2

It will be observed that Lieutenant-Governorships have obviously declined drastically in favour as patronage for federal members, the Bench and the public service have declined since 1911, and the number of members who retired has consequently increased proportionately. On the other hand, the number of members who became Senators or went into provincial politics has remained fairly constant, and the same is true of those who died while still members. These points are corroborated by Table XIV, which shows in percentages what happened to members whose House careers ended within each of three given periods: 1867-96; 1896-1911; 1911-35. This table, treating the members as individuals, shows clearly the decline in Lieutenant-Governorships, the more recent declines in the number of members reaching the Bench and public service, and the relative constancy in the proportion who die or return or go into provincial politics. It also reveals, however, that the percentage of those who become Senators is increasing substantially, while there is a much greater increase in the number of members who retire after a defeat than in those who retire undefeated. At least part of this trend may be accounted for because there are still living a group of Conservatives who are waiting their turn at the patronage appointments.

Despite the increase in the proportion of members who retire without obtaining patronage or returning to provincial politics, there remains a large group, comprising about 30 per cent of the total, which does receive federal patronage appointments.[1] Regardless of party, a member thus has a better than one chance in four of spending his latter days in some snug berth. His chances appear to be slowly declining, but they still remain substantial. Assuming that at least a majority of those who retire undefeated do so voluntarily, and that at least some of those who retire after a defeat are able to provide for themselves in some way, it can be argued that the number of members who are not the beneficiaries of patronage or who do not go into the provincial field (or die while members) and yet are unable to provide for themselves after retirement from politics, is certainly a minority of the total. The exact size of the group is indeterminable, but the evidence is fairly strong that politics in Canada is by no means as precarious an occupation as it is often assumed to be. Even if the statistics are complete, it is still true that, until very recently, only a small number of private businesses were in a position to provide excellent pensions for 30 per cent of their employees.

The most significant point which arises from more detailed analyses of the statistics is concerned with regions rather than parties, for the various kinds of patronage assume varying degrees of importance in the different provinces. There is a marked tendency for the two central provinces, but particu-

[1]This statement is made on the basis of excluding from the calculation the 10 per cent who die while members.

larly Ontario, to have comparatively fewer federal members receiving any of the various types of patronage. This means that the smaller groups of members from the western and eastern provinces have better chances of getting federal prizes than their central Canadian colleagues. Since the ratio of available patronage to the number of federal members is greater for the smaller provinces than the larger, this is hardly surprising. The importance for the present purpose is that the peculiar favouritism given to western and eastern members in regard to patronage, if it affects representation at all, cannot help but increase the unrepresentative nature of the House of Commons. When one considers that *all* patronage distributed to members, however small, comes from a government situated in central Canada and dominated by central Canadian interests, the temptation to western and eastern members to be "co-operative" with the central interests for purposes of obtaining whatever favours may be available must sometimes be strong. Certainly it cannot be dismissed as an irrelevant factor in the under-representation of some parts of Canada in the federal legislature. In addition, the greater availability of patronage to western and eastern members accentuates the turnover of representatives from these regions in the House, and hence must lessen their influence both there and in the caucus.

A final point of interest in regard to the subsequent careers of ex-members concerns the relationship between their length of service and the ultimate reward received. The figures for 1911-1935, a period selected as illustrative, are shown in Table XV, which reveals that the correlation between length of service and reward is not nearly so great as might be expected. It is true that there is a marked tendency for the proportion of members who retire alive but unrewarded to decrease with length of service (and for the death rate to rise with length of service), but a high percentage, and frequently a majority, of those who receive prizes do so after only one or two terms in Parliament. This is more true of some patronage appointments than others. An overwhelming majority of those who go from Ottawa into provincial politics do so after relatively short terms, and a member's chances of

TABLE XV

The Post-Parliamentary Careers of Members who Left the House of Commons Between 1911 and 1935, Inclusive, Expressed as Percentages of the Total Number of Members Whose Careers Ended as Indicated

Service	Bench	Senate	Lt. Gov.	Public Service	Prov. Pol.	Died M.P.	Defeated and Retired	Retired Undefeated
1 term.........	33.3	22.7	50.0	20.6	58.0	16.2	47.7	45.5
2 terms.........	30.7	14.7	—	14.7	11.6	28.0	25.0	18.2
3 terms.........	15.4	24.0	33.3	23.6	21.0	17.7	16.2	19.8
4 terms.........	10.2	20.0	16.7	14.7	9.4	25.0	8.8	6.4
5 terms.........	7.7	4.0	—	20.6	—	2.9	1.2	5.3
6 plus.........	2.7	14.6	—	5.8	—	10.2	1.1	4.8
	100	100	100	100	100	100	100	100

being forced to retire by defeat decline appreciably with his length of service. At the same time, there is no precise relation apparent between length of service and post-Parliamentary activities; there are frequent occasions when considerations of Parliamentary experience and party service appear to give way to special local or party circumstances, depending on tactics and expediency. The notion that patronage is a reward for prolonged and arduous labour is consequently subject to substantial qualification.

PART IV

ELECTIONS

CHAPTER VIII

NOMINATING AND VOTING PROCEDURE

FEW topics of legislation have received so much attention in Canada as the various devices and procedures which Canadian Parliamentarians have provided for their own election. As a tool for winning battles and for distributing petty patronage throughout the entire Dominion, the electoral machinery has been a continual temptation to the unscrupulous to seek party advantage by tinkering with it. It is, in addition, one subject in which every member of the House of Commons not only has an immediate interest, but is also to some degree an expert. Until a Chief Electoral Officer took charge in 1920, the result was exactly what might be expected: an endless tampering with the system, both as a whole and in details; prolonged, angry, and occasionally stirring debates, with charges and countercharges being bandied back and forth across the floor; and a continuous stream of ingenious ideas from private members, ranging from a ballot which contained candidates' pictures (as well as names) to a voting machine in which the elector recorded his considered decision by solemnly rolling a pea down a chute.

A detailed consideration of all the real and proposed changes in the electoral system since 1867 would result in a book of impressive proportions and aridity. It is not difficult, however, to select a few strategic aspects of the machinery and outline the main trends of development therein; while the description which follows is admittedly incomplete, it is a fair enough indication of the workings of Canada's democratic machinery to illustrate the chief problems which have had to be solved. The following have been selected as the most important topics to be considered: (a) the nominating procedure, (b) the voting procedure, (c) the choosing of election officials, (d) the compiling of voters' lists, and (e) the general election. Subsequent chapters deal with the franchise, controverted elections, and election expenses. All of these topics were conditioned at the beginning by sections 41 and

42 of the British North America Act, which prescribed that existing provincial electoral machinery was to be used until Parliament provided otherwise, but empowered the Governor-in-Council to appoint the returning officers for the first general election of 1867.[1]

THE NOMINATING PROCEDURE

The nominating process was open and straightforward in all four provinces in 1867. New Brunswick required no nomination whatever, for a sheriff was merely required to take "the names of all the candidates who shall offer, or be handed in by one or more freeholders of the County."[2] In Nova Scotia, any two electors could propose a candidate to the sheriff at the proper time and in the appropriate place,[3] which was the County Court House in both Maritime provinces. Ontario and Quebec offered a somewhat more picturesque display. In the words of one unusually eloquent statute:

Every returning officer shall, at the time and place by him fixed as aforesaid for opening the Election, proceed to the Hustings (which shall be held in the open air, at such place as that all the Electors may have free access thereto,) and shall make, or cause to be made . . . in the presence of the Electors there assembled at the Hustings, a Proclamation . . . and shall then require the Electors there present to name the person or persons whom they wish to choose at the said Election. . . .

The proclamation made was no less impressive: "O yez. O yez. O yez. All persons are commanded and strictly enjoined to keep silence while Her Majesty's Writ for the present Election is publicly read, under the pains and penalties in such case provided." At this cordial invitation the loyal electors then proceeded to choose their men, and not infrequently to riot. So bad was the situation in Kamouraska in 1867 that no election could be held; two nominations survived the bloodshed, but the returning officer had to make a special election return which held the seat open.[4]

[1]See Appendix A.
[2]*Statutes of New Brunswick*, 18 Vict., c. 37, s. 19.
[3]*Revised Statutes of Nova Scotia*, 1864, Appendix, p. 760.
[4]See *Canadian Parliamentary Companion*, 1872, p. 281. A graphic account of the affair in Kamouraska is given in the report of a House Committee which investigated it. (*Journals*, 1867-8, Appendix No. 1.) The seat was finally filled in 1869. Another reference to a violent election is given in *ibid.*, 1876, Appendix No. 6.

It must not be thought that abuses of this open system were confined to the electorates. The Prime Minister found it necessary to engage in public and violent altercation with an opponent during the election of 1872,[1] and a number of minor luminaries such as the returning officers distinguished themselves in less strenuous ways. The Liberals spoke intolerantly of a presiding officer who was able to hear the Conservative nomination but was deaf to Liberal shouts, with the subsequent return by acclamation of the Conservative; part of their complaint arose because the officer allowed hired bullies to surround the hustings so that the Liberals could not get near enough to nominate.[2] Further dissatisfaction was expressed over a New Glasgow returning officer who held the place of nomination in the woods at an immense distance from the centre of the district without bothering to inform the opposition.[3]

The Conservatives nevertheless thought highly of open nomination, which made Liberal resistance to it more or less obligatory. At the first opportunity, the Liberals substituted for it nomination by a petition containing twenty-five signatures, thus depriving the electorate of one of its most exciting social events.[4] At the same time, candidates for the Commons were required to make a deposit of $50. The purpose of this was to discourage frivolous candidatures, which were not uncommon in early years: ingenious souls sometimes set themselves up as candidates in the hope that more serious aspirants for Parliamentary honours would buy them off; and returning officers on occasion procured extra candidates at elections for the sole purpose of increasing their own fees.[5] The deposit of $50 was not refundable even to the winner, and was consequently a direct tax on candidature; this was an adaptation of a Nova Scotian statute which in effect required candidates to bear the expenses of holding an election.

[1]See Tuttle, *Popular History of the Dominion of Canada*, vol. 2, p. 356.
[2]*Debates*, 1885, p. 2188.
[3]*Loc. cit.*
[4]*Statutes*, 37 Vict., c. 9, s. 18. Even this method was not entirely foolproof. In 1900, the returning officer at Nipissing hid on nomination day so that no regular nominations could be held; he held an irregular nomination later. See *Debates*, 1901, pp. 1053-4.
[5]*Parliamentary Debates* (Scrapbook Hansard), April 21, 1874; *ibid.*, 1870, p. 543.

The Conservative opposition of 1874 had no particular objection on principle to the deposit, but they did assert, with some Liberals agreeing, that the sum demanded was too small to serve its purpose and that the deposit should be returnable at least to the victor.[1]   In 1882, when the Conservatives were in power, the deposit was increased to $200, but it was to be refunded to the successful candidate and all others whose vote exceeded half the winner's.[2]   At this point it has remained. Members have occasionally complained of the deposit as an unnecessary irritant and its abolition was moved in 1909-10 and again in 1910-11,[3] while a representative of the Trades and Labor Congress argued the same point before a Special Committee of the House of Commons in 1929.[4]   The C.C.F. party is on record as favouring its abolition.   It has not been an issue in recent years, and the latest committees on elections in the Commons have not discussed it.

Only once has the deposit been of particular significance in an election.   The returning officer in West Durham in 1900 accepted a cheque for a deposit and then, after the candidate concerned had won the election, decided that he was not qualified since a strict interpretation of the law required the payment of the deposit in cash.   On this technicality the loser of the election was returned as the sitting member.[5]

The only major alteration that has been made in the nominating procedure for decades occurred in 1920, when the number of signatures required for a nominating petition was reduced from twenty-five to ten with no great shock to the body politic.   This change seems to have given rise to a singular use of the nominating petition.   "The practice has been," the Chief Electoral Officer told a Special Committee in 1937, "to get a large number of these nomination papers and to circulate them throughout the electoral district, and bring them all to the returning officer.   Sometimes there have been as many as 200, and the returning officer does not know

[1] See *Debates*, 1878, p. 2118; 1880, p. 227, for suggestions to this effect.
[2] *Statutes*, 45 Vict., c. 3, s. 8.   During the debate, Liberal leaders admitted they had never favoured the deposit much.   See *Debates*, 1882, pp. 264 and 1467.
[3] E.g. *Ibid.*, 1909-10, pp. 1268 ff.
[4] *Report of Special Committee on Dominion Elections Act*, etc., 1929, pp. 44 ff.
[5] *Debates*, 1901, pp. 1053-4.

what to do with them." A member explained that the reason for this was that "in the local papers throughout the riding 150 names appear on one nomination paper . . . and are published, and another candidate has a miserable dozen.   It has an effect."   Discussion in the Committee made clear that most of the members approved of this practice, and the Committee rejected out of hand a suggestion that candidates be allowed to be nominated only once.[1]

Official nomination with a signed petition is not necessary to constitute a person a candidate.   By statutory definition every one becomes a candidate who is declared by himself (or others, with his consent) to be a candidate when there is a vacancy in the electoral district.[2]   Such a candidate is not entitled to have his name on the ballot unless he is formally nominated by petition and his deposit paid; nevertheless, he is legally responsible for violations of the laws concerning election expenses and corrupt practices.

THE VOTING PROCEDURE

The ballot as it is now known did not exist in Canada in 1867 except for certain local elections in Quebec.[3]   Open voting, by a simple declaration made in the presence of the appropriate officer, was the practice in three of the federating colonies.   New Brunswick alone had secret voting, and had had it since 1855;[4] but it was a curious form of ballot in which the voter merely wrote the name of his choice on a piece of white paper—any piece, and before coming to the poll if he chose— and handed it to the presiding officer.   This official had to satisfy himself that it was a single vote without reading it, and he then deposited it in the box.[5]   Under the terms of the B.N.A. Act, the first federal election was thus held openly in Nova Scotia, Ontario, and Quebec, but secretly in New Brunswick.

[1]*Report of Special Committee on Elections and Franchise Acts*, 1937, pp. 47-9. Official blanks for nomination are supplied to candidates, each being entitled to five copies.   Multiple nominations are still legal, but are discouraged in the *Election Instructions issued by the Chief Electoral Officer.*

[2]*Statutes*, 2 Geo. VI, c. 46, as amended by 11-12 Geo. VI, c. 46, s. 2 (3).

[3]*Debates*, 1870, p. 369.   A member here refers to the ballot being used as early as 1845.

[4]*Statutes of New Brunswick*, 18 Vict., c. 37, s. 27.

[5]*Ibid.*, s. 35.

The Conservatives were prepared to tolerate this situation indefinitely. The Liberals, for reasons that are not hard to discern, favoured the secret ballot, and every year after 1869 saw a Liberal motion for the adoption of the ballot fall by the wayside.[1] The opportunities for bribery of voters, the coercion of employees by their superiors and of civil servants by the Conservatives, and the open interference of the clergy in Quebec, were all cited as arguments by the Liberals. The Conservatives tacitly admitted the justice of the Opposition's case, but yielded nothing. One staunch party man went so far on one occasion as to observe with commendable frankness that, after all, elections could not be carried on without money, and "under an open system of voting, you can readily ascertain whether the voter has deceived you."[2] The Prime Minister thought the ballot "un-British." Another was critical of it on the ground that it would let a dishonest elector sell his vote to two or three different parties,[3] instead of just one. With these and other cogent reasons for preserving electoral purity, the open system of voting was allowed to last until 1874. That it was abused as the Liberals charged is undoubtedly true, for throughout the debates on the subject members on both sides spoke authoritatively from a striking wealth of background of corrupt electoral practices.[4]

Largely in self-defence, the Liberals adopted the ballot immediately on coming into power in 1874.[5] Since they were inexperienced in such things, their ballot was a poor but honest waif, devoid of counterfoil or official stamp, and printed by local printers on any paper available. The voter made his mark and inserted the paper in an envelope; the presiding officer then dropped the envelope into the ballot box.

The potentialities for abuse of this trusting enactment were almost as great as those of open voting, and it was not necessary for a general election to reveal its weaknesses.[6] Four years later the same Liberal Government, impressed by

[1]E.g., *Debates*, 1870, pp. 367 ff.; 1871, p. 583; 1872, p. 195.
[2]Quoted in W. Buckingham and G. W. Ross, *Alexander Mackenzie* (Toronto, 1892), p. 381.
[3]*Debates*, 1870, p. 545.
[4]See Chapter XIV.
[5]*Statutes*, 37 Vict., c. 9, s. 26 ff.
[6]See, for example, *Debates*, 1877, p. 311.

the number of empty envelopes cast as votes by the electorate in several by-elections, enacted a statute which added a counterfoil to the ballot and abolished the envelope. Hon. Mr. Laflamme, when introducing the bill, revealed another weakness of the law as it existed: illiterate voters at that time were allowed to obtain the assistance of others in the polling booth in making their cross in the proper place, and this provision was exploited not merely with the illiterate, but also with those who did not enjoy this disadvantage. Mr. Laflamme declared:

It had been found from experience that the liberty given to the voter in this respect was availed of for the purpose of detecting the voter, and of forcing on him this declaration. The party selected to act as agent for a candidate was sometimes one of the most influential men in the place, and this fact constrained the voter somewhat in regard to declaring that he could not make his cross.[1]

While Canadian electors were being initiated into the mysteries of the ballot, the more astute among them had of course discovered the convenience known as ballot-box stuffing, together with other useful expedients connected with ballots, ballot-boxes, and ballot counting. Hansard around this time began to bristle with references to these interesting though illegal practices.[2] Of these it can only be said that they undoubtedly existed; how widespread they were it is impossible to surmise, but judging from the general tenor of both debate and press report, it is a justifiable conclusion that they were by no means uncommon, and were certainly commoner than now.

The law itself continued for a while to facilitate certain types of abuse. Since the ballots for each constituency were printed locally, and there was no statutory regulation of the more technical aspects of both ballot printing and ballot marking, both the use of the ballot and judicial interpretation concerning it produced a number of ambiguities. One judge on a recount rejected ballots marked in a peculiar manner, while in an adjoining district another judge accepted exactly

---

[1]*Ibid.*, 1878, p. 1844.
[2]See *ibid.*, 1879, pp. 929 ff. for typical complaints. Also *ibid.*, 1891, pp. 5561-2; 1907-8, pp. 8425-6 and 11790. Also *infra*, Chapters IX, X, and XIV.

the same type of ballot, the total being sufficient to change the result of the election for that constituency.[1] Again, the ballot paper for many years was far from perfect. In 1887 a Liberal member complained that he had had personal experience in his constituency of a ballot so flimsy that any mark made on it showed through. He also cited other instances in which the ballot was thick enough, but the only surface in the polling booth that could be used for marking it was so rough that again the vote was visible, thus destroying its secrecy and opening the familiar doors to bribery.[2] The Conservatives were sufficiently impressed by these and similar complaints that in 1888 a precise weight of ballot paper and a hard, smooth, marking surface became statutory.[3] These advancements were still insufficient to prevent a determined presiding officer from numbering or marking the ballots himself, and complaints on this score continued for years.[4]

While gradual improvement in the ballot and related matters was thus being accomplished, the same could hardly be said for the electorate's use of the system. The Prime Minister observed in 1894 that "the proportion of spoiled ballots in rural districts was so large as to be somewhat serious,"[5] and introduced a new and foolproof paper in which the voter placed his cross in a large and clearly defined circle opposite his chosen candidate's name. This reform was quickly circumvented by the electors in a by-election, many of whom put their crosses everywhere but in the circle, and by a recount judge, who counted the ballots.[6] The Commons, thus frustrated, tried again with a more clearly defined circle. To this improvement the public gave a decisive if jocular answer, and in the general election of 1896 the percentage of

---

[1]*Debates*, 1879, p. 942. For a general discussion of such ambiguities, see *ibid.*, pp. 936 ff. The distinction between a valid and an invalid "cross" on a ballot is not easy to state. The general principle is that the ballot must not be identifiable in any way by the voter's mark, but "it does not matter whether a cross is irregular, shaky or ill-made, or what is its shape or position in the candidate's space." (*Election Instructions*, 1944, p. 168). See also *Memorandum from Chief Electoral Officer to Deputy Returning Officers*, Feb. 20, 1947.
[2]*Debates*, 1887, p. 204.
[3]*Statutes*, 51 Vict., c. 11, ss. 4 and 5.
[4]See *Debates*, 1891, pp. 106 and 994. Some of these markings by deputy returning officers were genuine errors, based on misunderstanding.
[5]*Ibid.*, 1894, p. 6479.
[6]*Ibid.*, 1895, p. 918.

spoiled ballots in a sample of twenty-two constituencies rose 500 per cent.[1]   The circle ballot was abandoned.

This genuine crisis in representation naturally turned men's thoughts to mechanical voting devices that could not be spoiled.   The House of Commons at the turn of the century gave some consideration to voting machines, on one occasion having several examples on display in the lobby.   But to persuade a majority of elected members that the system that had returned them was wholly bad proved impossible,[2] and neither party committed itself to any mechanical techniques.   Notwithstanding the fact that, as one member observed with awe, "it is marvellous that in most of the constituencies there should be enough spoiled ballots to elect or defeat a candidate,"[3] the House clung to its paper ballot. Some important changes were nevertheless accepted.   A new ballot adopted in 1900 had broad black lines separating the candidates' names, and an additional safeguard was provided in the form of a rubber stamp, provided by the Clerk of the Crown in Chancery, for use on the counterfoil by the returning officer.[4]   This stamp was to be specially made up for each election, and showed the name of the constituency and the year.   In addition, the ballot paper was to be sent to every district from Ottawa, although local printing of the ballot continued.   New protection was given to the printing, for the printer's name was to appear clearly on the face of the ballot; this provision was taken so seriously by one printer that in the 1900 election he received several votes.[5]

[1]*Debates*, 1900, p. 6714.   As an example of the type of problem that arose, one member produced evidence from a constituency where two candidates named Frankland and Maclean had run.   Frankland's name was long enough to leave no space other than the disc for marking purposes, but Maclean's shorter name did leave a blank space large enough for an "X," and this fact cost him several votes.   See *ibid.*, p. 6765.   The circle ballot reappeared as recently as 1947, when a committee of the House considered and rejected it, although unaware of its previous failures.   *Report of the Special Committee on Dominion Elections Act*, 1947, *Minutes of Proceedings and Evidence*, p. 111.

[2]*Debates*, 1900, pp. 472 ff.   On this occasion a bill for a voting device reached second reading.

[3]*Ibid.*, 1900, p. 4795.

[4]*Statutes*, 63-64 Vict., c. 12, ss. 41-8.

[5]*Debates*, 1901, p. 1053.   A curious point about this ballot and several of its predecessors was that the design for it was privately owned, and the government was obliged to compensate the copyright owners for use of it.   See *ibid.*, 1902, p. 4330; 1894, p. 6479.

The new ballot worked so well that it has not been sub-stantially changed since. Some trouble arose occasionally over the failure of returning officers to wield their rubber stamps on the counterfoil, which brought up the question of whether a valid vote should be rejected because of an official's negligence. In 1937 a Committee of the House recommended the abolition of the stamp and substitution of a printed mark which was also to be made by a piece of equipment provided from Ottawa.[1] This, combined with the extension of the solid black lines on the ballot to reduce to a minimum the chances of a voter showing too much originality, is the only major alteration to be made in the ballot in nearly fifty years.[2]

The same period has seen several interesting proposed changes, and a few real ones of a purely temporary nature. During the First and Second World Wars, the service vote was taken on a ballot which showed, in the first instance, parties instead of candidates' names, and in the second, both names and parties. Wartime circumstances also required a return to the "envelope ballot" which had been abolished in 1878.[3] In 1901 a private member seriously proposed a ballot containing candidates' pictures, for the benefit of the illiter-ate.[4] In 1917 the Government proposed an unusual ballot for Alberta and Saskatchewan (which were accustomed to it in provincial elections) whereby almost anybody could vote, with the condition that the votes of all refused or challenged voters be put in envelopes before going into the ballot box, to receive judicial consideration before being counted.[5] Both these schemes were abandoned.

Another proposal which received attention was compul-sory voting, which appeared as early as 1891. It was again introduced to Parliament in 1903 with the Conservative

[1]*Report of Special Committee on Elections and Franchise Acts*, 1937, pages ix, 296. Also *Statutes*, 2 Geo. VI, c. 46, ss. 27-8.
[2]In 1948, the ballot was altered to show the surnames of candidates more prominently. This was done on the advice of the Chief Electoral Officer.
[3]See *Statutes*, 7-8 Geo. V, c. 39; 8-9 Geo. VI, c. 26. This is as convenient a place as any to note that political parties in Canada are not unknown to the law, as is commonly supposed. Apart from the foregoing, Canadian electoral law recognizes parties in regard to the appointment of enumerators for the compiling of electoral lists.
[4]*Debates*, 1901, p. 2348.
[5]*Ibid.*, 1917, pp. 5415-18.

leader, Robert Borden, supporting it,[1] and once more in 1907. Interest in compulsory voting on these occasions was stimulated by the fact that it appeared to be a potential weapon against electoral corruption; presumably bribery and treating would be lessened if every elector had to vote whether he was induced to do so or not.   In 1934 a leading member suggested a penalty for failure to vote, as a means of persuading delinquent electors to exercise their franchise,[2] and the House became sufficiently disturbed over the matter to refer the topic to a Special Committee in 1936 and 1937.   After careful examination of compulsory voting in Australia and other places, the Committee rejected the proposal unanimously.[3]

A more serious suggestion for reform which was accepted in principle by both major parties arose in the twenties when the threatened rise of third parties led to agitation for some form of proportional representation.   The presence of three or more candidates in many constituencies naturally made it difficult for any one of them to gain a clear majority of the votes.   One party could thus obtain a sweeping majority of elected members on a minority of the total votes cast, while another could poll many votes without electing more than a few members.   Modern elections in Canada often produce such results, and they have become increasingly frequent as new third parties have appeared.[4]   These results cannot necessarily be regarded as a fundamental weakness in our electoral system, for, as two scholars have recently reported of the similar British system, "within reasonable limits, when the system is called upon to return to power that party which commands the most votes in the country as a whole, it will very rarely fail to do so."[5]

[1]*Ibid.*, 1891, p. 1030; 1903, pp. 13561 ff.

[2]*Ibid.*, 1934, p. 4526.   The penalty proposed was omission from the next voters' list, a provision which existed at the time in British Columbia.

[3]*Report of Special Committee on Elections and Franchise Acts*, 1937.   Harry Butcher, K.C., a former member, is deserving of special mention for the conscientious services performed in advising these committees.   In 1948, compulsory voting again arose, but few members supported it.   (*Debates*, 1948, pp. 5257 ff.)

[4]This has become so common in Canada as to need no elaboration here. See, e.g., R. MacG. Dawson, *The Government of Canada* (Toronto, 1947), pp. 370-1; H. McD. Clokie, *Canadian Government and Politics* (Toronto, 1944), pp. 81 ff.

[5]R. B. McCallum and A. Readman, *The British General Election of 1945* (Toronto, 1947), Appendix III, "The Relations of Seats to Votes."

Proportional representation was first aired in the House of Commons in 1877, when a committee was appointed to examine it; but no report was made. On that occasion, as indeed every time a debate arises on proportional representation, the discussion proceeded on the theory that the elected member from any constituency in some mysterious way represented only those who cast their votes for him on polling day. Again in 1909 proportional representation was discussed at some length without result.[1] It reappeared after the First World War and once more in 1948, but although such leaders as Mr. Mackenzie King have declared for it in unequivocal terms,[2] the House of Commons has not yet progressed beyond consideration of the proposal by a committee.

The single transferable vote, on the other hand, was endorsed unanimously by the legislature in 1923.[3] Liberal Government bills embodying it obtained first reading in 1924 and 1925, and it was proposed in the Speech from the Throne in 1926. The Conservatives indicated their acceptance of the idea in 1935 by obtaining first reading for a bill to try the system in federal elections in Saskatchewan only.[4] The alternative vote was again favourably spoken of in the Commons in 1948. Why the frequent government bills embodying it have never progressed farther is not readily explained, although as far as the Liberals are concerned, probably a

[1]*Debates*, 1877, pp. 816 ff.; 1909, pp. 2598-625. A resolution appointing a committee to examine proportional representation was passed in 1909, and the mover of the resolution proposed to have the Governor-General appear as a witness, because His Excellency had some experience as a proponent of electoral reform in England. See Earl Grey's evidence before the *Royal Commission on Systems of Election* (Great Britain), 1910.

[2]*Debates*, 1934, p. 4477. "I am in favour of the alternative vote and am also in favour of proportional representation." A former leading Conservative member who maintained a special interest in electoral matters, Mr. J. R. MacNicol, usually spoke against proportional representation and the alternative vote.

[3]The single transferable vote may be defined as a device whereby the elector votes for the various candidates in order of his preference for them. Instead of a cross, the ballot is marked with numerals 1, 2, 3, etc. The counting is so manipulated as to ensure that the candidate finally elected is the one most desired by a majority of electors, as indicated by their chief preference. This is effected by dropping, as defeated, the candidate who receives the least number of first choices, and redistributing his ballots according to the next choices. This is done until one candidate has a majority of votes.

[4]*Ibid.*, 1935, p. 3634.

sufficient degree of unanimity has never existed among them to force the issue in the House.[1] Another factor is the state of public opinion, and there has been no evidence at any time to suggest that Canadian citizens have been greatly exercised over proportional representation or preferential voting. A rare and convincing demonstration of Canadian interest in such devices was offered in 1892, when Sir Sandford Fleming became so concerned over the amount of electoral corruption in Canada that he donated $1000 to provide prizes for essays which developed a scheme of proportional representation for the country; this, he assumed, would in some way reduce corruption. Although the contest received wide publicity, only fourteen essays were submitted; and of these, a committee of leading citizens chose four as deserving prizes. Examination of the contestants' pseudonyms revealed the embarrassing fact that the four prizes had been given to three Americans and one Australian. The committee, on more mature consideration, concluded that none of the essays were really good enough to earn awards.[2]

To digress briefly, it should be added that there appears to be a close and logical connection between the alternative vote and compulsory voting which may be expected to receive attention in the House of Commons in the future. Unless the alternative vote is restricted by law so that electors must indicate their preference for more than one candidate on the ballot, the system can be no more satisfactory than the simple ballot now in use in Canadian federal elections. The outcome of the alternative vote when not coupled with compulsory use of the whole ballot can be shown by comparing election results in Canadian provinces which use the alternative vote with results in Australia, where compulsory voting is enforced,

[1]This suggestion is based in part on (a) the obvious stalling by Mr. King in 1924, when he evaded committing his party on no less than eleven occasions after the first reading of the bill; (b) the fact that the proposal was deliberately omitted from the Liberal Election Act of 1925, and brought in as a separate bill, and (c) conflicting statements on the topic by various Liberal leaders at various times. Recently the Liberal party has published some propaganda which is fairly critical of proportional representation and the alternative vote. See e.g., *The Liberal Bulletin* (National Liberal Federation of Canada) for Dec. 20, 1946, and March, 1947.
[2]Sir Sandford Fleming Papers, vols. 105 and 106.

and where a ballot is rejected as spoiled if all the preferences on it are not marked.[1]

	Number of general elections	Total number of electoral districts	Number of districts contested by three or more candidates	Number of districts in which ballot transfers were necessary	Number of candidates with most first choices who were defeated by ballot transfers
Manitoba	5	225	105	69	4
Alberta	5	246	186	67	6
Australia	4	296	220	101	30

The table shows that in all but a very small number of cases, the alternative vote in Alberta and Manitoba has produced the same result as the far simpler ballot used in federal elections, largely because the electors could use the ballot exactly as if it were to be marked with a cross—i.e., they could mark their first choice and no other. In elections in Manitoba and Alberta, as high a proportion as 57 per cent of the voters have used the ballot in this manner; the point of having a ballot transfer in such instances is frequently lost, for a candidate elected with transferred ballots may fall far short of a majority of the total votes. To expect the full benefits, if any, of the alternative vote, the electorate would have to be persuaded in some way to mark its preferences for every candidate on a ballot.

There is no immediate indication that the ballot marked with a cross is likely to be abandoned in Canada. Thus the only electors in Canada who will continue to have any choice in marking their ballots are the residents of the two remaining two-member constituencies; there two crosses are permissible but not obligatory, and some evidence exists to suggest that voters in these favoured areas have on occasion exercised the meagre discretion offered to them.[2] It remains only to be

[1]Figures supplied by Chief Electoral Officer of Canada. This aspect of the alternative vote was discussed briefly in the House of Commons on June 15, 1948 (*Debates*, pp. 5257 ff).

[2]Norman Ward, "Voting in Canadian Two-Member Constituencies," *Public Affairs*, Sept., 1946, pp. 220-3.

added that the ballot generally in use in federal elections in Canada is as safely guarded and as simple as human experience can make it, and that a small but determined proportion of citizens contrive to spoil their ballots at every election.

Election day is another part of the electoral machinery of which the present respectability has been reached only after an adventurous past. In early days, indeed, nothing was more easily taken advantage of than election day. Only Nova Scotia required simultaneous voting in all constituencies in 1867, with the result that the federal government could time elections in various parts of the country to its own convenience. The Conservatives extended the first general election over a period of six weeks, picking the soft spots first and working their way cautiously into the hard ones. The election of 1872 lasted nearly three months. To this sort of thing, needless to say, the Liberals took vigorous exception.[1] Again, the fact that election day extended over forty-eight hours in Ontario and Quebec facilitated certain abuses, for the law required that the vote be totalled officially at the end of each polling day.[2] The party which was behind after the first day's voting thus had ample opportunity to calculate exactly how many votes would be needed to carry the election on the second day, and also twenty-four hours in which to get them. Competition at the election of D'Arcy McGee in 1867 produced a serious riot on the second day of polling.

The Conservatives were not so firmly wedded to the two-day polling practice as they were to staggered elections, and considered abandoning the former in 1870.[3] This they accomplished the following year when provision was also made for the continued use in federal elections of most of the relevant provincial laws in force in 1867.[4] The arguments for the perpetuation of staggered voting, on the other hand, were very strong. In addition to its convenience for partisan purposes, staggered voting allowed men of property sufficient time to travel around to vote wherever they were qualified, and in a time when elections were frequently won by a mere

[1] E.g., *Debates*, 1870, p. 363.
[2] *R.S. Can. (Prov.)*, 1859, c. 6, s. 58.
[3] *Debates*, 1870, p. 357.
[4] *Statutes*, 34 Vict., c. 20, s. 2 (1).

handful of votes this was an important consideration.   A useful candidate defeated in one place, or elected but having accepted an office of emolument, also had time to move on to another constituency in the same election.[1]   Macdonald felt so keenly about three-month elections that he grouped simultaneous voting with the ballot as "un-British";[2] although the practice of holding all elections on one day was spreading among the provinces by 1872, he refused to take Liberal proposals on the subject seriously.

The Liberals came into power in 1873 before the dissolution of the second Parliament, and were thus able to establish the principle of simultaneous voting by dating the writs as they chose for the third general election.   In 1874 the holding of all elections on one day became statutory, with certain exceptions because of physical difficulties in some areas.[3]   At no subsequent time did the Conservatives propose to return to staggered voting, and with the exceptions mentioned, some of which lasted for many years, one-day polling and simultaneous elections have been accepted since 1874.[4]

The strategic point concerning polling day since then has been that the Government can spring an election whenever expedient,[5] provided that the electoral machinery is ready. The Government's freedom to choose election dates is limited by a section of the Dominion Elections Act which prevents, in effect, the holding of an election within three months after the passage of an amendment to the Act;[6] this is necessary to allow the Chief Electoral Officer time to alter the forms and

[1]Macdonald did this in 1878.   See p. 81.
[2]*Debates*, 1872, pp. 770-3.
[3]*Statutes*, 37 Vict., c. 9.
[4]A related issue is that of the advance poll.   Since 1920, workers such as railwaymen and fishermen who are away on election day can under some conditions vote on a day other than election day, but the proportion of votes so cast is infinitesimally small.   See *Debates*, 1909, p. 3468, when a member complained that railway companies were deliberately disfranchising workers by moving them around.
[5]See R. MacG. Dawson, *The Government of Canada* (Toronto, 1947), pp. 246-7.   This is true both of general elections and by-elections, although it has been suggested more than once that by-elections should be held automatically as vacancies arise.   See *ibid.*, pp. 385-6; *Debates*, 1888, pp. 1138-40; 1905, p. 9073.
[6]*Statutes*, 2 Geo. VI, c. 46, s. 110.   It is a valid conclusion that the more complicated the electoral machinery becomes, the greater will be the legal and circumstantial limitations on the government's choice of election day.

instructions given local election officials. The Government must also consider the fact that approximately sixty days are required for an election, and that communications are almost non-existent in many outlying parts of the country in certain seasons. The colossal electoral system, whose complexity grows apace, cannot under such circumstances be expected to operate as efficiently as usual. On one occasion, I was authoritatively informed, a government postponed a general election with considerable reluctance in the face of difficult weather conditions. Within broad limits, the choice of election day is nevertheless entirely with the party in power. This necessary consequence of the Cabinet system sometimes proves disconcerting to the Opposition (as in 1940) and may even prompt a private member to advocate that election day be fixed as in the United States. No party has yet taken this proposal seriously.

It has often been suggested that election day should be a holiday, which it used to be in fact although not by statute. This proposal, which first appeared in 1909, actually passed the House of Commons in 1925 as an accepted amendment to a government bill; but by a clerical error it was not in the copy of the bill sent to the Senate,[1] and consequently did not become law. In 1929, when election day was set by statute on a Monday, the proposal was again made but was rejected. The initiative for the holiday movement came largely from labour groups who claimed that, since there was no penalty to enforce it, employers were not giving workers their statutory two hours off with pay for voting purposes.[2] But Parliament has not yet been convinced of the necessity of compelling citizens to take a holiday on election day;[3] and as the early election holidays were often of the Roman variety, this may well be a beneficial example of the wisdom of parliamentary inaction.

[1]*Debates*, 1909-10, p. 1268; 1925, p. 4567; 1929, p. 3024.
[2]See *Report of Special Committee on Dominion Elections Act*, etc., 1929; evidence of Mr. Tom Moore, of the Trades and Labor Congress, p. 44 ff.
[3]The last committee to examine the electoral system in detail rejected the proposal flatly, but recommended that employers be penalized for not giving employees time to vote. This was done. See *Report of Special Committee on Elections and Franchise Acts*, 1937, p. xvi and *Statutes*, 2 Geo. VI, c. 46, s. 47.

Canadian experience with voting arrangements demonstrates that there is no such thing as a completely foolproof system. Quite apart from the tribulations of election day and the ballot, such innocent objects as ballot boxes have had a chequered and fascinating career, somewhat resembling that of an old-fashioned movie heroine. They have been lost, stolen, burned, delayed by the weather, carried off for weekends, and left in the snow while their custodians got drunk in an adjoining tavern, and yet despite these vicissitudes the course of Canadian democracy has rolled triumphantly on. They have, in addition, with regrettable frequency been stuffed, and on at least one occasion were provided with a mechanical gadget—in this instance a false bottom—that facilitated a more expedient distribution of ballots than the electorate might have deemed acceptable.[1] Since a modern election requires the moving around of five hundred tons of election material (including several million ballots) and the disposition of thirty-six thousand ballot boxes, it is hardly surprising that fragments of the whole should still on rare occasions go astray.

[1]An instance is mentioned in P. Bilkey, *Persons, Papers, and Things* (Toronto, 1940), p. 177.

CHAPTER IX

THE ELECTION OFFICIALS

AN election in any constituency is carried out entirely by local officials. Today there also exists a Chief Electoral Officer who exercises a general supervision; but in earlier days, no one was responsible for the work of the several hundred officers employed in an election. Efficient management of an election depended entirely on the integrity of these local workers, and the method by which they were selected was thus of major significance to representation in the House of Commons.

The officials for the first Canadian election were provided for by section 42 of the British North America Act. This statute empowered the new federal government, through the Governor-General, to "cause writs to be issued by such Person, in such Form, and addressed to such Returning Officers as he thinks fit." In all the provinces, the returning officers appointed their own deputies and assistants.[1] The first federal election was thus held under circumstances which allowed the whole electoral machinery to be established on a partisan basis.

There is abundant evidence that this was done. In view of the magnitude of the task and the fact that much of the machinery was being used for the first time, some confusion and misunderstanding were to be expected at the first election; but in several instances the conduct of returning officers was difficult to explain solely on the grounds of misunderstanding. The law, for example, gave returning officers no power to set aside properly compiled voters' lists for technical reasons, but in the first election parts of four counties were disfranchised

[1]See Appendix A. To dismiss a number of technical points briefly, it may be stated at once that the functions of returning officers have in their essentials changed hardly at all since 1867. The appointment of deputies, the procuring of voters' lists from the proper sources, the division of the area into polls, and the general direction of the election are the main duties of a returning officer, and the local machine is thus (and always has been) a highly autonomous one. Though essentially the same as in 1867, the burden of returning officers' duties has nevertheless increased greatly.

in this way.[1]   The law vested in returning officers no power to reinstate on voters' lists names struck off by a judge;[2] they were not empowered to return as elected anyone other than the winner of an election;[3] and they were not expected to prevent acclamations by securing candidates for the purpose of augmenting their own fees;[4] but instances of all these abuses were produced.   To what extent such activities were motivated by partisan reasons is of course impossible to determine, but their mere existence is indicative that the election machinery was by no means as complete and automatic as simple justice would require.

Opposition complaints regarding election officials were understandably frequent in the early years.   Edward Blake once cited an instance in which a returning officer had been appointed on condition that he retire from contesting the election as a candidate.[5]   Liberal leaders several times went on record as favouring the appointment of permanent non-partisan officers such as sheriffs and registrars, who were used for this purpose in pre-Confederation days.[6]   To this retrogression the Government was opposed on principle, and steps were taken in 1871 to retain in federal hands the appointment of returning officers.[7]

The Liberals, whose opinions on the electoral machinery undoubtedly contributed to their interest in provincial rights (and vice versa), abandoned this patronage after their election to power in 1874.   Their elections Act of that year provided that writs were to be issued to sheriffs or registrars, or, in the absence of such officials, to a federal appointee.[8]   Election

[1]*Parliamentary Debates* (Scrapbook Hansard), June 9, 1869; *Debates*, 1871, p. 459.   The Conservatives admitted the charge but attributed it to misunderstanding.   In one instance, an officer set aside a list because it was a copy, and not the original.

[2]*Journals*, 1867-8, p. 108.

[3]*Parliamentary Debates* (Scrapbook Hansard), April 2, 1873.   In 1872, a Muskoka returning officer refrained from making any return whatever, on technical grounds.

[4]*Debates*, 1870, p. 543.

[5]*Ibid.*, 1871, p. 980.

[6]*Ibid.*, 1872, p. 1001.

[7]*Statutes*, 34 Vict., c. 20, s. 7.   Macdonald's election bill of 1870, which was not passed, also proposed to keep the returning officers under control of the federal government.

[8]*Statutes*, 37 Vict., c. 9, s. 1.

writs for a time thereafter were not addressed to any individual by name, but to "The Sheriff of the County of . . . ." As before, the returning officers appointed their own assistants, who in turn appointed *their* assistants such as poll clerks. All the officials were paid out of the Consolidated Revenue Fund through the returning officer, a provision which gave rise to many complaints in later years, as some officers were reluctant to reward their hirelings.[1] The Liberals also gave a degree of permanence to the machinery by appointing in a large number of constituencies the same returning officers for the 1874 and 1878 elections.[2]

The procedure adopted in 1874 seems to have evoked less complaint than its predecessor, but there was some grumbling. One Liberal admitted that, "the returning officer was, generally, a man of respectable character, and . . . fraud was possible without his connivance at all;" while a Conservative member, who did not deny the truth of the statement, replied that "as a rule, deputy returning-officers were partisans—it was almost impossible to appoint non-partisans. . . . As a rule, they were men of little education, and of no judicial experience of that character which was required to decide the really difficult question as to whether a ballot was properly marked or not."[3] Again, complaints were heard after the 1878 election about officers who sealed ballot boxes improperly, miscounted ballots, and identified ballots by numbering them.[4]

Little happened in the 1874 and 1878 elections to warrant returning to the system of federal appointment of officers on the grounds of greater efficiency, and the Conservatives made no attempt to persuade the Liberals to do so. They bided their time, and before the 1882 election the appointment of returning officers by the Government was re-estab-

[1]See, e.g., *Debates*, 1900, p. 6733. As late as 1937 the Chief Electoral Officer told the Special Committee on Elections and Franchise Acts (*Report*, p. 99): "In my experience, there have invariably been two or three [returning officers] who would grab the money and beat it."
[2]Statement based on a comparison of lists of returning officers given in *Public Accounts* for 1875 and 1880.
[3]*Debates*, 1877, pp. 902-3. The Conservative member here had a grievance, for the improper counting of ballots by officials had kept him out of the House for more than a session.
[4]*Ibid.*, 1879, pp. 929, 935-7.

lished as a section of the great gerrymander Act.[1]   Sir John
had his own good reasons for making the change.

In the first place the returning officers provided for the present law are not
in any way the servants or officers of the Dominion, but . . . of the Provinces.
They are in no way under the control of the Dominion Parliament, except
that they may be brought to the Bar of the House and punished for mis-
demeanors.   They are not obliged to perform this duty; they can refuse
to do it, and more than that; I mean to say I have no confidence in a certain
number of these officers.   They are the creatures of the Local Government,
and if the Local Government chooses to put pressure on them there is
great danger of their being governed by those who appointed them. . . . I
think the returning officers should be considered in every respect as Dominion
officers.[2]

These were forceful arguments, although possibly not all of
equal validity,[3] and point was given them by the fact that
Liberal governments existed in several of the provinces.
Conservative members had no difficulty in pointing out that
electoral fraud was far from unknown therein, so that the
resumption of the appointment of returning officers from
Ottawa could be justified as a method of protecting federal
politicians from the machinations of provincial ones.[4]

The Liberals of course again objected to the appointment
of returning officers by the Government and harked back to
previous abuses, some of which were not without humorous
aspects. "In my own constituency," David Mills complained, using an argument based on the fact that all election
officials were for a time disfranchised, "the hon. gentleman
appointed as returning officer one of the most violent partisans. . . . He went outside of the constituency for deputies,
so that the Tory party might not lose a vote in the election,
and he appointed Reformers as poll clerks, and in this way
prevented twenty or thirty persons from voting."[5]   As a

[1]*Statutes*, 45 Vict., c. 3, s. 6.
[2]*Debates*, 1882, pp. 1462-3.   For an instance in which an officer was examined
at the bar of the House, see *Parliamentary Debates* (Scrapbook Hansard), March
26, 1873.
[3]It seems possible, at least, that the Courts would hold that provincial
sheriffs etc., were federal officers *to the extent to which the law required*.   See
Debates, 1898, pp. 4383 ff. for an analogous point in regard to using provincial
franchises and voters' lists; here a Privy Council decision is quoted which suggests that the foregoing point may be a valid one.   It was never tested, so far
as I can determine.
[4]E.g., *ibid.*, 1882, p. 1463.
[5]*Ibid.*   Election officials have now been enfranchised for years.

final indignity, these Liberal poll clerks were not even paid.
Blake had a similar story which turned on a statutory provision making it an offence to refuse an appointment as an
electoral official: "A most active supporter of mine . . . was
chosen the day before polling. He was the gentleman upon
whom I mainly depended for organization in that particular
township, and the £10 [fine] had to be paid in order to release
him."[1] The use of Liberals as election officials by the
Conservatives nevertheless occasionally backfired: "The
Deputy Returning Officers in important places were nearly
all Grit," a supporter wrote to explain a defeat to Macdonald
in 1883, "and . . . one or two bad votes in each division
were got in early in the morning. This meant 50 or 60
votes against us which we did not count on."[2]

Not all of the complaints against the electoral system
in the first decades could be discounted as party prejudice.[3]
It is a fact, to take a single instance, that in 1887 the returning
officer in Algoma was a collector of customs in the employ
of the Government.[4] The Government tacitly admitted in
the same year the existence of a curious practice based on
an ambiguity in the law concerning candidates' agents.
There were supposed to be only two agents in a polling
division for each candidate, but a member declared:

In one particular district in my constituency where five polls were held,
some sixty-six agents voted. To my mind, that is contrary to the election
law, and the returning officer held the same view until within twenty-four
hours of the polling being held. . . . He had made out some seventy-two
certificates for agents, men coming from Winnipeg to vote in the town of
Portage la Prairie. These men did not act as agents, and I believe the
returning officer was forced into the position he took by the advice of Winnipeg lawyers, that any man could be appointed an agent and go and vote,
*provided there were not two men holding agents' certificates in the booth at the
same time.*[5]

[1]*Ibid.*, p. 1466.
[2]G. W. Elliott to Macdonald, Nov. 28, 1883 (Macdonald Papers, vol. 65).
[3]E.g., *Debates*, 1883, pp. 57 ff.; 1885, p. 2233. The most remarkable case
during this decade occurred in 1887, when a returning officer returned the loser
of an election on a technicality (*ibid.*, 1887, *passim*). In this instance, the
returning officer was summoned before the bar of the House.
[4]*Ibid.*, 1887, p. 1240.
[5]*Ibid.*, pp. 888-9. (Italics added.) See also *ibid.*, 1891, p. 3244. Even
the mere establishment of polling booths has been abused for party advantage,
according to members' claims. See *ibid.*, 1890, p. 4664; 1920, p. 1995.

Thus after twenty years of active use, the operation of the electoral machine was still not clearly defined and virtually automatic. A major reason for this was that the complex nature of an election in a large country with poor communications and an expanding frontier was enough to tax the ingenuity of any government even if it had the best will in the world. Certainly a substantial proportion of the inadequacies most frequently criticized in the electoral system arose as much from honest trial-and-error methods of legislation as from wilful manipulation.[1]

Many abuses were perpetrated by local partisans over whom the Government had no real control. Regarded solely as an administrative machine, the electoral organization was poor; for the use of provincial laws, provincial officials and provincial voters' lists for federal purposes, when added to the serious difficulties imposed by slow communications, hopelessly complicated an already disordered situation. "Be careful to consult the Statutes of your local Legislature," the clerk of the Crown in Chancery advised returning officers in one form letter, "to ascertain the qualifications of Voters, the Oath or Oaths to be taken by them, and the Electoral Lists to be used."[2] Since the modern Chief Electoral Officer administers only federal law, and finds a 350-page book of instructions to election officials to be indispensable,[3] it will be appreciated that the undirected and irresponsible returning officers of the early decades worked under extraordinary difficulties, which would increase in direct ratio to their own conscientiousness.

This is not to say that all election officials in the past discharged their duties as best they knew. But there is considerable evidence that partisan officers were not appointed in every constituency, but only where they would do the most good. "I am glad," one Liberal leader declared, "to say that, with one or two unfortunate exceptions, the Government have not introduced the vicious system of appointing

[1]See Sir John Thompson's remarks, *ibid.*, 1891, p. 741, for a case in point.
[2]A copy of this letter is in the Macdonald Papers, vol. 66.
[3]"I am convinced that without the elaborate instructions . . . the present electoral machinery would break down." *Report of the Chief Electoral Officer to the Speaker*, 1926, p. 2. In 1892, returning officers received one and a half pages of written instructions.

partisan returning officers into the Maritime Provinces."[1] The credit for this belonged as much to private members of Parliament as to government policy, for the convention naturally developed that the appointment of a returning officer in any one constituency was to be made on the recommendation of the government candidate. A partial list of returning officers in Sir John Macdonald's correspondence establishes this fact, and reveals in addition that one person recommended that sheriffs be appointed in fourteen New Brunswick constituencies.[2]

The weaknesses of allowing members to appoint returning officers were clearly stated by Sir Richard Cartwright in 1891:

They are, it is well known, appointed by him, not with reference to their experience, not with reference to their standing in the county, not with reference to their general capacity, but for the strictest party reason, and because they have power to appoint a number of minor officials by whose hands, perhaps, more than by those of the returning officers, any improper results that may occur in the course of the election can be manipulated.[3]

When this statement was made, the Liberals were urging once more the use of sheriffs and registrars as permanent returning officers. They supported their case with multiple references to instances in which the Government or election officials had been (to take the most charitable view) amazingly careless, and pressed their suit with such conviction that Sir John Thompson admitted that he was not averse to the principle of permanent officers. Among this welter of complaints, the Liberals produced one unique grievance: the returning officer in Algoma was unable to distinguish between male and female Indians. The Indians were herded like sheep to the polls, declared a member, and after the braves had voted, the squaws changed clothes with them and went in and voted too.[4]

Liberal eloquence about election officials was stilled by the party's return to power in 1896, and the Franchise Act

[1]*Debates*, 1891, p. 5578 (Louis Davies). See also *ibid.*, 1898, p. 2792.
[2]Macdonald Papers, vol. 66.
[3]*Debates*, 1891, p. 5576. See also *ibid.*, 1888, p. 1140; *Parliamentary Debates* (Scrapbook Hansard), Mar. 13, 1873.
[4]*Debates*, 1891, *passim*. There was, to cite another example, no election whatever in Huntingdon in 1887, because of the failure to appoint a returning officer.

of 1898 continued the appointment of returning officers from Ottawa. The party's policy was not acceptable to everybody, for one member, in whom a fit of despondence coincided with a charitable impulse, subsequently suggested that the post of returning officer be confined to clergymen. "They are deserving individuals," he said; "If there are a few dollars to be spent, I do not know of any individuals more worthy to receive it."[1] A Liberal member advocated in a private bill the use of provincial officers.[2] The Government, for its part, paid lip-service to the principle it had advocated for so long by showing a tendency to use permanent provincial appointees as returning officers. The Liberal record in this regard after their victory of 1896, compared with the Conservative, was for several elections as follows:[3]

Election	Party in Power	Number of Provincial Appointees used as Returning Officers
1900	Liberal	66
1904	Liberal	68
1908	Liberal	63
1911	Liberal	46
1917	Conservative	35
1921	Conservative	17
1925	Liberal	32
1926	Conservative	15

It will be noted that even during the period when these officials were in greatest use, the total did not exceed 30 per cent of the number of constituencies, although it is perhaps significant that the lowest figures in the table are for elections held under Conservative auspices. The decline in the use of provincial employees as returning officers may be partly explained by the growing complexity of elections; for the extra burden placed on a sheriff or county registrar who had a full-time job of his own to perform became increasingly unreasonable. Even at the turn of the century, an election

[1] *Debates*, 1900, p. 7335.
[2] *Ibid.*, 1903, p. 13562.
[3] Figures supplied to *Special Committee on Dominion Elections Act etc.*, 1929, by Chief Electoral Officer.

official did not necessarily hold a sinecure. Hansard records a case of a western officer who in the course of his duties travelled 1500 miles, eighty of which required him to break a new trail in sub-zero weather, and then spent two weeks in hospital suffering from exposure. An austere Government, through the Auditor-General, subsequently cut his expense account for the trip.[1]

The last decade of the nineteenth century (one hesitates to date this from the decease of Sir John A. Macdonald in 1891) saw the beginnings not merely of a decline in the complaints about the electoral machinery, but of a change in the spirit exhibited by the two parties in discussing them.[2] Serious dissatisfaction with election officials was rarely expressed in this century until the khaki election of 1917; and then the complaints were more concerned with the powers given to the officials than with the men themselves. Borden, it is true, reminded the House of Commons in 1906 and again in 1908 of the dangers of using the electoral system as patronage,[3] and occasional examples to prove his point were conveniently provided by appointees.[4] But on the whole the machinery seems to have started to work fairly well. Since the first four elections of this century were held under Liberal auspices, a tribute paid it by a leading Conservative is fairly reliable evidence, and it is worth recording that in 1917 Arthur Meighen told the Commons that in his experience he had found no partisanship by returning officers, though they were Liberal appointees.[5]

Into this fairly settled system was injected the wartime election of 1917. This occurred more or less in the usual manner as far as the civilian vote in Canada was concerned,

[1]*Debates*, 1903, p. 13593.
[2]See *infra*. In 1896, nonetheless, election frauds in Manitoba led to the conviction of a deputy returning officer. See *Report of Select Standing Committee on Public Accounts*, 1899, pp. v-vi. Also *Report of the Select Standing Committee on Privileges and Elections*, 1899. This committee examined the conduct of elections in Brockville and Huron West, and although some remarkable evidence was taken, reached no conclusions.
[3]*Debates*, 1906, p. 236; 1907-8, p. 7859.
[4]E.g., *ibid.*, 1907-8, pp. 8302, and 11790. In the former instance, a deputy received assistance with his voters' lists from a Liberal organizer, which Sir Wilfrid admitted was "certainly injudicious, most injudicious;" in the latter a deputy, confusing provincial and federal law, marked some ballots.
[5]*Ibid.*, 1917, p. 5668.

although under a strange franchise,[1] but it gave to election officials sweeping powers which even Sir John A. Macdonald would scarcely have suggested. As part of a general disfranchisement of certain naturalized aliens, for example, it was proposed to allow deputies to refuse a ballot to anyone who *"by his manner shows that he was born in an enemy country."* (This may have been a misprint, as the clause was subsequently repaired by the substitution of "answer" for "manner."[2]) The vote of overseas servicemen was to be taken by government appointees, who through further appointees of their own were empowered to be present at the marking of every ballot, although "in such manner as not to disclose to them or to any other person any marking thereon."[3] Inadequate provisions were made for scrutineering at the polls.[4] In addition, the act contained two clauses which gave at least an opportunity for the "massing" of soldier votes in any constituency in which they might be needed, although the actual massing might be illegal unless the soldier voters could not state where they had resided in Canada.[5]

There are two major facts to be noted for the purposes of this chapter: the strategic officials for taking the service vote were almost to a man commissioned officers in the forces, so that the possibilities for intimidation of privates under the "open voting" procedure were inviting; and the instructions given to officials were admittedly poor.[6] Add to this the manipulation of the franchise at home, and the power given an enumerator in compiling voters' lists to refuse

---

[1]See *infra*, for further discussion of the 1917 election.

[2]*Debates*, 1917, p. 5621; *Statutes*, 7-8 Geo. V, c. 39, s. 21 (f).

[3]*Ibid.*, 7-8 Geo. V, c. 34, s. 9 (e).

[4]The Act provided for six scrutineers (three from each party) who could appoint deputies to be at the polls, but these latter officers, it was specifically provided, were not to be paid. See *ibid.*, s. 4, 1 (e), and 4 (2).

[5]*Ibid.*, s. 3 (4) and s. 12 (2). See *Debates*, 1919 (2nd session), p. 534 ff. for a debate in which the Liberals charged that this was actually done. From personal interviews with veterans of the First World War I have concluded that the smoke raised by the Liberals was not without fire.

[6]A Conservative spokesman in 1918 admitted that "a widespread impression prevailed among the soldiers that they could elect what constituency they should vote in." (*Debates*, 1918, p. 2440.) At least part of this, it was argued, was the Liberals' fault, for they had harped a good deal on this particular point (*ibid.*, p. 2463). Whatever the reason, part of the result was a huge percentage of spoiled soldier votes, reaching nearly a third of the total in Canada (*ibid.*, p. 2466).

even a statutory declaration of qualification from a potential elector,[1] and the resulting electoral machine at least appears open to enormous abuse.   The Liberals certainly thought so; and they produced in 1918 an indictment which took four hours to deliver.   The Government, displaying a profound faith in the virtue of their appointees in general, the honour of the soldiery in particular, and the long arm of coincidence, treated it as a motion of want of confidence and refused even an inquiry.   An investigation, they admitted frankly, would be extremely inconvenient.[2]

The Conservatives, perhaps by way of compensation, enacted a most salutary reform of the electoral machinery in 1920.   In that year they established a Chief Electoral Officer, with the status of a deputy minister and the tenure of a judge of the Supreme Court, who was to be a general overseer of the system.   The returning officers remained political appointees; and they were provided with a new system of compiling voters' lists which greatly enhanced their patronage by requiring some two to three hundred minor officials in each constituency.[3]   For the first time these minor officials were all to be paid directly from Ottawa, a provision which threw upon the Auditor-General's office the work of scrutinizing and honouring well over 100,000 separate accounts in every election; this proved to be so large a task that the payment of many election workers was delayed for months.[4]

Although the Liberals revived in 1920 their old objections to the continued appointment of returning officers by the Cabinet, they thought well enough of the system to maintain it after coming into power in 1921.   Before the 1925 election, in accordance with a recommendation from the Chief Electoral

[1]See *ibid.*, 1919, p. 4631.   This power was given in instructions to the officials, rather than in explicit terms in the statute.   The statute (7-8 Geo. V, c. 39, s. 1 (r)) authorized an enumerator to accept statutory declarations of qualification as *prima facie* evidence of qualification, while the instructions added that he need not do so, and in fact could refuse to do so "if he deems it not credible or is in doubt."
[2]*Debates*, 1918, pp. 2400 ff.
[3]*Ibid.*, 1920, pp. 1574 ff.
[4]See *Statutes*, 10-11 Geo V, c. 46, ss. 76-7.   Also *Report of Special Committee on Elections and Franchise Acts*, 1937, pp. 96 ff.   On the recommendation of this Committee, the paying process was improved in 1938 after evidence of very long delays in payment had been presented to the Committee.

Officer, they varied its form by proposing to give the appointing power to the Secretary of State; this the Senate amended by giving the authority back to the Cabinet on the recommendation of the Secretary of State.[1] The Senate also amended the Act to make the returning officers permanent during pleasure, instead of mere one-year appointees.[2] An unexpected weakness of the electoral machinery came to light in the same bill when the Liberals proposed to establish means to force returning officers to take action when writs were sent them. "In one or two constituencies," said Hon. A. B. Copp, "there was barely time to carry on the election after the returning officer refused to act."[3]

The patronage system for the electoral machinery was thus continued. At its best it seems to have worked very well, but, as the Chief Electoral Officer reported in 1926, "the fact that appointments are generally made from among supporters of the party in power naturally inclines supporters of the opposite party to think that unfair administration tactics are intended to be or are in fact resorted to. . . . The present mode of the selection of election officers does induce on the part of appointees a mistaken idea that they owe a duty to the party to which they belong rather than to the state."[4] A ready example of this was at hand. A chaotic election had been held in Athabaska in 1925, and a Select Standing Committee of the House of Commons, appointed to consider a report on the affair by a judicial commission, had decided that the trouble was directly attributable to the "partizanship, ignorance and incompetence of certain election officials."[5]

[1]*Debates*, 1925, pp. 4567 and 5064. The Senate has never hesitated to interfere with election laws, though these concern only the House of Commons. One reason given by Mr. Mackenzie King for not pressing the alternative vote further in the twenties was that the Senate would not have allowed it. See *ibid.*, 1932-3, pp. 22-3.

[2]See *Statutes*, 15-16 Geo. V, c. 42, s. 3. This permanence of course did not survive the change of government in 1926, when the existing returning officers were replaced almost in entirety. *Report of Chief Electoral Officer to the Speaker*, 1926; quoted in *Debates*, 1934, p. 4540.

[3]*Debates*, 1925, p. 3539; *Report of Chief Electoral Officer*, 1922, p. 10. This amendment, with most of the others in the Act, was suggested by the Chief Electoral Officer, who was required to make an annual report on the electoral machinery. Not only did some officers refuse to act in 1921, but a few tried to hold up the Government for more money.

[4]Quoted in *Debates*, 1934, p. 4542.

[5]*Select Standing Committee on Privileges and Elections, Second and Final Report*, June 1, 1928.

No one was legally responsible for these officials. Although the Chief Electoral Officer was empowered to "direct all returning officers," and to "exercise general direction and supervision over the administrative conduct of elections," his jurisdiction was severely limited by the circumstances governing the appointment of returning officers, who were the officials responsible for the election in any one constituency. The Chief Electoral Officer wrote accurately in his 1922 report that his duties did not extend "to administrative intervention in any electoral district so as to relieve the returning officer of the responsibility for the conduct of the election therein when he either fails to ask for instructions or to comply with the instructions he receives. . . . No other position is possible consistently with the appointment of election officials . . . (by) the government of the day."[1] Before a Special Committee in 1929, the same official deposed that while he might remove an incompetent or partisan returning officer whose conduct was brought to his attention, it was a "physical impossibility" to control all the local functionaries from Ottawa.[2] The returning officer in each electoral district was thus beyond the reach of authority.

The electoral administrator, despite this fact, thought in 1929 that "it would be very hard to improve upon the machinery."[3] A Special Committee of the House of Commons in the same year nevertheless took evidence which indicated substantial dissatisfaction with the electoral system. Several members of Parliament proposed the use of municipal officials in cities as returning officers, and also advocated the appointment of permanent deputy returning officers by the Chief Electoral Officer. A brief from the Trades and Labor Congress requested that *all* election officials be non-partisan appointments under the same official. On this point the chairman of the Committee, Mr. C. G. Power, added indignantly that "the experience of every one of us

[1]*Report of Chief Electoral Officer to the Speaker*, 1922, p. 8.
[2]*Report of Special Committee on Dominion Elections Act and Corrupt Practices Inquiry Act*, 1929, p. 2. There have been two removals of returning officers since 1920.
[3]Despite the Officer's optimism concerning the machinery it was improved in 1929 by *requiring* him to make inquiry in any suspected cases of abuse, and endowing him with the powers of a commissioner (*Statutes*, 19-20 Geo. V, c. 40, s. 5), and in 1931 by giving him as legal adviser his own predecessor.

has been that we do not know who the poll clerks are until the morning of the election. We have quite a time finding them. The returning officer himself has a time finding them."[1] The Chief Electoral Officer recommended that the Government be limited in its choice of returning officers to provincial officials, and his predecessor suggested that the Officer should make recommendations for each constituency, from which the Government must select.[2]

The Committee passed over the two administrative experts to adopt the suggestion of the Trades and Labor Congress that the Chief Electoral Officer appoint all returning officers. These officials in turn were to continue to appoint their own assistants. This recommendation was subsequently adopted by the Liberal party, though not without a great backstage battle,[3] and finally by Parliament. There the proposal met with almost no trouble whatever.

The election of 1930 was consequently held under an administrative machine which was, on paper, at the highest point of development it had ever reached. The Chief Electoral Officer travelled from coast to coast appointing a returning officer in each constituency, and in his 1930 report was able to state:

The number of administrative difficulties and complaints against returning officers showed a notable decrease. From only twenty electoral districts was any complaint received against the conduct of a returning officer, and in most of these cases, as well as in the few additional cases in which complaints were made to me against the conduct of subordinate election officers, the making of the complaints appeared on inquiry to have been due to misunderstanding.[4]

The apparent satisfaction afforded by the appointment of returning officers by the chief administrator of elections

[1]*Minutes of Proceedings and Evidence, Special Committee on Dominion Elections Act*, etc., 1929, no. 1, p. 22; no. 4, pp. 44-6.
[2]*Ibid.*, no. 4, p. vii; p. xiii. The turnover of returning officers during the twenties was remarkable. Of the 241 who acted in the 1926 election, only 3 had acted in the two previous elections, and only 42 in either one of them. *Ibid.*, no. 2, p. 32.
[3]"Day after day I was obliged to fight the men of my own side of the House, some of them very important men, in order to press the amendment through." (Mr. Power in *Debates*, 1934, p. 4540.)
[4]*Report of the Chief Electoral Officer to the Speaker*, 1930. The status which the post of returning officer had reached at this time is indicated by the fact that the Department of Justice appears to have ruled that it was not an act of political partisanship for a civil servant to act as one. *Debates*, 1931, pp. 2134-5.

turned out to be illusory. The fundamental weakness of the technique was that it imposed upon the Chief Electoral Officer an impossible task, that of appointing a nation-wide string of officials who had to be reasonably competent, on the one hand, and tolerable to local party organizations and candidates on the other. Since he could not conceivably be expected to have a detailed knowledge of local conditions in over 240 constituencies, he had to rely on interested persons for advice. The only interested individuals to be found in most instances were partisans.

Thus the Chief Electoral Officer's appointments were certain to be unsatisfactory to many people. After the 1930 election, a Special Committee of the House of Commons treated itself to a spectacle which is fortunately rare in Canadian politics, the "grilling" of a public servant for a policy he has pursued. As the plan followed in the appointment of returning officers had been to allot a minimum of thirty positions to the Conservative Opposition before the election, the triumphant victory of that party in 1930 did not enhance the Officer's chances of avoiding criticism.[1]

A second major weakness of the Chief Electoral Officer's appointments was that they were permanent. The Conservative Government elected in 1930 was thus presented with the unpleasant prospect of having very little electoral patronage to dispense at the next election. But the remedy was at hand; and in 1934 the choosing of returning officers by the Cabinet was re-established, although their "permanence" remained. "The offices of all returning officers heretofore appointed," read the Act, "shall be deemed to be vacant, and the Governor-in-Council may appoint to such offices either the same persons as now hold them, any of such persons, or any other persons."[2] There was consequently a total turnover of returning officers before the 1935 election.[3] The Liberals repealed and then re-enacted

[1]See *Report of Special Committee on Dominion Elections Act* etc., 1930, *Minutes of Proceedings and Evidence*, no. 2 and no. 6; before the Committee, the Chief Electoral Officer at first declined to state whom he had consulted in regard to appointments, but the information was tabled in the House.

[2]*Statutes*, 24-25 Geo. V, c. 50, s. 8.

[3]The Conservatives re-appointed some former officers, as a comparison of lists shows. See *Report of the Chief Electoral Officer on the 17th General Election, 1930*, p. 544; *and the 18th General Election, 1935*, p. 640.

this clause in 1938,[1] so that there was again a total turnover in 1940. It is a sobering commentary on our legislative processes that the turnover of electoral officers has been at least as great since they were made permanent as in the bad old days when they were temporary.

The turnover of returning officers naturally declines when one party is in power for several consecutive elections. On June 1, 1948, the number of times returning officers had served in both general and by-elections was as follows:[2]

Number of Elections	Number of Officers
None	25
1	96
2	104
3	1
4	3
6	1
7	1
9	2

It will be noted that the largest group of officials had served in two elections, which would date their appointment in most cases as following the Liberal return to power in 1935, but preceding the election of 1940. Despite the continuance in office of one party, the turnover of officers is nevertheless high.

The quality of the returning officers has naturally varied. A civil servant concerned with the paying of election officials testified in 1929 that some returning officers conscientiously visited every poll to explain matters to their subordinates; but in 1937 the Chief Electoral Officer stated that in some districts, "the returning officer is nothing but a figurehead and the election clerk does all the work."[3] The attainments of the local officials must also vary with the requirements of the constituency. While the conducting of an election is generally a routine though complex procedure, there are not lacking in Canada ridings populated by a rough-and-ready

[1]*Statutes*, 2 Geo. VI, c. 46, s. 8.
[2]Figures supplied by Chief Electoral Officer.
[3]*Report of Special Committee on Dominion Elections Act* etc., 1929, p. 14: *Report of Special Committee on Elections and Franchise Acts*, 1937, p. 42.

citizenry who are unlikely to be awed merely by a returning officer's authority. In such rare instances, I am informed on unimpeachable authority, the returning officer must not only know the law, but also be able to hit with both fists and run like a deer.

Recent references to the electoral machinery in the House of Commons have reflected credit on it, notwithstanding the strategic role still played by patronage.[1] The Athabaska election of 1925 demonstrated the dangers of unsupervised appointment of minor election officials; but the invidious position into which the Chief Electoral Officer was forced in 1930 gave an equally convincing demonstration of the difficulties of centralized control of the electoral system. The high degree of efficiency which the election machine has achieved over the years, as evidenced by the competent handling of the overseas serviceman's vote in 1945,[2] is a strong indication that the patronage involved is ordinarily harmless. It is a safe generalization that political parties can be relied upon to make good appointments in their own interest; but at the same time, the fact that no legal qualifications whatever are required of returning officers is a continuing source of potential trouble.

The existence of a permanent Chief Electoral Officer with substantial authority gives to the machinery a measure of automatic operation that would be otherwise impossible. But the strategic positions, so far as the efficient holding of an election in any one constituency is concerned, are the local ones, and the degree of local autonomy enjoyed by each district remains very substantial. As a matter of policy (the efficacy of which has been apparent for many years) the staff of the Chief Electoral Officer discourages constituency officials from relying upon Ottawa for assistance in every difficulty; the primary assumption is that a general election consists of two hundred and sixty local elections.

[1]*Debates*, 1943, pp. 5095-158. In that year a returning officer discharged two enumerators who had been padding the voters' lists, and in the same constituency the returning officer was replaced for one election because he was the uncle of one of the candidates.

[2]See *Report of Special Committee on Dominion Elections Act, 1938 (Armed Forces)* 1944; *Debates*, 1944, pp. 3693 ff.

Smooth working of the electoral system thus requires either that the returning officers be permanent or that they be appointed long enough in advance of an election to give them ample time to learn the problems of their constituency. The Special Committee on Elections and Franchise Acts, 1937, significantly recommended "that a longer period of time should be given to the various returning officers to revise the arrangement of polling divisions of their respective electoral districts, and with that purpose in view the proposed new Dominion Elections Act should be passed not later than the year 1938."[1] This suggestion, considered in relation to the history of the electoral machinery, points a clear moral: any parties intending to manipulate the system for patronage purposes in the future should at least be considerate enough to do it early.

[1]*Report of Special Committee on Elections and Franchise Acts*, 1937 (Second and Final Report), p. vii.

CHAPTER X

THE VOTERS' LISTS

A voters' list, on the face of it, is an innocuous thing. It comprises the names and addresses of qualified electors, so that the only apparent problems are to discover what persons are entitled to vote, and to write down their names in alphabetical or possibly geographical order.

Canadian experience with voters' lists is a far cry from this routine procedure. Until roughly 1900, the opposing parties frequently fought longer and more bitter battles over lists than they did over actual elections. The real franchise in Canada during that period was not necessarily what the law said it was, but the presence of one's name on an accepted voters' list; whether or not this coincided with statutory provisions might depend primarily on the political circumstances in one's own riding. The local situation of course varied greatly with the integrity of constituency election officers, but the franchise law was in general for many years a poor source to which to turn for information on the extent of the suffrage in Canada.

Voters' lists at Confederation were easily compiled. Since all the provinces then required a property qualification for electors, an assessment list could be used as the basis for the accumulation of voters' names. This was done in all the provinces, although the details varied considerably; revision and correction of the lists took place before a county court judge in Ontario, and various municipal officials in Quebec, Nova Scotia, and New Brunswick. In addition, the lists were "closed" in each case; once properly compiled and revised, they could not be changed before polling day. Omission from a list thus automatically disqualified an elector, whether he was entitled to vote or not. This fact explains much of the party strife over voters' lists.

The administrative organization concerned with the first Canadian lists was local or municipal, free of official interference from federal and provincial governments in nearly all areas. In terms of practical politics, this involved the waste of a vast amount of valuable petty patronage, and Sir John Macdonald, motivated nominally by the disparity in the qualifications of electors in the several provinces, was early led to propose that the federal government should look after voters' lists. In 1870, for example, taking the reasonable line that it was "out of the question" to leave the federal franchise and voters' lists in the hands of provincial and local governments, Sir John introduced a comprehensive bill to provide a uniform franchise and a system of list-compilation by appointed Boards of Registrars in each district; judges were to be ultimately responsible for revision of the lists.[1]

The proposal that federal machinery for voters' lists should be created was by no means devoid of merit. There was some evidence of inefficiency on the part of local officers; it appeared in a committee of the House of Commons that in some instances lists used in 1867 had not been revised since 1861.[2] The Conservatives were also able to make the usual references to the wickedness of the existing method in general, and the total depravity of certain municipal officials in particular.[3] The arguments for federal control were strong, and might well have appealed more to the Liberals had Macdonald not been so intent on converting the electoral system into both a pool of patronage and an instrument for winning elections. But since the parochial nature of the system in use allowed Liberals as well as Conservatives to hold strategic local positions as assessors and county clerks, it was impossible to persuade the Opposition that a list machinery administered solely by Conservatives was in any sense an improvement. The Liberals committed themselves to the perpetuation of the entire local and provincial system for national elections, while the Conservatives were satisfied to adopt in 1871 the federal appointment of all returning officers.[4]

The compilation of federal voters' lists between 1867 and 1885 was a large and uncontrolled enterprise whose operation,

[1]*Debates*, 1870, pp. 355 ff. A similar bill was introduced in 1869. See *Parliamentary Debates* (Scrapbook Hansard), May 18, 1869.
[2]*Debates*, 1870, p. 713.
[3]*Ibid.*, p. 536; pp. 711-12.
[4]See previous chapter.

considering the magnitude of the task, produced surprisingly few serious complaints.[1]   Possibly because of this, Sir John pressed with great caution towards his goal, and bills to establish federal lists were introduced but not proceeded with on several occasions.   Beginning in 1882, indeed, such bills made annual appearances.   The parliamentary session of 1885 opened with yet another proposal, but as week followed week with no indication that the Government intended to force a bill through, Liberal suspicions were lulled into quiescence.   The diversion of both Parliament's and the public's attention to the North-West troubles provided a second major reason for the Liberals' failure to anticipate so important a government measure as a fundamental change in the electoral machinery.[2]

The Conservative strategy, if it was expected to produce an Act of Parliament after a short but sharp discussion, was a total failure.   The motion for second reading of the franchise bill of 1885 touched off one of the greatest debates ever heard in the House of Commons, and so obstinately did the Opposition obstruct that the Government finally conceded several changes.   The bill occupied the legislature from April 16 to July 6; day after day saw adjournment come well after midnight, and not infrequently at four and five A.M.   One memorable sitting lasted from a Thursday afternoon to Saturday midnight, as the Government sought by a variation of its tactics to force through a repugnant clause by sitting out the Opposition.   One reformer declared:

They found that their ribaldry, their songs of merriment and their disorderly conduct would not do. . .   They held a caucus, and the Fiat went out from the leader of the Government that silence was henceforth to be the order of the day and . . . they came here with their pillows, and went to sleep. . . They provided themselves with beds and couches, and a gentleman who ought to know better . . . was actually engaged in dancing the Highland fling.[3]

[1]*The Week* recorded on April 30, 1885, during the debate on the Franchise Act, that "from wilful tampering they (the present lists) are as free as lists prepared under this bill could be expected to be."
[2]*Debates*, 1885, pp. 1133 ff.   The Liberals moved in amendment at this time that "in the opinion of this House it is not possible at this late stage of the Session, and having regard to the present conditions of public business, to discuss the said Bill satisfactorily."
[3]*Ibid.*, p. 1549.   Also pp. 1473 ff.   The long sitting was from April 30 to May 2, 1885.

Some of the provisions of the bill were as remarkable as the means used to secure its passage. The essentials of the original proposals were: (1) The varied provincial franchises were to be abandoned for a single federal franchise.[1] (2) The foregoing proposal necessitated a change in the procedure for preparing lists, and the Conservatives intended to have these compiled and revised in each district by a government appointee called a "revising officer." (3) From this compilation and revision there was to be no convenient and readily accessible system of appeal. (4) Names could be removed from or added to the list virtually at the discretion of the revising officer. The Act, as finally passed, charged this officer with comparing "the list of voters of the preceding year . . . with the last assessment rolls, and (he) shall, with all the information that he can obtain from that *or any other source*, proceed to revise the list of voters. . . ."[2] It hardly seems necessary to add that the Liberals were particularly dissatisfied with these third and fourth points. Truly, as one Opposition member said, speaking perhaps more prophetically than he knew, this meant that "a Conservative vote, by their machinery, can be got on the list with the greatest possible ease, upon statements or information and any wrongs can only be set right at great expense. . . ."[3] *Grip* suggested gravely that a good deal of time, trouble, and money could be saved in future elections if the revising officers did all the voting.[4]

In the face of tremendous Liberal opposition, the government side of the House was notably silent for several weeks. Presumably the hope was that the Liberals would talk themselves out. Sir John himself appears to have been in great good humour during most of the debate:

Well, I must really despair of coming to any arrangement with hon. gentlemen opposite. The question of appeal was discussed, and hon. gentlemen opposite came to me from the opposite side and stated, if there be an appeal from the revising officer who was not a county judge much of the objection would be removed. It was distinctly understood that . . . in case the revising officer was the county judge, then his decision was final. That is the

[1]See Chapter XII.
[2]*R. S. Can.*, 1886, c. 5, s. 15. (Italics added.)
[3]*Debates*, 1885, p. 2306.
[4]*Grip*, May 2, 1885. See also *The Week*, May 14, 1885.

position I proceeded upon, and upon which the whole discussion proceeded, and I am quite surprised and rather indignant at the attempt to get rid of that.[1]

As the Liberals denied the existence of any such agreement, Sir John's statement is useful not only as an example of his amiability, but of the sort of "misunderstanding" that marked the debate.

The essentials of the franchise bill survived the storm in the Commons.[2] One important concession was made when Sir John decided to accept his own version of the above misunderstanding and provide for a convenient method for electors to appeal to a judge if the revising officer was not himself a judge.[3] But the fundamental principle of having voters' lists compiled and revised by a government appointee remained unchanged.

These appointments were limited by the statute to judges or lawyers of five years' standing at the provincial bar.[4] Macdonald's avowed policy was to appoint judges where possible, and a glance at a list of his first appointees suggests that this aim was conscientiously pursued. The first revising officers selected were as follows:[5]

	Judges	Non-Judges
Ontario	80	11
Quebec	7	58
Nova Scotia	4	14
New Brunswick	12	3
Prince Edward Island	3	–
British Columbia	3	2
Manitoba	3	2
Totals	112	90

The fact that judges were used in more than half the constituencies was nevertheless misleading as an indication of

[1]*Debates*, 1885, p. 2349.
[2]Changes connected with the franchise, but not related to the lists, are discussed in Chapter XII.
[3]*R. S. Can.*, 1886, c. 5, ss. 33-5.
[4]*Ibid.*, s. 11.
[5]Compiled from *Auditor General's Report*, 1887, pp. 788 ff.

the actual policy followed in making appointments.[1]   Further examination of the eleven Ontario constituencies where judges were not appointed reveals that eight of them were fairly doubtful Conservative seats; seven of these remained Conservative in 1887.   A majority of the seven Quebec constituencies where judges were used were safe seats for one party or the other, so that a non-partisan revising officer could do no harm.[2]   That this aspect of the revision of the lists was not entirely overlooked in 1885 is suggested by many letters in Macdonald's correspondence.   "At the last contest we were only beaten by 32," wrote one stalwart, "and with a little assistance we certainly can change that.   Our junior county judge has always favoured the Reform party, and if he was appointed it would be difficult to work up the riding so as to elect a Conservative."[3]   "To appoint him," wrote an opponent of another judge, "would amount to a virtual surrender of the counties named to the Grits."[4]   In South Perth, strong representations from the local organization resulted in the appointment of a barrister; the judge was rejected because he was allegedly a partisan.[5]

A surprising number of judges seem to have been partisans in the eighties.   Even before the statute of 1885 had passed the Commons, Macdonald's correspondence shows that he was being importuned on all sides by applicants for the post of revising officer.   Some of the letters were from judges;[6] others were from party supporters for or against particular judges. One of the most interesting of these was from a staunch Conservative who urged the appointment as revising officer of a judge who was a former staunch Grit, and a colleague of the prominent Liberal, Louis Davies.   "If he leans at all," the Tory told Macdonald, "it will be away from the Grits as he prides himself on his impartiality, and moreover has a

---

[1]In passing, it may be noted that this new electoral machinery required the appointment of extra junior judges, mainly in Ontario, and thus provided the strange anomaly of judicial appointments being created for political purposes.
[2]Quebec appointments were made on Hector Langevin's advice; Macdonald looked after Ontario.   See Macdonald Papers, vols. 9-11.
[3]W. F. Roome to Macdonald, October 3, 1885 (*ibid.*, vol. 9).
[4]G. Moore to Macdonald, August 1, 1885 (*ibid.*, vol. 10).
[5]See *ibid.*, vol. 9.   In other cases, Macdonald was obdurate in insisting that judges be appointed.   See *ibid.*, vol. 10, p. 124.
[6]E.g., Judge Burnham to Macdonald, May 19, 1885; Judge McDonald to Macdonald, July 13, 1885 (*ibid.*, vol. 9).

personal dislike to Davies."[1] The limitations of the celebrated independence of the judiciary can rarely have proved more efficacious than immediately after the passage of the Franchise Act of 1885.

Dissatisfaction with the employment of judges to revise voters' lists was not confined to their real or suspected partiality. The statute which the judges were to administer was so loosely worded in part that trained legal minds could show considerable originality in interpreting it. Making due allowance for party prejudice, the following statement by George Casey, Liberal member for Elgin, contained a great deal of truth:

Some revising officers have accepted applications for the insertion of a long list of names, authenticated by one declaration, made by the person who compiled the list. Other revising officers . . . required individual declarations made by each person who claimed the right to have his name placed in the list. Some revising officers, I am informed, in other Provinces than Ontario . . . have refused to accept any applications or to pay any attention to any declaration of qualification until after the publication of the first list, saying that the proper time to make these declarations is at the preliminary revision. . . Others have received such applications. . . Of those who have accepted and dealt with those applications, some have simply given no notice whatever to the applicant, whether his application has been successful or not. Others have returned the rejected applications, with reasons endorsed, directly to the applicants. Others . . . have returned the rejected applications in batches to the persons through whom they were sent in. . . . Unfortunately these acts of the revising officer, who happens also to be a judge, cannot be questioned; his rule is absolute; no appeal can be had from it; and it is all the more necessary that his action should be criticised in this House.[2]

Another point which Casey criticized was that an elector omitted from the lists had to obtain legal advice before he could apply for inclusion when, Casey argued, he belonged there as of right. Even hiring a lawyer guaranteed nothing, for Casey proceeded to produce several applications, drawn up by lawyers, which had been rejected by judges on legalistic technical grounds. "I found a great difficulty in coming to

[1] I. T. Jenkins to Macdonald, September 21, 1885 (Macdonald Papers, vol. 10). This judge was appointed.
[2] *Debates*, 1886, p. 44. This is a good example of a not infrequent occurrence; the peculiar position in which judges were put by the electoral laws of this period did little to enhance the prestige of the judiciary. See *ibid.*, 1890, p. 3196; 1934, pp. 4469 ff.

any conclusions as to the information I should take," a former revising officer admitted. "For instance I got letters and lists of twenty or thirty names asking to be put on. .... I believe the uniform practice throughout Ontario was to insist upon evidence, such as a statutory declaration."[1] This process, while undoubtedly fair, introduced into the system a rigidity and an emphasis on legalistic procedure which put the individual voter both to inconvenience and expense.

Where judges' activities were causing concern, the work of revising officers who were mere lawyers of five years' standing could hardly escape censure. Some added names to lists without any proper application whatever being made;[2] others put disqualified voters on the lists in the expectation that pending legislation would qualify them;[3] others allowed dead and removed voters to remain on the lists in large quantities and added the names of minors;[4] one acted when he had already been disqualified for corrupt practices;[5] and some rejected applications on even more frivolous grounds than fine points of law.[6] All these were referred to by the Liberals in uncomplimentary terms and with proof which carried varying degrees of conviction.

The blame for these variations on a familiar theme cannot all be charged to the revising officers. Apart from the vagueness of the law, they were in too many instances at the mercy of local party organizations. In a revealing letter to the Prime Minister in 1886 Dalton McCarthy wrote:

From what I can learn, I am beginning to think that it may not be at all impossible that we shall find that the Grits will get more of their men on the Voters' Lists ... than we will. Our friends are enthusiastic enough, but ... it will require solid and careful work on the part of the organization to have the vote put on. For my part I have come to the conclusion that the only sure way of getting the names on is to employ some intelligent man who understands the new law. .. My belief is that if the proper men could be secured to do this, that many of the closer ridings could be made secure.

[1]*Ibid.*, 1889, p. 1012. The Ontario revising officers (they were almost all judges) at least took their duties seriously, for they held a meeting in Toronto on December 27, 1886.
[2]*Ibid.*, 1886, p. 50.
[3]*Ibid.*, p. 1499.
[4]*Ibid.*, 1887, p. 1223. The constituency was Kent, Ontario, where the revising officer further sinned by refusing to hear appeals.
[5]*Ibid.*, p. 1226. Montmagny, P.Q., was the constituency here.
[6]*Ibid.*, 1886, p. 49.

It would cost $2000 or $3000 for each constituency, but how much wiser to make that investment now, when it can be properly and legitimately spent, than to be squandering money at the election time.[1]

That McCarthy's suggestion was adopted in principle by both parties was evident in many statements made in Parliament. A Liberal member testified in 1889, for instance, that a revision of the lists cost him personally $750 in legitimate expenditure for applications and legal charges.[2] A Conservative admitted in 1890 that "nobody will deny that a revision involves a great deal of anxiety, trouble and expense, both to members already representing constituencies, and to the would-be candidates."[3] *The Week* denounced the statute as "one of the most expensive, cumbrous, and generally unsatisfactory ever put upon a statute book."[4]

The expense was not confined to candidates and other interested persons, and the total official expenditure on voters' lists exceeded one million dollars between 1885 and 1896.[5] While this sum is perhaps small when compared with present election expenses, it was enormous when considered in relation to the smaller electorate of that period, the additional expenditure by candidates which the act necessitated, and the singularly unsatisfactory nature of the lists when prepared.

The worst result of the statute's expense was that the Government did not hesitate to suspend its operation as often as was expedient. Revisions of lists, instead of being annual, were made only in 1886, 1889, 1891 (too late for the election of that year), and 1894. The general election of 1891 was thus held on a closed list that disfranchised everybody under twenty-three and some under twenty-four, though they were otherwise legally qualified; and the same thing happened again in 1896. In addition, persons moving to another constituency after the last revision and before an election were disfranchised in their new district; this was a serious weakness

[1]McCarthy to Macdonald, January 29, 1886 (Macdonald Papers, vol. 228). Another supporter wrote, "If we don't look after [the lists] thoroughly we may be hoist with our own petard . . . I will prepare some 'hints' for our friends which I will send you so that they may be printed and disseminated." (J. A. MacDonnell to Macdonald, September 2, 1885, Macdonald Papers, vol. 11).
[2]*Debates*, 1889, p. 1278.
[3]*Ibid.*, 1890, p. 3896. See also p. 1159, where another member states that a revision cost him approximately $700.
[4]*The Week*, April 12, 1889. See also *ibid.*, June 10, 1889; April 12, 1889.
[5]*Debates*, 1897, pp. 89-90.

in view of the tremendous turnover of population in some urban areas and in frontier agricultural districts.[1]

The Franchise Act of 1885 was in fact a failure insofar as it was intended to provide a solution to the problem of the voters' list. *The Week* summarized its shortcomings in 1892:

The Act is very complicated and expensive in operation, it affords facilities for "stuffed lists", it tempts strongly to perjury, it works wholly in favour of the wealthier party, and in practical operation it undoubtedly results in the omission from the lists of many good citizens whose right to vote is beyond question, and in placing and retaining on the lists many who are without a shadow of qualification.[2]

Many of these strictures the Government soon admitted: tacitly by frequently suspending the Act and making what economies they could in its administration;[3] openly by confessing that they had underestimated the time and trouble the Act involved;[4] and finally by proposing in 1894 to abandon the federal franchise and return to the provincial one.[5] This proposal was still linked with federal control of the voters' lists, but by the nineties the Conservatives were obviously becoming wary of the scheme they had introduced in 1885.

The Liberal victory of 1896 consequently gave that party a unique opportunity to develop with Conservative co-operation a new and better way of obtaining voters' lists. Their solution to the problem was a simple act of retrogression; they put the whole burden back on the shoulders of the local governments. This proposal, which included the use once more of provincial franchises as well as provincial lists, was first introduced as a government bill in 1897, and finally enacted in 1898.[6] It was undoubtedly a part of the Liberals' belief in provincial autonomy,[7] and since it required the new federal government to divest itself of a large amount

---

[1]Sir Richard Cartwright stated in 1896 that in one county, 2600 names of a total electorate of 5000 changed between the 1891 and 1894 revisions. *Debates*, 1896, p. 6605.

[2]*The Week*, March 18, 1892.

[3]Thus at one stage the printing of all lists was transferred to Ottawa, where lists for the entire Dominion were maintained by the Queen's Printer. This did not add to the Act's flexibility. The main Conservative amendment to the Liberal Franchise Act, 1898, admitted the expensiveness of the 1885 statute.

[4]*Debates*, 1890, p. 3897; 1898, p. 2785.

[5]*Ibid.*, 1894, pp. 4300 ff. The bill did not go past second reading.

[6]*Ibid.*, 1897, pp. 718 ff.; 1898, pp. 2270 ff., 2532 ff., etc.

[7]See e.g., *ibid.*, pp. 2705 ff.

of desirable patronage in each constituency, there is strong
evidence that the Liberals' belief in this regard was sincerely
held.

The bill also brought up two constitutional questions:
whether it involved a delegation of power by the federal
government; and whether in any case the federal government
could require local and provincial officials to work for it.[1]   To
both of these questions the Liberals had answers satisfactory
to a majority of the House of Commons.   Finally, and most
oddly, the Liberal act necessitated the adoption of varied
provincial laws and machinery of which even the Liberal
ministers were substantially ignorant.   This fact provoked
Borden to protest: "We are not only invited to pass upon
legislation which we do not understand, but to pass an act
providing that everything which these provincial legislatures
shall enact in the future will be all right."[2]   He might have
gone further to point out that using the provincial machinery
would involve the Liberals in a serious inconsistency for in
1885 the Liberals had fought a pitched battle for the right of
electors to appeal from a revising officer's decision.   The reversion to provincial lists meant that there would be no such
appeal permitted in the Maritimes.[3]

The original bill of the Franchise Act of 1898 was passed
with a few concessions,[4] and the essentials of the scheme thus
adopted were not disturbed for a decade.   The administrative
aspect of voters' lists consequently forced once more a close
connection between the two separate fields of federal and local
politics (such as had existed between 1867 and 1885) for
federal candidates would in their own interest again be required to keep a sharp watch on the preparation of provincial
lists.   Since the provincial governments at the turn of the
century were predominantly Liberal, disputes between the
federal and local governments over lists were rare;   the

[1]See *ibid.*, pp. 4383 ff., 4045.
[2]*Ibid.*, p. 2991.   See p. 2955 and pp. 4121-2 for admissions by Liberal leaders
that they were unacquainted with the details of provincial law.
[3]This point was brought up later when Laurier promised to *ask* the offending
provinces to change their laws in this regard.   See *ibid.*, pp. 4407 ff., 5664 ff.
[4]See *ibid.*, 1898, pp. 5664 ff., 7467 ff.   The former are concessions to the
House, the latter to the Senate.   The most important of the former was that
accepting the principle of adding to the provincial lists the names of those who,
though qualified for federal purposes, were disqualified in the provinces.

Conservatives, at the same time, were not deprived of the customary opposition role of fighting elections on voters' lists prepared by their opponents.

By 1908 more than one of the provincial governments had deserted to the Conservative camp, and in two of these the voters' lists were found to be unsatisfactory for federal purposes. The Liberals therefore proposed to restore federal lists in British Columbia and Manitoba. In Manitoba at least, their hand was forced by the provincial party organization, which had been embarrassing the federal government for years by loudly desiring federal supervision of provincial lists.[1]   A bill embodying the Government's lopsided plan was entrusted to Hon. Mr. Aylesworth who, being somewhat deaf, was able to thread his way through a thunderous Conservative Opposition with a singleness of purpose which did little to allay the latter's indignation.   The Conservatives, thrust by a strange irony into a position of defending provincial lists, obstructed to the point of refusing supply,[2] and finally the Government surrendered most of its bill.   It insisted on one provision, however, which is interesting because it constituted the first use in a general election act of what has since been recognized as the most efficient way of obtaining voters' lists: compilation by enumerators.[3]

This principle was extended to the entire country for the first time by the Wartime Election Act of 1917, which empowered the Governor-in-Council to appoint enumerators in each province; provincial lists, however, remained as the basis of the enumerators' compilation in most of the Dominion.[4]   The Liberals not unnaturally objected to the appointment of such important officers on a patronage basis, particularly in view

[1] J. W. Dafoe, *Clifford Sifton in Relation to his Times* (Toronto, 1931) pp. 343-5.
[2] E.g., *Debates*, 1907-8, p. 9225.
[3] This principle was applied here only to the unorganized parts of Ontario. Before this, enumeration had been used in the old North-West Territories and continued in Alberta and Saskatchewan after 1905.   These Ontario enumerators were to be appointed by judges, which provoked yet another protest about judges and politics.   Said a member: "I generally find that the judges have politics in Ontario as well as other people.   I do not say that they exhibit any political feeling offensively, but no man can get rid of the idea that he was once a Liberal or a Tory, and there can be no doubt that in appointing these enumerators the judges will have to appoint Grits or Tories." (*Ibid.*, p. 13229.)
[4] *Statutes*, 7-8 Geo. V, c. 39, s. 1, and ss. h-u, inclusive.

of the powers given them to omit names from lists,[1] but as the bill was passed under closure, they had little opportunity to expand their case.   This revolutionary change in the procedure of compiling voters' lists was such a minor matter in the general furor that accompanied the khaki election of 1917 that it received only passing notice.

The reform of the whole electoral machinery by the Conservative Government in 1920 saw those great champions of federal lists returning to provincial lists.   Certain reservations were made, however, if the existing lists in any province were over two years old.[2]   In that event a cumbersome machinery was adopted whereby in all centres of over one thousand population the voters had to register personally at a registrar's office to have their names put on the list; judicial revision was provided; and these lists, once made, were final.   In rural areas the list was prepared by enumeration, but without judicial appeal:[3] here the lists were "open"—i.e., qualified voters omitted from the list could swear themselves in on polling day, as long as they were vouched for by another elector.[4]

This complicated experiment worked well enough at first to satisfy the newly appointed Chief Electoral Officer.[5]   But succeeding years showed the profound difficulty of holding federal elections on provincial lists for whose accuracy no federal officer was responsible.   In 1922 the Electoral Officer's annual report to the Speaker listed four major weaknesses of the scheme: the law on occasion required the use of provincial voters' lists that the province itself regarded as obsolete; provincial and federal polling divisions did not coincide, so that creating lists for one purpose from lists compiled for another was extremely difficult; the accurate transfer of names from one list to the other in areas having a high turn-

[1]See *Debates*, 1917, p. 5831, and section 1 (0) of the statute. Also *supra*, pp. 180-1.
[2]The original reservation was on lists over one year old.
[3]*Statutes*, 10-11 Geo. V, c. 46, s. 32.   The provisions relating to the rural enumerators, it is curious to note, refer to them consistently as "registrars" because the word "enumerators" was not popular after 1917.   The revising judges received extra pay in 1921 for their work on the lists.
[4]*Ibid.*, s. 62.
[5]See *Debates*, 1921, p. 3093; 1922, pp. 184-5; *Report of the Chief Electoral Officer to the Speaker*, 1921.

over of population was virtually impossible; and the law did not allow for the removal of dead or disqualified electors from provincial lists.[1]   In 1926 the Chief Electoral Officer reported:

While the system of preparing Dominion lists continues to depend upon the ever-changing practice in the nine different provinces of Canada, difficulties are bound constantly to arise, and it is only by attempting, often in great haste and with insufficient information, to adapt the provisions of the Dominion Elections Act to the local and temporary situation in a given area as this develops . . . that it is possible to hope to make these provisions operate to the satisfaction of candidates and the public.[2]

During the twenties the principle of open lists and enumeration by door-to-door workers was slowly extended.   In 1921 it was applied to all towns below 2500 population; in 1925 the limit was raised to towns of 5000; and in 1929 to towns of 10,000.   The cumbersome machinery which required electors to register in larger centres was abolished in 1929, and all lists were prepared by enumeration.[3]   At the same time, the Liberal Government then in power abandoned the use of provincial lists even as a basis for federal lists; the electoral wheel had made a full turn.

The election of 1930 was thus held on the basis of the most carefully prepared lists yet compiled.   In essence, the names for the lists had been taken as in a census; enumerators worked in pairs, each major party being represented; and citizens had every opportunity to get their names on a list if by any chance the enumerators had missed them.   "I have been connected with the administration of the last eight general elections," declared the Chief Electoral Officer in 1937, "and I have no hesitation in saying that in my opinion the system for the preparation of lists adopted in the 1930 election

[1]*Report of the Chief Electoral Officer to the Speaker*, 1922.
[2]*Report of the Chief Electoral Officer to the Speaker*, 1926, p. 4.   In this report the Officer advocated the use of closed printed lists, to be kept up-to-date and available at all times.   A major difficulty with this, he admitted, was that a voter would have to notify somebody every time he changed his residence.
[3]*Statutes*, 19-20 Geo. V, c. 40.   This gradual extension of enumeration and open lists was not made without opposition.   In 1925 Mr. Meighen objected to the widespread extension of the "swearing-in" process on polling day because of the possibilities of fraud in larger towns where not everybody was known to everybody else.   He was joined by a leading Liberal, Mr. Power, who argued that the Chief Electoral Officer was "not aware of the extent to which certain people carry their patriotism . . . through their willingness to vote more often than the law considers judicious." (*Debates*, 1925, p. 4540.)

was by far the most satisfactory system used during that period."[1]

Unfortunately the Conservative Government elected by the 1930 system did not appreciate its benefits and scrapped its principles almost entirely in 1934. In that year a Dominion Franchise Commissioner, whose position was analagous to the Chief Electoral Officer, was appointed to be in charge of lists; both parties agreed in his choice. The basic voters' list was still to be made by enumeration, but once more revising officers (called Registrars) for each constituency were established; once more the lists were to be revised annually; and once more all lists were to be closed, so that only those whose names were actually listed could vote even in rural areas.[2] The Dominion Franchise Commissioner, pursuing a policy that was more commendable for its impartiality than for its grasp of political realities, appointed half of his franchise registrars from each major party, and placed them with no great regard for the leanings of any particular constituency.

This stratagem was not popular. The Chief Electoral Officer reported cautiously after the 1935 election that "it cannot be said . . . that the new list-making procedure proved to be an improvement on the old."[3] The Special Committee on Elections and Franchise Acts, 1937, unrestrained by any professional consideration for a colleague, denounced the 1934 scheme in no uncertain terms:

Your committee is unanimously of the opinion that the system of the Annual Revision of lists of Electors, as provided in the Dominion Franchise Act, 1934, has proved unsatisfactory. Experience has shown that the basic lists prepared in 1934 were almost obsolete within six months . . . and that the Annual Revision held in the year 1935 was inadequate to remedy the situation. The conclusion arrived at is that the yearly revision . . . could not produce satisfactory results, and that only through voluntary efforts on the part of Members of Parliament, candidates and political organizations involving great cost in time and money, could the lists of electors be brought up-to-date

[1] Report of Special Committee on Elections and Franchise Acts, 1937, p. 194.
[2] Statutes, 24-5 Geo. V, c. 51. Mr. King's seconding of the appointment of the Dominion Franchise Commissioner is a noteworthy one. "I for one," he said, "am prepared to believe that the qualities of character which have made him somewhat rigid in the work of the particular commission over which he presides are characteristic of a strict impartiality and honesty which may give him a special fitness for this particular post." (Debates, 1934, p. 4556.)
[3] Report of the Chief Electoral Officer to the Speaker, 1936.

and thoroughly purged. Your Committee is unanimously of the opinion that it would be advisable to return to the system of preparation and revision of the lists of electors immediately after the issue of the Writs of Election, with closed lists in urban polls, and open lists in rural polls, as in 1930.[1]

The Committee's recommendations were accepted in the Dominion Elections Act of 1938.[2] The essentials of the scheme have not since been changed, so that contemporary lists in Canada are compiled entirely by enumeration. The enumerators in an urban constituency work in pairs and are appointed by the returning officer on a patronage basis which recognizes the claims of the party which last won the riding in a contest; the second enumerator of each pair is selected by the party which was the runner-up in the last election.[3] The system thus minimizes the possibilities of unfairness and abuse, and is in general a most satisfactory development from the long history of trial-and-error methods of compiling lists in Canada.

So discursive an experience can hardly point a clear moral. But the chronicle of Canadian voters' lists at least indicates two conclusions which may act as guides for future policy. The first is that any scheme of "standing" lists, which are kept up-to-date by regular revisions, apparently cannot work in a country which has heavy internal movements of population.[4] The Canadian experiments of 1885 and 1934 were both total failures, and put the ultimate burden of compiling accurate lists not on the state, but on interested individuals and organizations. The second conclusion augments the first: any system which puts the onus on individuals and organizations is certain to produce inaccurate and unsatisfactory lists, for the circumstances governing the actual compilation of the lists will inevitably tend to be irrelevant to the lists' purpose. Eighty years of Canadian experience have furnished conclusive evidence that the making of voters' lists is a proper state function; seventy of those eighty years were required to prove the point.

[1]*Report of Special Committee on Elections and Franchise Acts*, 1937, pp. vi-vii (Fourth and Final Report). See also p. 177 for some objections to the open list system, and p. 183 for some objections to the 1934 system.
[2]*Statutes*, 2 Geo. VI, c. 46.
[3]The rural procedure requires only one enumerator.
[4]Nevertheless, standing lists work acceptably in Australia and New Zealand.

CHAPTER XI

THE ELECTION

THE modern electoral system is a loose-limbed colossus which lies dormant most of the time.[1] Once every few years, on the occasion of a general election, it springs to life and it will then employ an army of over one hundred thousand persons over a period of nine or ten weeks and involve the expenditure of two to three million dollars. Between elections, only the staff of the Chief Electoral Officer at Ottawa, comprising less than a dozen civil servants, is steadily at work.

In each constituency is a single returning officer, a permanent appointee of the Governor-in-Council, who, if he is experienced and already has his constituency organized into polling divisions properly mapped out, has little to do between elections but hold his position. This inactivity provides him with no sinecure, for he is not paid for it. If he is a new incumbent, the Chief Electoral Officer sends instructions and supplies to him at the earliest possible moment; he is expected to prepare his constituency for an election that might be announced any day. He must allow a polling station for every 300 or 350 electors, and divide his district geographically so that ballot boxes are fairly distributed and easily accessible to the populace. He must also dispose of the large quantities of supplies sent him, familiarize himself with their content and significance, and be ready to use them rapidly and accurately when a writ of election arrives.

A general election begins with the issuance of writs by the Chief Electoral Officer, ordering each returning officer by

[1]Throughout this chapter, the word "election" refers to a general election. This chapter is based entirely on material supplied by the Chief Electoral Officer; it is an adaptation of the Prefatory Summary to the *General Election Instructions issued by the Chief Electoral Officer*, 1948, supplemented by information given in correspondence. The chapter is necessarily a gross over-simplification of the procedure followed. The Election Instructions, a detailed book of 376 pages which alone can give an accurate survey of the electoral system, is obtainable from the King's Printer, Ottawa.

name to hold an election on a date determined by the Governor-in-Council. The writs are issued in the name of the King, and in part read: "We command you that notice of the time and place of election being duly given, you do cause election to be made according to law of a member to serve in the House of Commons of Canada, for the electoral district of. . . ." Ordinarily the writs go forth roughly sixty days before polling day, as that is the minimum time in which the huge administrative organization can perform its task.

The returning officer in each constituency then sets about the one hundred and sixty jobs he must accomplish before polling day. He publishes a proclamation to tell the public what it already knows: that an election is going to be held. The proclamation names nomination day, polling day, the place in which nominations will be received, and sundry other items of interest to those interested. A copy of the proclamation is sent to every postmaster in the district, and must be placed in the post office where the public can see it.

This accomplished, the electoral juggernaut is in full train and cannot be stopped until a member is returned. Arrangements must therefore be made forthwith for the holding of a contest. The returning officer appoints an election clerk for the constituency, who is in effect his executive assistant. He opens an office in a central location. He appoints, assuming his district is an urban one, up to three hundred enumerators, in consultation with the party organizations which ran first and second at the last election. These enumerators must be instructed and set to work on the Monday which is the forty-ninth day before polling day; one week later they bring to the returning officer two copies of the lists which they have compiled by going from door to door in the constituency.[1] They have in the intervening week left a notice with each elector to let him know whether or not he is on the voters' list.

[1]In rural areas, only one enumerator is used, and door-to-door visitation can be replaced by "such other sources of information" as the enumerator may secure. The rural procedure is generally different from the urban procedure described above, though it is based on similar principles.

The lists, which in each constituency may contain as many as fifty thousand names, must be printed at once and in any case before the Wednesday which is the twenty-sixth day before polling. Twenty copies of the list for the whole riding go to each candidate; each elector receives a copy of the list for his own polling division. The lists must then be revised either by a judge or a substitute appointed by him. Each revising officer holds public sittings for the revision of lists on the eighteenth, seventeenth, and sixteenth days before polling. Any qualified elector omitted from the list, may be registered on personal application at these sittings; sworn applications made by agents (on a prescribed form) on behalf of electors will also be dealt with, as will applications for the correction of errors. The revisor may also remove names from the lists, provided the elector concerned has been notified so that he can object to the removal of his name. The final corrected lists are then reprinted, and again copies go to each candidate. No one whose name is omitted from the reprinted lists can vote. A different procedure in rural areas allows electors, though omitted from the list, to vote if an oath is taken and the applicant is vouched for on oath by a second elector.

While all this is proceeding, the returning officer has received nominations and deposits from candidates.[1] These must be carefully checked to ensure their compliance with the law, and a candidate must consent in writing to his nomination unless he is absent from the constituency. Nomination day is set at fourteen days before polling day in all but one constituency where local conditions necessitate a gap of four weeks; if by two o'clock in the afternoon of nomination day only one petition has been received, the returning officer makes a return by acclamation and the election is over. Should an election be necessary, the returning officer must at once acquaint the world with the fact: he arranges for advance polls (if any); he secures the printing of ballots on paper supplied from Ottawa, and he distributes ballot boxes among perhaps two hundred polling stations. In anticipation of a poll, he will already have

---

[1] The deposit is $200. See *supra*, pp. 155-6.

appointed his deputy returning officers to officiate over each ballot box; these must be briefed for their work on election day. In addition, the returning officer must obtain from each candidate a list of the persons working on the candidate's behalf for pay, and communicate these to his subordinates; he must send countless copies of lists, forms, and notices to everyone who is interested, and to some who are not.

On polling day, the emphasis shifts from the returning officer to his deputy in each polling station. Before the poll, the deputy returning officer will have checked his supplies of ballots and other forms, and appointed a poll clerk; he must also examine the proposed polling station to ensure that it is satisfactory and properly furnished, complete with screened booths for voting purposes; and he must swear in the candidates' agents, of which there may be two at each poll for each contestant. Ballots must be counted before the poll is opened, and the ballot box must be scrutinized sharply; the box is then locked, placed on a table in full view of all present, and the electors are invited to vote.

Each elector receives a ballot initialled on the back by the deputy; the elector's name is checked against the voters' list; he is told how to fold the ballot so that the deputy's initials can be seen without the vote being disclosed; and he is warned that the ballot will be rejected if he marks it with any other sign than a cross, or with any other implement than a black pencil. He steps into a booth, marks his ballot on the hard surface by law provided, and brings it back to the deputy. The deputy checks, removes and destroys the counterfoil on the ballot, marks "Voted" against the elector's name in the poll book, and deposits the ballot in the box in the presence of the voter. The voter must then leave at once; his active participation in his country's affairs is ordinarily finished for another four or five years.

This procedure takes place possibly two hundred and fifty times in any one polling station; across the country as a whole, it occurs over six million times. When polling closes at six P.M., each of the thirty-six thousand deputy returning officers, attended by a candidate or his agents and anybody else invited, counts the ballots in his box. He packages them, adds to the pile various statements concerning the day's polling, puts the lot in the ballot box, seals this and despatches it to the returning officer. The votes cast in the constituency are in due course totalled; but as candidates and their agents receive statements from each deputy returning officer of the results in the several polling stations, the unofficial result is known well before the final count. A formal addition is made by the returning officer, who declares one candidate elected, stores the ballot boxes against another day, sends quantities of material to the Chief Electoral Officer, and certifies various accounts so that he and his subordinates may be paid. Later, if the candidates are so disposed, the returning officer receives statements of their election expenses; he publishes a summary return of these, and six months later returns or destroys the relevant material.

Throughout the election, the Chief Electoral Officer and his staff must work literally night and day. Copies of all important documents, including voters' lists, are transmitted to Ottawa; complaints from candidates must be quickly checked and the R.C.M.P. set to work if the circumstances warrant it; and a general supervision must be exercised over the whole machinery. After the election is concluded, the Chief Electoral Officer arranges for the publication in the *Canada Gazette* of the names of the new members of Parliament; and he also sends the comptroller of the Treasury a certified statement of votes polled in each district, so that every candidate entitled to a refund of his deposit will receive it.

The routine aftermath of an election occupies the Chief Electoral Officer for several months; but life between elections is somewhat calmer for him. He supervises occasional by-elections, studies possible amendments to the Dominion Elections Act for the improvement of the system, prepares reports for committees of the House of Commons, supplies information to party organizations and various individuals, and keeps himself informed of developments in electoral machinery elsewhere in the world. Several hundred tons of forms must be printed and stored for the next election; if there have been amendments to the law, both the forms and the detailed instructions sent to local election officials may require substantial revision. It may be necessary to visit returning officers personally.

These are routine performances, perhaps, and can be handled by a few people working steadily within regular office hours. Nevertheless, the central office must have a tremendous flexibility, for at any moment it may be required to produce the effort called forth by a general election. The organization must be ready to expand in a matter of days from a tiny handful of permanent public servants to a vast nation-wide machine operated by 260 returning officers, 36,000 deputies, 36,000 poll clerks, and 40,000 enumerators. The occurrence of this phenomenon every few years involves one of the major administrative feats performed by the government of Canada.

CHAPTER XII

THE FRANCHISE

THE qualifications required of electors in Canada have varied as much as most parts of the representative machinery. While the general history has been one of gradual enlargement of the electorate, the extension of the suffrage has not proceeded at a uniform rate, nor has it affected all parts of the community equally. There are three great landmarks, in 1885, 1898, and 1917-20. The history of the franchise since Confederation is thus divided into four main periods.

1867-1885

It was intended from the beginning that the federal franchise would be the concern of the federal government. Section 41 of the British North America Act, 1867, provided for the continued use of provincial franchises, but this was a temporary expedient, to last only until Parliament provided otherwise. The mere presence of this qualification in the act is *prima facie* evidence that a federal franchise was contemplated, and indeed John A. Macdonald's remarks on the topic during the Confederation debates of 1865 left little room for doubt as to his own wishes.[1]

For the first Canadian Parliament, however, it was impracticable to use anything but existing provincial franchises. The general election of 1867 was thus held with an electorate which varied among the four provinces. The common denominator in these franchises was property. In Ontario and Quebec, the right to vote in cities and towns was confined to males who owned, occupied, or rented real property which was assessed at $300, or had a yearly value of $30; in rural areas the qualifications were $200 and $20

[1]See *Confederation Debates*, 1865, p. 39. See also a letter to Hon. Charles Tupper, November 14, 1864, in which Macdonald refers to a resolution to leave the related topic of constituency boundaries in the hands of the provinces as "an obvious blunder, and must be corrected." J. Pope, *Correspondence of Sir John Macdonald* (Toronto, 1921), pp. 14-15. Relevant sections of the B.N.A. Act are given in Appendix A of this volume.

211

respectively. New Brunswick gave the suffrage to every male subject over twenty-one, not otherwise disqualified, who was assessed for real estate worth $100, or for personal property (or real and personal together) worth $400; regardless of property, an annual income of $400 carried with it the franchise in New Brunswick. Nova Scotia's laws were similar to New Brunswick's but included no income qualification; here the requirements were real estate worth $150, or personal property (or real and personal property together) valued at $300.

The qualifications in effect constituted a householder's franchise which allowed most heads of families to vote. These citizens did not compose a large portion of the total population, for figures based on a random sample of constituencies from the four provinces show average electorates to approximate 15 per cent of the population of the constituencies:[1]

	Constituencies in Sample	(1) Average Electorate	(2) Average Population	(1) as per cent of (2)
Ontario........	12	3,164	19,184	16.5
Quebec........	10	2,836	17,656	16.1
Nova Scotia....	4	3,206	22,856	14.0
New Brunswick.	4	2,833	18,616	15.2

The Speech from the Throne in 1867 forecast a change in the franchise, but the pressure of more important business during that session of Parliament led to a postponement of any alterations. Sir John explained that the new franchise bill would be found "so complete and comprehensive as properly to occupy the attention of an entire session;"[2] but he made it clear that a franchise act would be passed as soon as was expedient, for comprehensive draft bills began to appear as early as 1869.[3] A factor in Sir John's plans

[1]Table computed from figures for 1872 general election, and 1871 census. See *Sessional Paper* no. 60, 1873. The total electorate in each constituency at that time did not approximate the total of males over 21. Thus Addington, for example, had 3200 voters out of 5000 adult males; Bothwell had 3650 out of 4900; Brant South had 3600 out of 4900.

[2]*Debates*, 1868, quoted in *ibid.*, 1885, p. 1177.

[3]See *Parliamentary Debates* (Scrapbook Hansard), May 18, 1869; Macdonald Papers, vol. 73.

was that shortly after Confederation Ontario and Nova
Scotia began to change their franchise laws.   The intention
in Nova Scotia was plainly to interfere in federal elections,
and this was effected simply by the disfranchisement for
provincial purposes of all federal employees.   The latter
were thereby automatically disqualified for voting in federal
elections.   In 1868 Sir John wrote to a colleague:

It is impossible, of course, that the elective franchise should be at the mercy
of a foreign body.   I had hoped that they would have let the law alone
for three or four years, and that the franchise might have remained undisturbed until near the next General Election.   This cannot be, however,
now, so we must deal with it. . . .   Personally . . . I have rather a fancy
for fancy franchises, but I do not think we can educate our people up to it.[1]

A new franchise was not proceeded with immediately, and
Sir John circumvented provincial tinkerings with the suffrage
by enacting that for federal purposes the provincial franchises would be used as they had existed in 1867 regardless
of subsequent changes.[2]   The use of contemporaneous provincial franchises was not accepted until the accession to
power of a Liberal Government in 1874.[3]
    The draft bills introduced by the Conservatives between
1867 and 1874 were interesting indications of that party's
reluctance to extend the franchise.   Proposed statutes in
1869 and 1870 would have established an income qualification of $400 but "it did not apply to day labourers, who
might as a matter of fact earn $400 in a year . . . because
they had no abiding interest in the country."[4]   Sir John
proposed at the same time to disfranchise owners of mort-
gaged farms, and rural tenants who did not hold their
property on a five-year lease; and since long leases were
unknown in many parts of Canada, this would have wiped
out a substantial part of the rural electorate in some areas.
The Liberals, who relied a good deal on rural support, disapproved of all such alterations.

[1]Macdonald to Brown Chamberlin, M.P., October 26, 1868 (Pope, *op. cit.*,
p. 75).
    [2]Interim Election Acts in 1871 and 1873 did this.   An exception to the
general rule was made for Ontario, for which an 1869 provincial statute was
accepted.
    [3]*Statutes*, 37 Vict., c. 9.
    [4]*Debates*, 1870, p. 356.

The national franchise became increasingly diverse as new provinces entered the federation and old ones changed the qualifications required of voters. A member thus summarized the situation for the House of Commons in 1882:

In Ontario . . . in cities, the franchise is real estate to the value of $400, in towns, to the extent of $300; and in municipalities and villages, to the extent of $200; besides which there is an income franchise of $400. In addition to this, we have the farmers' sons, who enjoy the franchise without having any property qualification. In Quebec, the franchise is $300 in cities, or a rental of $30; in other municipalities it is $200, or a rental of $20. In Nova Scotia, the franchise is $150 of real estate, and $300 of personal or real property, or $300 of personal property alone. In New Brunswick, the franchise is $100 real estate; $400 personal property or income, while in Prince Edward Island . . . any man between twenty-one and sixty enjoys the franchise, while over the age of sixty a voter must be assessed for property to the value of $6.40 a year. In Manitoba, a residence of a short time is required, with property to the value of $100. In British Columbia, the franchise amounts to manhood suffrage.[1]

The member found this not merely confusing, but unfair. "The man who has no property pays the heaviest taxes you can levy on any man," he cried, "and yet you give him no voice in the government of the country."[2]

Changes in provincial franchises between 1867 and 1885 appear to have extended the suffrage appreciably only in Ontario. The last federal election held on the provincial suffrage during this period, that of 1882, showed the following proportions of the population to be enfranchised.[3]

	Constitu-encies in Sample	(1) Average Elector-ate	(2) Average Popula-tion	(1) as per cent of (2)
Ontario........	12	4,109	20,309	20.2
Quebec........	10	3,300	19,897	16.6
Nova Scotia....	4	3,654	24,159	15.1
New Brunswick.	4	3,536	20,849	16.9
British Columbia	3	974	8,831	11.0
Manitoba......	2	3,872	11,119	34.8

[1]Ibid., 1882, p. 255. This was not an exhaustive statement of provincial franchises.

[2]Ibid., p. 256. This is the earliest statement of this type in the House that I have come across. Both Liberal and Conservative leaders for many years after 1867 continued to regard the franchise as a trust going with the ownership of property, rather than as a right belonging to citizens. (See

The remarkable variations shown by British Columbia and Manitoba reflect special circumstances in those two provinces. Manitoba had not merely a generous franchise, but a population containing a large proportion of adult males; British Columbia had a very small number of white settlers as compared with its total population, and only whites were allowed to vote.

The franchise in the two largest provinces between 1867 and 1885 was not markedly biased towards either the rural or urban areas. In Ontario, the electorates of Hamilton, Ottawa, and Kingston closely approximated the average given in the table; Toronto and London had electorates substantially larger. In Quebec, Montreal was well above the average, while Quebec City was appreciably below it. In the Maritimes, on the other hand, a strong rural bias was shown in New Brunswick, where voters in Saint John comprised only 11 per cent of the city; a less marked rural prejudice was shown in Nova Scotia, where the electorate of Halifax was proportionally smaller than the average in the sample. However, in none of these instances is the evidence conclusive.

Members of the Conservative party, who seem at first to have been but lukewarm supporters of Sir John Macdonald's plans for a federal franchise, had by the eighties begun to agree with him. His Ontario colleagues were particularly anxious for a national law, for the Liberal Government of the province led by Oliver Mowat had shown a natural tendency to enfranchise people who were expected to vote Liberal. "Extend the suffrage to city artisans to counterbalance the farmers' sons given the vote by Mowat," one of Macdonald's supporters wrote his leader in effect; others

Debates, 1870, pp. 530 ff., 754 ff.) During the great franchise debate of 1885, a motion for manhood suffrage was rejected 86 to 33, at which time several Liberal leaders came out for the principle. With many of them, however, this position was dictated by strategy in the particular debate going on, and it is significant that several of the most prominent did not commit themselves at all. (Ibid., 1885, pp. 1939 ff.)

[3]Computed from Sessional Papers, 1883, no. 77. P.E.I. did not use voters' lists at this time. The British Columbia and Manitoba samples include the only constituencies with usable returns for this purpose in 1882. The figures in both the foregoing tables, it should be noted, are inflated because a person owning various parcels of property would be listed as a voter for each one.

made various suggestions for a wider suffrage; and all expected that the newly enfranchised would be so carried away
by gratitude as to vote Conservative.[1] Other provinces
besides Ontario had Liberal governments in the eighties,
and the distrust by the Conservatives of federal electoral
law controlled by provincial Liberals was not only understandable but often justified. In addition, the glorious
opportunities for patronage in a nation-wide electoral system,
combined with the relative failure of the gerrymander act
of 1882 to accomplish its purpose,[2] no doubt quickened Sir
John's interest in a project which he had openly favoured
for two decades.

His hand was forced to some degree by the Government
of Ontario. In 1885, before the federal franchise act of that
year had begun its journey through the Commons, Mowat's
Government extended the provincial franchise to include
urban artisans and wage-earners;[3] in a word, the Ontario
law was timed to steal some of Macdonald's potential
thunder. Ontario also had now a substantially wider
franchise than the Conservatives, as evidenced by draft
bills prepared for the House of Commons, were prepared to
accept for federal purposes.

1885-1898

The most striking point about the Conservative franchise
bill of 1885 was that it was not a general extension of the
franchise, but rather the opposite. It was, moreover, not
a uniform franchise for the whole country, and it became
progressively less so as it passed the House of Commons
clause by clause. The main theme of the proposed franchise
was a property qualification, and this was adhered to as

[1]See Macdonald Papers, vol. 64.
[2]See *supra*, Chapter II.
[3]*Statutes of Ontario*, 48 Vict., c. 2. The essentials of this statute were a
property qualification of $200 property in cities and towns; $100 elsewhere; an
income franchise of $250; a wages franchise of the same amount; landholders'
sons and householders were also included. The act is interesting also in that it
gave Toronto a mild form of proportional representation (viz., the limited vote).
The city was made into a three-member constituency for provincial purposes,
and each elector had only two votes. While the act was passing the Ontario
legislature, the leader of the Conservative Opposition moved for the adoption
of manhood suffrage.

consistently as was expedient even where substantial concessions to particular interests were made. The property qualification was to be $300 in cities and towns, and half that amount in rural areas; an income qualification of $400 that did not include wage-earners was also added. The bill included a special concession that allowed fishermen to use the value of their equipment towards the minimum property requirement; this clause actually established a separate franchise for important sections of the Maritimes. Two genuine extensions of the franchise were also proposed, in that widows, spinsters, and Indians with the property qualification were to be allowed to vote, and a low rental qualification might add new voters in the tenant class.

The proposed property qualification was higher than the existing one in all provinces except Quebec. In view of the slovenly way in which voters' lists were often compiled in those days, this was no guarantee that the number of persons enfranchised for practical purposes would necessarily be affected. A noteworthy feature of the 1885 Act was that it was introduced in the legislature without a word of explanation as to its probable or possible effect on the constituencies, and indeed the entire debate ran its course with neither party in the House of Commons having any real knowledge of what the bill was going to do.[1] Liberals spoke feelingly and at length of tens of thousands being disfranchised; Sir John's supporters, when they spoke at all, concentrated on those hordes of citizens who were about to receive the marvellous boon of the suffrage. Sir John's intentions at least were clear: "The proposal to enfranchise the Indians," recorded *The Week*, "speaks for itself; these poor pensioners of the commonwealth must needs vote with the meal bag, which is in the hands of the agents of the Government. . . . The aim of the Female Suffrage clause was revealed by Sir John Macdonald himself."[2]

The suggested enfranchisement of certain classes of women (who were expected to vote Conservative) was dropped from the bill almost as soon as it entered the committee

[1]*Debates*, 1885, pp. 1133 ff.
[2]*The Week*, May 14, 1885. Earlier drafts of the bill did not enfranchise Indians (see Macdonald Papers, vol. 64).

stage in the legislature. Sir John spoke strongly in favour of the section as it stood, but made it so clear that he expected the proposal to be removed from the bill that it would have been surprising had it remained.[1] An amendment rejecting female suffrage in Quebec passed the House, and this was taken by the Government as an indication that a majority disapproved of female suffrage generally, so the clause was withdrawn entirely. There thus existed a situation involving the defeat of a Government on a fundamental proposal which had been accepted in principle on second reading of the bill, and was favoured strongly by the Prime Minister; yet the defeat was not taken seriously by the Cabinet, and had been almost requested by them.[2] The obvious explanation was that the issue of female suffrage in a bill already full of controversial clauses was too dangerous to force upon the House. The tactics followed suggest that the clause was a ready-made concession put in to draw fire away from other parts of the bill.

The fundamentals of Sir John's franchise survived passage through the legislature, but not without concessions both to the Opposition and to Conservative groups from particular regions. "Tory delegations," *The Week* declared, "give a party assent to equalization (of the franchise) only on condition that their own Province shall be left out."[3] This was an accurate statement; the bill emerged a more liberal statute than it began, but the liberality (as well as some illiberality) was gained at the expense of uniformity. The final franchise agreed upon was in fact an astonishing hodge-podge that discriminated between provinces, social classes and racial groups. On balance, the uniform federal franchise of 1885 may be fairly described as more diversified than the varied provincial qualifications it supplanted, a situation which Sir John drily explained away by a desire not to insist on "pedantic uniformity."[4]

So complicated was the suffrage adopted in 1885 that only a partial summary of it is possible. Essentially it

[1]See *Debates*, 1885, p. 1388, "I believe a majority of this House is opposed to female suffrage," he said, in the face of members loudly denying it.
[2]*Ibid.*, pp. 1388 ff.
[3]*The Week*, May 14, 1885.
[4]The Franchise Act is *Statutes*, 48-49 Vict., c. 40. See *Debates*, 1885, *passim.*

emerged, as it began, a property franchise. The requirement in cities (except Hull and St. Hyacinthe, P.Q.) was $300 for owners and occupants,[1] and $2 monthly rental or $20 annual rental for tenants provided the rent was paid up. In towns, the requirement was originally set at $300 but a reduction to $200 was conceded; in rural areas the requirement was $150 for owners and occupants, and for tenants— to whom it was conceded that rent could be paid in kind— the provisions were the same as for cities. Sons of property-owners, though not of tenants and occupants, were qualified to vote if their father's property was valuable enough to enfranchise them at the rate of $300 per son, starting with the oldest. Income and wage earners were enfranchised if they made $300 annually; although the original proposal had been to include only income-earners who made $400.[2]

Special concessions were made for the Maritimes, for fishermen who owned real property and fishing equipment together worth $150 were qualified. This was the only compromise allowed for owners of personal property, and the Government refused to concede either the principle it involved to any other group of artisans or workers, or to extend to fishermen the opportunity to enfranchise their sons on the same basis as land-owners. The special interests of British Columbia and Prince Edward Island were recognized by the adoption of provincial franchises for those persons qualified by them in 1885; but future generations of voters in these two provinces came under the new federal act. "The happy expedient of preserving the votes of those who have already exercised them is a brilliant idea," a supporter wrote Macdonald. "It takes away every reasonable ground of complaint without at all interfering with the principle of the bill."[3] Further concessions to British Columbia were made in the definition of the word "person." This

[1]The value of the property, it is worth noting, was not its assessed but its *actual* value, in the determination of which the revising officer was given some discretion. He was empowered to determine a property's value "upon the best information in his possession . . . provided that the assessment rolls as finally revised . . . shall be *prima facie* evidence of the value." (*Statutes*, 48-49 Vict., c. 40, s. 1.)

[2]This particular concession, Sir John admitted, was by no means approved by all his supporters (*Debates*, 1885, p. 2000).

[3]E. Hodgson to Macdonald, July 15, 1885 (Macdonald Papers, vol. 10).

harmless term was, in effect, so determined as to exclude Mongolians and Chinese, but to include all Indians except those living west of Ontario; an application which excluded most of them. Originally the plan had been to enfranchise all Indians, although in what way was not made completely clear. Since the redskins were not merely wards of the Government but also good Orangemen in many areas, the Opposition was happy to take the lead in forcing restrictions on the Indian franchise.[1]

As the 1885 suffrage was primarily based on property, it is necessary to digress briefly to note that it involved, as a corollary, plural voting. The Ontario act of 1885 had adopted the "one man—one vote" principle, but an attempt to amend the federal act to forbid voting by non-resident property owners was rejected. Residence, however, was strictly insisted on for tenants, occupants, and income and wage-earning voters. Plural voting, as the Liberals pointed out, discriminated between land owners generally, because one owner could exercise his several votes only if his properties were close enough together to let him get around to the various constituencies on election day. It also discriminated between landowners in a particular area, because a man might have $1,000,000 in property and still have only one vote if his real estate were all in one constituency, whereas a mere $1,000, properly distributed, would give him three votes in city districts and five votes in towns. Logic and consistency, the Liberals suggested, assuming the principle of plural voting was to continue, would require every property owner to have as many votes in each district as he had multiples of the property qualification. This the Conservatives were not prepared to accept.

The Liberals' objections to plural voting were not merely academic. A Conservative member testified that in his

[1]The Opposition's fears that the Government would exploit the Indian vote were not without basis, as the following Conservative election circular of 1887 showed: "To the Indians: The Queen has always loved her dear, loyal subjects, the Indians. She wants them to be good men and women, and she wants them to live on the land they have, and she expects in a little while, if her great chief, John A., gets into Government again, to be very kind to the Indians, and to make them very happy. She wants them to go and vote, and all vote for Dr. Montague, who is the Queen's agent. He is their friend, and by voting for him every one of the Indians will please Queen Victoria."

riding there were 269 non-resident voters[1] (a figure large
enough to carry most elections in those days) and other
members gave even higher numbers for their areas. The
practice also facilitated impersonation, and encouraged the
importation of voters from the United States into border
constituencies; a useful trick which was given a guise of
legality by the fact that the names of many American
citizens holding property in Canada appeared on Canadian
voting lists.[2] Plural voting was not infrequently expensive
to members, for many non-resident voters expected the
member to pay their travelling expenses.[3]

The remarkable franchise of 1885, coupled with the wide
powers given to the revising officers who were to make up
the voters' lists, could hardly fail to provide grounds for
dissatisfaction. George Casey, for example, spoke irritably
in 1886 of an officer who refused to admit to the lists men
who "earned wages," instead of "derived an income from
his earnings," (as the Act stated)[4] and other Liberal members
gave frequent examples of abuses that reflected usually more
on the revising officers than on the franchise qualification
itself.[5] The franchise can be tested only on the basis of
what it did to the electorate, and a survey of constituencies
in 1891, comparing the election of that year with the 1891
census, gives the following results:

	Constitu-encies in Sample	(1) Average Elector-ate	(2) Average Popula-tion	(1) as per cent of (2)
Ontario........	12	5,624	21,247	26.4
Quebec........	10	4,125	20,546	20.1
Nova Scotia....	4	5,367	24,288	22.1
New Brunswick.	4	4,486	20,537	21.1
P.E.I.*........	3	8,022	36,359	22.1
British Columbia	3	2,947	22,094	13.3
Manitoba......	4	10,461	34,259	30.3

*P.E.I. includes the whole province, which consisted of three double
constituencies. This accounts for the large size of the constituencies there.

[1]*Debates*, 1885, p. 1769.
[2]*Ibid.*, 1886, p. 1672.
[3]*Ibid.*, 1898, pp. 2305-6.
[4]*Ibid.*, 1886, pp. 43 ff.
[5]See Chapter x.

It is apparent that the "uniform" federal suffrage of 1885 produced a general extension of the franchise, but that the extension varied greatly among the provinces.[1]   The change did not, moreover, apply equally to the population throughout any one province.   Thus while the Ontario electorate as a whole, judging from the sample, increased roughly 25 per cent between 1882 and 1891, that in the urban area of Toronto increased just half that amount; the Quebec electorate grew 17 per cent while Montreal's remained almost stationary; the Nova Scotia electorate increased roughly 45 per cent, while that of Halifax went up only 30 per cent; while in New Brunswick, by contrast, the total electorate grew only 25 per cent, and that in the city of Saint John actually more than doubled.[2]   Considering the unreliability of both voters' lists and the early censuses, comparisons based on statistics cannot be pushed very far; but it is at least clear that the 1885 Act affected the country unevenly.

Not all the extensions of the suffrage after 1867 can be credited to statutory alterations.   Changes in the age-structure of the population must be admitted as a factor, for obviously a high proportion of people below voting age would affect the ratio which the qualified electorate bore to the total.   Again, the maintenance of a rigid property and income qualification for a prolonged period during which prices, incomes, and property values would naturally fluctuate, might involve either a gradual extension or contraction of the franchise.   The trend seems to have been towards expansion, and even between 1867 and 1885 slight franchise extensions appear to have taken place in Quebec and New Brunswick, where the statutory requirements remained unchanged; the development of the country generally must he reckoned as a factor in this regard.[3]   Another consideration

[1]An analysis of the 1887 election made for Macdonald by Pope showed that a general increase of 23.62 per cent in the electorate was effected by the 1885 Act.   This varied from 19 per cent in Quebec to 54 per cent in British Columbia and 66 per cent in Manitoba.   Pope's method of calculation is not apparent (Macdonald Papers, vol. 154).

[2]Comparisons based on General Election returns for 1882 and 1891, and the census of 1881 and 1891.

[3]I am not assuming that incomes and price levels were rising steadily and uniformly in the period concerned.   A brief debate in the House in 1890 (pp. 3720-2) suggests on the contrary that the $300 income required of wage earners was just high enough alternately to enfranchise and disfranchise them as local working conditions fluctuated in some areas.

is that during this period elections were becoming better organized, from the point of view of both the Government and the parties. Improvements in the techniques for accumulating names of electors, combined with the clarification of party lines and the development of party organizations, inevitably increased the opportunities for names to be put on lists. The 1885 Act in particular made it ridiculously easy for partisan workers to get the lists extended almost without limit.

The Franchise Act of 1885, except for routine amendments and Liberal motions for total repeal, remained almost in its original form until 1898. However, increasing dissatisfaction with the administrative aspects of the statute turned even the Conservatives' attention to some alternative system, and in 1894 Sir John Thompson proposed a return to the provincial franchises. While denying that any principle was being surrendered, Thompson said somewhat inaccurately:

The number of differences which exist between the provincial franchises and the Dominion franchise . . . are so few as not to be worth the contest and expense involved in keeping them up, and the adoption of a general system which will apply both to the Local and Dominion Legislatures, has recommendations as regards simplicity and facilities for economy, which cannot exist under a dual system. . . .[1]

The bill was dropped after almost no discussion, so that the 1885 Act was used again in the general election of 1896.

1898-1917

The Liberal Government elected in the eighth Parliament wasted little time in returning to the provincial franchises. After receiving an airing in 1897, the proposal to revive the use of provincial laws was pushed through in the following year,[2] and had the anomalous result of producing a more uniform franchise than its predecessor. This was because manhood suffrage, with minor local variations as to residence requirements and payment of poll-tax, had by this time become accepted in all the provinces except Nova Scotia and Quebec; there the property qualifications remained essentially as they had been since 1867. Provincial qualifications

[1]*Debates*, 1894, p. 4301. This idea had been suggested during the 1885 debate by the premier of Nova Scotia, who urged a Dominion-provincial conference on the franchise. *Ibid.*, 1885, p. 2170. See *supra*, p. 198.
[2]*Statutes*, 61 Vict., c. 14; *Debates*, 1898, *passim*.

were assumed without exception in 1898, but to prevent a recurrence of an old problem—the manipulation by a province of its electoral law for the purpose of affecting federal elections—provincial disqualifications were not adopted.[1] Special safeguards were established to guarantee that federal lists be as comprehensive as possible. The use of provincial laws involved incidentally the abolition of plural voting everywhere except in Quebec.[2]

The reasons for the Liberal policy are easily found, for the party had consistently supported the principle of provincial electoral machinery since 1867. This, as suggested elsewhere, was part of their faith in provincial autonomy. The knowledge that, with one exception, the provincial governments were Liberal in 1898 made such faith justifiable and safe. Furthermore, the failure of the Franchise Act of 1885 was a most convenient excuse for scrapping the whole machinery connected with it.

The reversion to provincial laws evaded a problem which was threatening to become embarrassing for a federal government led by either party. The adoption of manhood suffrage in most of the provinces by 1898, had resulted in a rise of pressure to force the wider franchise on the federal government. That government, on the other hand, had to consider the fact that Quebec was opposed to manhood suffrage. The perpetuation of a property qualification for federal purposes was thus becoming increasingly difficult in most of the provinces, yet the national adoption of manhood suffrage was a political impossibility. The Prime Minister himself stated explicitly his opposition to manhood suffrage, though he was willing to accept it for any particular province that already had done so.[3] The easy way out of the dilemma was to resort to provincial franchises once more.[4]

[1]*Statutes*, 61 Vict., c. 14, s. 6. The particular point covered here, it will be remembered, was one of the reasons Macdonald advanced for a federal franchise between 1867 and 1885.
[2]Plural voting in federal elections in Quebec did not disappear until 1920, when provincial franchises were finally abandoned. See *Debates*, 1920, pp. 1158-9.
[3]*Ibid.*, 1898, pp. 4010-11.
[4]The Liberals made few concessions in reverting to provincial law. The Senate proposed several sweeping amendments, notably one to continue the federal law in Nova Scotia, New Brunswick, and Manitoba, but the Liberals refused to accept any but a few comparatively minor changes relating to Prince Edward Island. See *Debates*, 1898, pp. 7467 ff., 7527 ff., 7792.

The Liberal franchise of 1898 thus produced the curious spectacle of the adoption of manhood suffrage for most of the country by a Government whose leader was against it as a matter of principle. But except for a few observations from Quebec members, no serious stand against manhood suffrage was taken on either side of the House. It is a fair statement that some time between 1885 and 1898 the notion that the franchise was a trust accompanying property, rather than a right normally accompanying citizenship, all but disappeared in federal politics. The shift to popular democracy was effected quietly and painlessly.

The election of 1900 was held on the widest franchise yet adopted for federal purposes. Its results were as follows, taking the 1900 election and the 1901 census:

	Constitu-encies in Sample	(1) Average Elector-ate	(2) Average Popula-tion	(1) as per cent of (2)
Ontario........	12	5,530	20,420	27. 1
Quebec........	10	4,905	23,262	21. 1
Nova Scotia....	4	5,802	23,382	24. 8
New Brunswick.	4	5,328	19,730	27. 3
P.E.I.*........			20,652	
Manitoba......	3	11,282	40,443	27. 9
British Columbia	3	5,443	24,903	21. 9

*Under provincial law, there were no voters' lists in Prince Edward Island at this time. There was no need for them, as open voting still obtained there, although it was not adopted for federal purposes.

Manhood suffrage, as might be expected, produced electorates of almost identical proportions in the provinces where it prevailed. The sole exception was British Columbia, whose disfranchised citizens were sufficiently numerous to cause the qualified electorate to be a comparatively small percentage of the whole population. The wider franchise brought much greater change in some provinces than in others. In Ontario, for instance, the Franchise Act of 1885 produced nearly as many voters as did manhood suffrage; in New Brunswick, on the other hand, the new franchise helped to raise the electorate for federal purposes from 21.1 per cent to 27.3 per cent of the total population.

By 1900, with manhood suffrage existing in all but two provinces, the franchise could be greatly extended only by the adoption of female suffrage. In the thirty years since Confederation, the Canadian electorate as a whole had grown roughly from 15 per cent to over 25 per cent of the total population, an increase of nearly 70 per cent in the electorate itself; for this, as the figures for Quebec and Nova Scotia show, by no means all the credit could be given to statutory extensions of the franchise. But the gradual abolition of property and income qualifications, combined with improvements in the techniques of compiling voters' lists, meant that the limits of franchise extensions which depended in any way on economic and administrative developments were being reached, so that future changes would have to be largely by legislative enactment.

There was no general rush towards the adoption of female suffrage. Except for areas where women held municipal franchises, no province adopted woman suffrage until 1916; in several provinces, prior to that time, bills had been introduced and defeated.[1] The House of Commons, whose members were elected on provincial franchises after 1898, was happily free of responsibility for all problems connected with female suffrage, and the issue was not forced in federal politics until 1917. When in 1916 and 1917 female suffrage was granted in the five provinces west of Quebec, the national administration could no longer ignore the matter, and it was forced to take a stand.

1917-1948

The first solution to the problem of woman suffrage, introduced by the Conservative Government in 1917, produced the most remarkable franchise act ever passed in Canada, and very possibly in the democratic world. The Government, in addition to establishing a unique machine for the 1917 election,[2] not only adopted a special franchise which was frankly biased in its own favour, but also openly admitted the fact.

[1]See C. L. Cleverdon, *The Woman Suffrage Movement in Canada* (Toronto, 1950); I. H. Harper (ed.), *The History of Woman Suffrage* (New York, 1922), vol. VI, pp. 753-66.
[2]See Chapters IX and X.

The wartime franchise of 1917 could hardly fail to return a majority in Parliament for the party which enacted it. Women were enfranchised, for example, but only those women who had, or had had, husbands, sons, brothers, or fathers in the Canadian or British armed forces.[1] Men were enfranchised who might be disqualified by provincial property or income qualifications but who had sons or grandsons in the services.[2] The franchise was granted, under the Military Voters Act, to virtually all members of the Canadian armed forces, whether or not they were ordinarily resident in Canada, were minors, or Indians.[3] On the other hand, the following categories were disfranchised: conscientious objectors and those who applied for certificates as such; Mennonites and Doukhobors; and not only all naturalized British subjects born in an enemy country and naturalized *after March 31, 1902*, but all who even spoke an enemy language habitually and were naturalized after that date.[4]

On the positive side, the newly enfranchised soldiers and their sisters and their cousins and their aunts were expected to vote for the Government; on the negative side, the disfranchised group (most particularly the naturalized aliens) were those who would, on their record between 1900 and 1911, be likely to vote Liberal. These facts were so obvious that little attempt was made to hide them; and to give the Government due credit, it must be recorded that its spokesmen made no consistent attempt to pretend that the dice

[1]*Statutes*, 7-8 Geo. V, c. 39, s. 1 (d).
[2]*Ibid.*, s. 1 (e), and 2. This applied in fact only to Quebec and Nova Scotia.
[3]*Ibid.*, 7-8 Geo. V, c. 34, s. 2 (c).
[4]*Ibid.*, c. 39, s. 2 (d). These disfranchised classes were of course enfranchised again if in the armed forces. This particular section of the bill brought up an interesting constitutional point concerning the taking away of a civil right from persons who have already been admitted to full citizenship, including the franchise, under naturalization laws. The Privy Council had already held in 1903, when a British Columbia Japanese-Canadian appealed to that tribunal for the franchise, that the franchise and citizenship do not necessarily go together: "Such a right is not inherent in the respondent either as British born or as a naturalized British subject. It is a right and privilege which belongs only to those . . . upon whom the provincial legislature has conferred it." (*Cunningham and Attorney-General for British Columbia* v. *Homma and Attorney-General for Canada*, [1903] A.C. 151.) The Government in 1917 thus found no legal difficulty in depriving enfranchised citizens of their votes, although some expansion of the principle laid down in 1903 was involved.

were not being heavily loaded. Thus Sir George Foster, a
veteran Cabinet Minister, remarked: "I have viewed it along
the line, which I consider the proper line, of putting as
much punch and power behind the war government of this
country, whatever Government it may be, as it is possible
to put."[1]   Mr. Meighen, a rising Privy Councillor, stated:
"I do believe that the majority of those in the trenches . . .
[and] of those whose near relatives are overseas fighting the
foe would rather support this Administration than support
one formed by the leader of the Opposition."[2]   "Are the
men who have died and given their lives in Flanders, to
have made that sacrifice in vain?" cried a backbencher,
making it clear that he and his colleagues regarded the
wartime franchise as the only way of guaranteeing the
proper answer.[3]   Even if the excitement engendered by the
war is allowed for, these were remarkable statements to
make about a statute whose general purpose was to provide
for a registration of public opinion.

A perusal of the 1917 debates leads one to think that,
unscrupulous though the wartime elections acts were, the
Government did well to guarantee its own return; for the
alternative Government on the opposition benches has rarely
appeared in a poorer light than did the Liberals in that year.
Split by the conscription act of a few weeks previously,
lacking the services of their aging leader, who was absent
throughout most of the debate,[4] hampered by a rigid application of the closure at both second and third reading, and
finally, manœuvered into an awkward position where they
might appear both unpatriotic and opposed to woman suffrage if they criticized the Conservative bill, the Liberals
could hardly have been more ineffective.   They obstructed
as well as they could, but the Government had little difficulty
in securing the act's passage; the final amendments were
pushed through while the House was awaiting summons to
the Senate for prorogation.

[1]*Debates*, 1917, p. 5854.
[2]*Ibid.*, p. 5586.
[3]*Ibid.*, p. 5841.
[4]As the bill was entering *third reading*, Laurier said, "I have had no time
to look at it myself."   See *ibid.*, p. 5806.

As an instrument for winning an election, the acts of 1917 may be regarded as an unqualified success. As an extension of the franchise, the instrument operated in the highly discriminatory manner which was intended. Unfortunately an unprecedented number of acclamations (for which no voters' lists were prepared) occurred in the election of 1917, and this, combined with a redistribution of constituencies in 1914, makes accurate comparison with previous elections impossible. The electorate of Ontario, where reasonably valid comparisons between the elections of 1911 and 1917 can be made, jumped from 27.5 per cent to 39.4 per cent of the population, primarily as a result of statutory changes. On the other hand, the electorate of Alberta (where a complete comparison between 1911 and 1917 can be made) merely increased from 28.6 per cent to 32.5 per cent of the population.[1] In Quebec and Saskatchewan, where acclamations took place in one quarter of the constituencies, the electorate on the voters' lists naturally declined.

Not all this decline can be attributed to the high proportion of acclamations. In the Saskatchewan constituency of Humboldt, for example, whose population of 52,195 included 16,363 persons of German and Austrian-Hungarian birth, the number of eligible voters dropped from 182 to 22 in the polling division of Englefeldt; from 53 to 7 in Florek; from 63 to 1 in Forner; and from 63 to 6 in St. Meinrad.[2] The disfranchisement of alien-born clearly took a heavy toll of former electors in the West. "If it were only confined to Austrians and Germans," a frank Alberta Cabinet Member wrote to a federal colleague in 1919, "it wouldn't be worth raising a row about, but American citizens of long standing were harassed."[3]

The franchise acts of 1917 nevertheless produced a general extension of well over 20 per cent in the electorate, as shown in Table XVI. Having accomplished their purpose,

[1]There were two acclamations in Ontario in 1911, and one in 1917. In Alberta there were no acclamations in either election, and the comparatively small increase in the electorate must be charged to the peculiar franchise of 1917.

[2]See *Sessional Papers*, 1912, no. 18; 1920, no. 13.

[3]G. R. Reid to Hon. Chas. Murphy, February 7, 1919 (Murphy Papers, vol. 27-4-c.).

they did not have to be used again. A comprehensive extension of the franchise to all women was enacted in 1918, provided they had the same qualifications as male electors in their respective provinces. The only exceptions to this wide suffrage were alien-born women who had become British subjects by marriage or through the naturalization of their parents; these were until 1922 put to the singular inconvenience of having to obtain a certificate from a judge before they could vote.[1]

TABLE XVI

Percentage of Total Population Enfranchised
at Selected General Elections,
by Provinces[2]

	1911	1917	1921	1930	1940
Ontario..............	27.4	39.4	58.6	55.2	61.8
Quebec..............	22.7	20.6	44.8	47.0	54.0
Nova Scotia.........	27.8	29.7	56.2	53.8	58.1
New Brunswick......	28.7	29.9	52.7	50.7	55.1
Manitoba...........	21.4	29.3	41.8	46.9	58.2
British Columbia.....	21.2	38.4	44.0	48.0	57.8
Prince Edward Island.	—	33.3	52.9	53.4	58.2
Saskatchewan.......	28.9	22.9	44.0	44.5	53.8
Alberta.............	28.6	32.5	46.5	41.6	53.2
Total.............	25.2	30.6	50.6	49.7	57.3
Number of Acclamations........	3	31	0	2	0

The adoption of female suffrage raised hardly a stir in the federal legislature; only a few Quebec members, taking their cue from the sanctified nature of woman's place in the home, recorded somewhat lyrical objections to the extension of the

[1]*Statutes*, 8-9 Geo. V, c. 20. This act enfranchised women in Quebec for federal elections, although they remained disfranchised for provincial purposes. A limitation on alien-born citizens, both men and women, was continued in the election Act of 1920 (*ibid.*, 10-11 Geo. V, c. 46) and finally removed in 1922 (*ibid.*, 12-13 Geo. V, c. 20).
[2]The total figure for this table includes the Yukon. The 1917 figures include both civilian and military voters; since many military electors were on lists at home as well as having a vote overseas, the statistics for 1917 are somewhat inflated. They are further inflated by the fact that the 1917 election could be compared only with the 1911 census. Other general elections in the table are compared with the census of the nearest census year.

franchise. Isolated pockets of resistance to the subjection
of women to the franchise appeared in Parliament from time
to time thereafter.[1]

The Conservative election act of 1920, which created the
post of the Chief Electoral Officer, established for the first
time a genuinely uniform federal franchise. Provincial
franchises were abandoned entirely, and with the only major
limitation that on alien-born citizens, the election of 1921
was thus held on the widest suffrage so far accepted. The
electorate (as Table XVI shows) increased to half the total
population. The restriction on alien-born citizens was abolished in 1922, so that since that date the electorate in Canada
has been based on a universal suffrage.

Despite this fact, the electorate since 1920 has varied
widely in extent in the several provinces. A major factor
in this has been the different age distribution of the provincial
population in each case, for where everyone over twenty-one
is enfranchised, it is of immediate significance whether the
society concerned is "old" or "young." The inconvenience
to which alien-born citizens were put during the 1921 election
might also account for some of the variations between
provinces in that year. Another major element until 1930
was the method of compiling voters' lists. As has been
shown elsewhere, the 1920 election act on occasion required
personal and voluntary registration of voters in all towns
of more than 1,000 population; this principle was restricted
to towns of 5,000 and over in 1925, and not finally abandoned
until 1929.[2] The voters' lists during this period were therefore not necessarily indicative of the total qualified electorate in
any but rural areas. Particularly in Quebec, where local prejudice prevented for years the adoption of female suffrage in
provincial elections, voluntary registration of female electors
could hardly fail to produce incomplete lists in urban areas.

All these possible explanations do not account for the
fact that universal suffrage, applied on an efficient and non-
partisan basis, still produces a varying electorate in the
provinces. The use of enumeration for all voters' lists in

[1] E.g., *Senate Debates*, 1923, pp. 76-85. A bill to limit the vote to women
over thirty received sixteen votes.
[2] See Chapter x.

1929, which resulted in voters' lists as complete as human ingenuity can devise, yielded an electorate substantially equal to that of 1921; the election of 1940, held on the same franchise, revealed an electorate proportionately much larger than its counterpart of a decade before.

The Canadian electorate has thus grown in eighty years from a small fraction to over half the total population. Any great increases in the future can result only from a lowering of the voting age below twenty-one, a development which has already appeared in the provinces. Considering the history of the franchise in Canada since 1867, provincial experiments with the voting age may be expected in due course to affect federal policy; that the time is not yet at hand was indicated by the rejection of a lower voting age by a House of Commons Committee in 1947.[1]

Historically, as with so many parts of the electoral machinery, the major steps in the development of the franchise were taken first in the provinces. The Dominion franchise between 1885 and 1898 was based on a property qualification, while in that same period all but Quebec and Nova Scotia adopted some form of manhood suffrage. The return to provincial franchises in 1898 thus included the adoption of manhood suffrage for most of Canada, yet the issue was really settled in the provinces. Again, the use of provincial franchises between 1898 and 1917 diverted to provincial arenas almost the whole struggle for woman suffrage. The success of that movement in the provinces in a sense committed the Dominion government to it, for the issue could not be evaded by the federal legislature once a majority of the provinces had accepted such an important extension.[2] If, as is often claimed, a major function of the component parts of a federal system is to act as laboratories for the testing of new political ideas, the Canadian provinces, as far as the franchise is concerned, may rightly be regarded as having proved their worth.

[1]*Report of the Special Committee on the Dominion Elections Act*, 1947, *Minutes of Proceedings and Evidence*, especially no. 7.
[2]According to the Minister of Justice in 1917, the law officers of the Crown ruled in that year that the enfranchisement of women for provincial purposes did not enfranchise them for federal purposes, even though the Dominion was using the provincial franchises at the time. See *Debates*, 1917, pp. 5574 ff.

CHAPTER XIII

THE DISFRANCHISEMENT OF CITIZENS

A SURVEY of the franchise in Canada would be incomplete without a sketch of disfranchisement. The negative side of the franchise has two aspects; there are those to whom the suffrage has never been granted (i.e. the unenfranchised), and those who might ordinarily have the vote but have been deprived of it for a particular reason. Thus the number of unenfranchised persons immediately after 1867 included an overwhelming majority of the population; but eventually this situation was reversed with the successive adoption of manhood and universal suffrage. The proportion of disfranchised people, on the other hand, though still but a small part of the total population, has until very recently tended to increase rather than decrease.

There have been in Canada three main causes of disfranchisement: deliberate action by the legislature; accidental disfranchisement by special circumstances; and voluntary abnegation of the vote by electors. Deliberate action by the legislature has been taken for four primary reasons. The first is to keep free of politics those who hold strategic judicial or administrative offices. Thus judges are disfranchised, and have been by federal statute since 1885;[1] before that, when provincial franchises were in force, Nova Scotia and New Brunswick allowed judges to vote. The Chief Electoral Officer and his assistant are not allowed to vote; nor is the returning officer in any constituency unless the popular poll results in a tie, when he casts the deciding ballot.

All election officials were disfranchised during a large part of the period after 1867. The practice in this regard varied in the provinces at Confederation, but the Franchise Act of 1885 specifically disqualified election officials in the constituency where they were employed, thus presumably leaving

[1]R. S. Can., 1886, c. 8, s. 42. In this chapter, the term "disfranchised" is sometimes used loosely. Strictly speaking, those who voluntarily refrain from voting on election day are not disfranchised; they still have the *right* to vote, but have failed to exercise it.

them free to vote elsewhere if they were qualified. The
Liberal act of 1898 continued the essentials of this provision.
The statute at present in force does not disfranchise officials
below the rank of returning officer so long as their employment is legal; unofficial election workers who assist candidates and are remunerated for their work are not disfranchised,
but the total of such assistants cannot exceed one in each
five hundred electors.[1] The disfranchisement of election
officials thus exists today in a most restricted form. Abuse
of this generosity is virtually unknown.[2]

A second reason for deliberate disfranchisement is the
commission of an offence, either against the state generally,
or the election laws in particular. Criminals, for example,
have been disfranchised since 1898; but before that time,
they were not specifically deprived of the vote in the Elections
or Franchise Acts, although they were in practice because
they could not get to a poll. Voters found guilty of bribery
have been disfranchised since 1894,[3] and corrupt practices
generally have been a reason for disfranchisement in federal
law since 1885. In all these cases the disfranchisement is
a limited one. Criminals are not deprived of the suffrage
after they have served their term, while persons found guilty
of illegal or corrupt practices in elections are today disfranchised for five or seven years, depending on the nature
of the offence.[4]

Statutory disfranchisement is also applied to persons who
are not competent. A fairly broad view of what constitutes
competence has been taken, for literacy or intelligence tests
for electors are unknown in Canada; on at least two occasions
suggestions along this line have been rejected.[5] In practice,
disfranchisement of incompetents is consequently confined to

[1]*Statutes*, 2 Geo. VI, c. 46, as amended in 1948.
[2]See Chapter ix for examples of abuses in earlier days.
[3]*Statutes*, 57-8 Vict., c. 14, s. 1.
[4]*Ibid.*, 2 Geo. VI, c. 46, s. 81. The distinction between corrupt and illegal
practices, which was not made until 1920, is that the former concerns such
grosser matters as bribery and personation, while the latter is concerned with
more minor offences in regard to the administrative aspects of elections, such
as interfering with election lists.
[5]Blake went on record in favour of a literacy test in 1885 (*Debates*, 1885,
p. 1254) but his proposal received no serious consideration by the House. In
1937, the Special Committee on Elections and Franchise Acts rejected without
discussion a proposal that illiterates be disqualified (*Report*, p. 53).

lunatics who are actually in institutions, a provision in force since 1898. A somewhat allied requirement in operation from 1898 to 1948 denied the suffrage to inmates of charitable institutions in those provinces where they were disqualified for provincial elections. This negative remnant of the property qualification, which did not apply to war veterans, in practice affected the franchise only in Ontario, Nova Scotia,[1] and New Brunswick; it was repealed in 1948. The setting of the voting age at twenty-one seems to involve the assumption that minors are incompetent to vote, as does the disfranchisement of Eskimos and Indians who are wards of the government. Minors may vote if they are war veterans or in the armed forces, and the franchise was extended in 1948 to wives of Indian veterans; in general, the status of war veteran is sufficient to overcome all disqualifications cited in the Dominion Elections Act.

A fourth reason for specifically denying the suffrage to citizens that reflects rather less credit on Parliament than the foregoing is the manipulation of the franchise for purely political purposes. The disqualification in 1917 of certain citizens naturalized after 1902 provided one instance of this. Another major example is the disqualification of Orientals. These immigrants, so far as the franchise is concerned, have always been given special treatment in Canada. The first federal franchise act in 1885, as a concession to British Columbia members, disfranchised the major groups then in the country by the novel expedient of defining the word "person" so that it excluded Chinese and Mongolians.[2] In 1898, when the provincial franchises were once again adopted for federal purposes, the Government creditably accepted an amendment which rejected existing provincial disqualifications. The Liberal Franchise Act of 1898 stated that the federal franchise would extend to all persons who had been provincially disqualified merely because of their

[1]Nova Scotia disfranchised paupers well before Confederation, so that this disqualification obtained for federal purposes between 1867 and 1885. (*Statutes of Nova Scotia*, 1863, c. 28.)

[2]*R.S. Can.*, 1886, c. 5, s. 2. Of this Act it can at least be said that Sir John had the courage to name those he was disfranchising. Subsequent disfranchisements of this sort have usually evaded the actual naming of the group by round-about phrasing.

belonging to some special class. This provision remained in force until 1920, so that there was no legal obstacle to Japanese or Chinese Canadians voting in federal elections during that period. However, the use of provincial voting lists as the basis for federal ones no doubt in practice deprived many Orientals of their rights as electors.

The federal government in 1920 again disfranchised most Orientals by providing that persons disfranchised by any province because of their racial origin were disqualified for federal elections unless they were war veterans.[1] This general disfranchisement applied mainly to Japanese, Chinese, and East Indians in British Columbia, and Chinese in Saskatchewan, as they were disqualified by provincial law; all these restrictions in provincial law have since been removed, although not without friction in some instances. Notwithstanding the generality of the restriction while it was in force, the Liberal Government in 1944 enacted a somewhat startling provision, retroactive to 1938, which not only disfranchised all such persons already disqualified by the province concerned, but had the effect of disfranchising them even if since 1938 they had moved to a province where they were ordinarily not disfranchised. The practical effect of this was that Japanese Canadians resident in British Columbia in 1938, who moved to Ontario in (say) 1942, were still disfranchised because they had been disfranchised in British Columbia back in 1938!

The disqualification of Japanese Canadians provoked a heated discussion in the Special Committee on the Dominion Elections Act, 1947, and the Committee declined on a division to recommend the lifting of the ban.[2] In 1948, however, the franchise was extended to Japanese Canadians for federal purposes almost without discussion.[3]

The only group apart from Eskimos and Indians which is disfranchised today is the Doukhobors. These people are not specifically disqualified by name; but a section of the

[1] *Statutes*, 10-11 Geo. V, c. 46, s. 30.
[2] *Special Committee on Dominion Elections Act, 1947, Minutes of Proceedings and Evidence*, especially pp. 241-9.
[3] See *Debates*, 1948, pp. 5257 ff.

Dominion Elections Act applies obviously to nobody but Doukhobors:

In any province, every person exempted or entitled to claim exemption or who on production of any certificate might have become or would now be entitled to claim exemption from Military Service by reason of the Order in Council of December sixth, 1898, because the doctrines of his religion make him averse to bearing arms, and who is by the law of that province disqualified from voting at an election . . . of that province.

The Doukhobors, by mutual consent, thus remain without the franchise in some areas. It appears probable that even if that privilege were available to them, not all would take advantage of it.

An appreciable number of persons are in effect disfranchised by accident at every election. Even if perfect voters' lists are assumed, and due allowance is made for the fact that at any given time a certain number of citizens will be away from their homes on business or vacation, problems are continually recurring which are extremely difficult to cope with because the making of special provisions for particular instances may easily open the doors to widespread abuse. The concentration of people from many constituencies into a large hospital is one example of this type of difficulty, for it raises such questions as the following: which constituency shall list any one patient as a voter; how long should he be resident in the hospital before he can qualify there; how can the franchise be guaranteed to those who leave the hospital and return home between enumeration day and the polling day?

A similar instance of great moment in 1948 was the attendance of thousands of student veterans at universities throughout the country; all of these were qualified to vote, yet very few had homes in the constituency containing their university. The arrangements for voting by students thus had to take account of the fact that much depended on whether an election was held during the school term, or during the vacation periods. Since in many cases there were enough student votes to swing an election one way or another, it was of immediate interest to all concerned (and not least to the members of Parliament) to provide an efficient machinery for recording student votes with the least trouble and the most fairness.[1] The solution finally accepted in this case was to allow students to be listed as voters both at their homes and at the university, and to let them choose in which district they would vote. But a midsummer election might easily have disfranchised hundreds who were neither at home nor at school, but on vacation or working in another part of the country.

From one-quarter to one-third of all those able to vote voluntarily disfranchise themselves, in effect, by staying away from the polls. The statistics in this regard can be readily presented in tabular form (Table XVII).[2] At the lowest point, Saskatchewan and Alberta have seen 43 per cent of their electors refrain from voting; at the highest, Prince Edward Island, whose citizens on election day appear to descend upon the polls in droves, has established a record of 89 per cent of the voters voting. This is almost equal to the proportion normally attained in Australia under a compulsory ballot.

TABLE XVII

PERCENTAGES OF ELECTORS ON VOTERS' LISTS
WHO VOTED AT ALL GENERAL ELECTIONS
SINCE 1921, BY PROVINCES

	1921	1925	1926	1930	1935	1940	1945
Ontario.............	63	65	64	69	74	69	75
Quebec.............	75	72	71	76	74	66	73
Nova Scotia.........	69	70	72	83	76	70	72
New Brunswick......	64	61	68	78	77	68	78
Manitoba...........	68	68	77	72	75	74	76
British Columbia.....	67	75	71	73	76	76	80
Prince Edward Island.	79	76	84	89	80	78	81
Saskatchewan.......	67	57	70	81	77	77	85
Alberta.............	63	57	57	66	65	63	73
Canada.............	67	66	68	76	75	70	76

[1]See *Report of the Special Committee on Dominion Elections Act*, 1947, *passim*, for an example of how seriously a House committee worked at this particular problem.

[2]Table compiled from figures in *Reports of Chief Electoral Officer*, 1920-1945.

Weather conditions are, of course, a major factor in keeping electors at home. It is significant that the elections of 1930, 1935, and 1945, which drew forth the largest numbers of voters, were held in the summer and autumn; but the three lowest points on the table (1921, 1925, 1926) include only one winter election, so that weather alone cannot be blamed for this "disfranchisement" of citizens.[1] Illness, business trips, other absences from home, and the degree of excitement engendered by election campaigns must all be reckoned as factors whose effects unfortunately cannot be measured. But it would require a long stretch of credulity to believe that at least one Canadian in every four on election day is rendered *hors de combat* by circumstances beyond his control. The only conclusion is that some citizens voluntarily avoid the polls.

The existence of so many non-voters makes it virtually impossible for one party to secure the support of a majority of the electorate. A party which received the very high proportion of 60 per cent of the votes polled on election day would still have the approval of only 60 per cent of roughly 75 per cent of the voters, or 45 per cent of the total. Whether or not one accepts the theory, popular among proponents of proportional representation, that an elected member represents only those who cast their ballots for him on election day, there remains the impressive conclusion that the election of a Government positively approved by a majority of the qualified electorate is barely within the realm of practical politics in Canada. For this phenomenon the non-voters are responsible; in effect, absence from the polls plays the same role in upsetting election results as does a major third party.[2]

[1]The dates of the general elections in the table are as follows: Dec. 6, 1921; Oct. 29, 1925; Sept. 14, 1926; July 28, 1930; Oct. 14, 1935; Mar. 26, 1940; June 11, 1945.

[2]This paragraph was written before the presidential election of 1948 in the United States, when all the major public opinion polls were in error in forecasting the results of the election. Before all the returns were in, Dr. Gallup, of the Institute of Public Opinion, was explaining the error made by his poll as caused in part by the large proportion of electors who did not vote.

CHAPTER XIV

ELECTORAL CORRUPTION AND CONTROVERTED ELECTIONS

CORRUPT electoral practices and controverted elections are topics which might normally be expected to go hand in hand, for the latter usually result only from the former.[1] To some extent, the number of controverted elections is a useful criterion by which to measure the prevalence of electoral corruption; but it may be highly misleading, since the corruption must be discovered and proved before any election result can be affected. The criterion is therefore trustworthy only insofar as the relevant legislative devices are effective. To the degree that laws providing for the investigation of electoral malpractices are operative, bribery and personation are discouraged; weakness in these laws, on the other hand, will inevitably stimulate unscrupulous candidates and election agents to utilize any opportunities which may be turned to their advantage.

No one who has even a nodding acquaintance with the tolerant attitude taken towards political behaviour generally in the years immediately after 1867 will be surprised to hear that for some time after Confederation the whole problem of corrupt practices and controverted elections was handled in a haphazard fashion. The four provinces which came together in 1867 agreed in general terms on a definition of corrupt practice: it included the giving and receiving of bribes, whether of money, employment, or anything else; the real or threatened use of violence; treating; personation; and in some cases payment for the hauling of voters to the

---

[1]Apart from corrupt practices, an election could be controverted: (a) in the case of a double return. For several years after Confederation, returning officers did not have a deciding vote in case of a tie, so that no candidate could be returned as elected in that eventuality. This happened in Marquette in 1870. (J. G. Bourinot, *Parliamentary Procedure and Practice*, Toronto, 1892, p. 185.) (b) If undue influence could be proven. E.g., see the *Canadian Monthly*, September, 1875, for a report of a petition charging that priests had influenced an election by branding one party as "infamous and dangerous" and threatening supporters with the "punishments of another life." See also O. D. Skelton, *Life and Letters of Sir Wilfrid Laurier* (Toronto, 1921), vol. I, pp. 136 ff.

polls. They also had similar views how that action for corrupt practice should be begun (by a simple petition signed by either an elector or candidate), and had adopted somewhat similar ways of trying the actual election cases, though their procedures varied in detail. Thus the assembly of the province of Canada had a general committee of elections, appointed by the Speaker subject to the sanction of the House, which was charged with preparing two panels of chairmen and members from which election committees consisting of a chairman and four members were finally chosen. Nova Scotia and New Brunswick sent controverted elections directly to a Select Committee. Manitoba and British Columbia, when they entered the federation, used the ordinary judicial system and tried election disputes like other cases.[1] In the provinces where committees of the assembly were used, the procedure was similar to that of a court: the committee members were sworn to uphold justice; witnesses were examined under oath; and the parties concerned were represented by counsel.[2] It is to be feared, however, that judicial impartiality was noticeably absent in the rendering of verdicts.

The adoption of provincial electoral laws for federal purposes in 1867 compelled the House of Commons to choose one of these systems for trying election cases, and the lot appears to have fallen on that used by Ontario and Quebec. This choice was presumably made because it met the criterion of the greatest familiarity to the greatest number[3] and not on grounds of intrinsic merit, for the assembly of the province of Canada had earlier entertained many bills for the repeal of the Controverted Elections Act.[4] The acceptance of this Act for federal purposes created an extraordinarily cumber-

[1]R. MacG. Dawson, *The Principle of Official Independence* (London, 1921), p. 53; Bourinot, *op. cit.* (1884 ed.), pp. 117 ff. In the case of Manitoba, there was at first considerable dispute over the matter in the federal House.

[2]Bourinot, *op. cit.*, p. 118.

[3]*Journals*, 1867-8, pp. 26, 37, 42. See *Parliamentary Debates* (Scrapbook Hansard), April 30, 1873, for an example of a New Brunswick member complaining that a petition had not been properly disposed of according to New Brunswick law. He withdrew his objection when it became apparent that, regardless of New Brunswick law, the House was satisfied.

[4]See, e.g., *General Index to Journals*, Assembly of Canada (Prov.), 1850-66. By 1872, New Brunswick and Ontario had adopted trial by judges.

some piece of machinery which put a heavy burden on honest petitioners, who had to travel to Ottawa to fight their cases, and on members of the Commons, who were usually interested persons and had to share the expenses. In many instances the procedure consumed a great deal of valuable time.[1] It was also palpably unfair, since the partisan majority in the House could usually capture the chairmanship of the election committee together with at least half the membership, with the result that election cases were often settled on grounds irrelevant to the main issues. "Some of the proceedings in Election Committees," a member asserted in 1873, "have been a scandal to the country."[2]

Finally, there is ample evidence that the scheme was extremely inefficient. During the first Parliament, twenty-one petitions in twenty-one separate constituencies resulted in one Conservative member being unseated, five members being confirmed in their seats, and two petitions being withdrawn, while the remaining thirteen either were discharged on technicalities or disappeared without trace. The short second Parliament handled the remarkable total of fifty-five petitions with no unseatings whatever. Thirteen members were confirmed and four petitions were withdrawn, while of the residue of thirty-eight petitions roughly half were discharged or rejected, and half were lost in the maze of Parliamentary procedure. One case, particularly worthy of note, occurred in Hochelaga, P.Q., where the trial of a petition was dragged out over four sessions of the House.[3]

The inefficiency of the system was further illustrated during the third Parliament, when all election cases were referred to the judiciary. Through the initiative of Sir John A. Macdonald in 1873, an Act was passed which assigned election petitions to the courts of only those provinces whose Lieutenant-Governors, with the consent of the Executive Council, authorized such procedure.[4] In other cases, barris-

---

[1]Bourinot, *op. cit.*, p. 118; *Debates*, 1872, pp. 798-807.
[2]*Parliamentary Debates* (Scrapbook Hansard), March 18, 1873.
[3]Figures computed from index to *Journals*, for appropriate years. In a majority of the cases, the petitioner was the losing candidate. The few decisions in which members were confirmed in their seats benefited Liberals and Conservatives almost equally. Partisanship seems to have played its main role in the discharging and disappearance of petitions.
[4]*Statutes*, 36 Vict., c. 28, s. 6.

ters of ten years' standing could be appointed judges *ad hoc*. These unusual provisions, though they may have reflected a desire on Macdonald's part to keep the trial of contested elections under his own control, were based in part on a genuine doubt whether the Dominion government had the jurisdiction to impose the necessary duties on courts administered by the provinces. Macdonald's opinion that it did not was shared by several judges.[1] Some years later, this view was held to be erroneous by the Judicial Committee of the Privy Council,[2] but in the meantime the Liberals in 1874, perhaps exercising a degree of foresight which was not generally characteristic of their first régime, repealed the 1873 law and established the provincial supreme courts as election courts.[3]

Since the statute of 1874 is the basis of the existing procedure for handling contested elections, it is worth describing in some detail. Briefly, it provided for the trial of election cases before a single judge, who was required not only to report his decision to the House of Commons, but also, if circumstances seemed to warrant it, to make a special report on corrupt practices naming the parties concerned. As the House might then proceed with or forget these special reports, judges were put in the invidious position of making decisions which might possibly be reviewed in the legislature. Petitions had to be presented within thirty days after the publication of election returns in the *Canada Gazette*, and petitioners had to deposit $1,000 as security. The deposit was also intended to discourage frivolous protests. Once presented, petitions could not be withdrawn except by leave of the court, and a proposed withdrawal because of an improper bargain or corrupt consideration was to be reported to the Speaker—an attempt to prevent "saw-offs," which are discussed below.[4] An action once begun on a petition could not be stopped because of the resignation of the

[1]*Debates*, 1872, p. 802; Bourinot, *op. cit.*, pp. 85-7, 119.
[2]*Valin* v. *Langlois* [1879] 5 A.C. 115.
[3]*Statutes*, 37 Vict., c. 10.
[4]A saw-off is an arrangement between two opposing parties whereby they agree to withdraw petitions against each other, thus saving trouble and expense. In addition, saw-offs also involved on occasion the mutual yielding of seats, riding for riding, an arrangement which vacated seats but forestalled investigation into corrupt practices on either side.

respondent from his seat or his acceptance of an office of emolument; but at the same time, a section of the House of Commons Act prevented a member from resigning if a petition had been entered against him.

The operation of this Act produced results strikingly different from those of the former committee system. The years 1875-8, inclusive, produced election petitions against the representatives of no less than sixty-five constituencies, or substantially more than one-third of the whole House. Only two of these were discharged, as compared with the record of rejections under the old scheme; only fourteen members were confirmed in their seats; while forty-nine members were unseated, a fact which gives some indication of the extent of corrupt election practices in those early days. These figures, it must be remembered, cover only cases which actually came into court; undiscovered corruption, and saw-offs which occurred before a petition was brought to trial, are undisclosed in these court cases which unseated nearly 30 per cent of the members.[1]

The heavy casualty rate was not necessarily any reflection on the members concerned, for in only three of the sixty-five cases did judges make special reports implicating members in corrupt practices. An election could be set aside if the bribery or other offence was committed by anybody acting on behalf of the candidate, not only without the candidate's knowledge or consent,[2] but even contrary to his instructions. The opportunities for Liberals to ensure the unseating of successful Conservatives (and vice versa) by the roundabout device of bribing electors to vote for their opponents must have been very tempting indeed.

Electoral corruption was, in fact, so widespread at this time that one of Her Majesty's learned judges, accustomed as he must have been to the coarser side of human nature, commented on its prevalence in giving a decision,[3] and

[1] Figures computed from *Journals* for appropriate years. A convenient reference to many of the court cases concerned is found in *Canadian Encyclopedic Digest* (Ontario Edition), vol. 4, under "Elections". Cases tried in Ontario courts are given in detail in T. Hodgins, *Election Cases* (Toronto, 1883). As to the general prevalence of electoral corruption; see the files of *The Week, The Canadian, Grip*, etc.

[2] W. D. McPherson, *The Law of Elections in Canada* (Toronto, 1905) p. 76.

[3] Hodgins, *op. cit.*, p. 567.

another justice asked in all gravity, "Is not bribery the corner-stone of Party Government?"[1] Bribery, indeed, seems to have been the most efficacious of the various corrupt practices, as it spread the desired influence as widely as possible throughout the constituency. Since a single and trifling act of bribery could void an election,[2] the common attitude seems to have been that one might as well be hung for a sheep as a lamb. Thus one candidate through agents spent the sum of $3 per vote polled for him, while another, faced by purely local economic laws, spent over $7.[3]

Treating was also a useful, popular, and comparatively cheap way of influencing the electorate, and there is considerable evidence to suggest that a large portion of the history of Canadian politics could be written in terms of its alcoholic content. Oddly enough, treating *per se* was not necessarily an offence. One justice laid down the interesting doctrine that whether treating was a corrupt practice depended on whether one was or was not a habitual treater at a constant rate. The habitual treater, who treated at his usual rate without perceptible acceleration during an election, was not guilty of an offence, though a known teetotaller who ordered drinks for the house at the wrong time was clearly asking for trouble. There was thus, the judge ventured to suggest, "a great inducement . . . to would-be candidates to look out in each constituency for men who are habitual drinkers . . . and then to send them out to cause the electioneering of the country to depend to a great extent on the popularity aroused by these means . . . The door is thus very widely opened to the introduction of drink as a means of quietly, yet surely, affecting an election."[4] A glance at newspaper files of the period suggests that the judge must have led a singularly sheltered life to be able to think that drink affected elections quietly.

This temperate view of intemperance was indicative of the fact that not all problems of electoral corruption were solved by sending petitions to the courts. On the contrary,

[1]Quoted in *The Week*, Dec. 11, 1884 (Mr. Justice Armour).
[2]Hodgins, *op. cit.*, p. 567.
[3]*Ibid.*, pp. 547, 560.
[4]*Ibid.*, p. 778.

to follow up the preceding example, other justices took a very strict view of treating, with the disconcerting result, as a member explained, that while some candidates might be floated into office "upon a perfect sea of beer," others were unseated by the ill-timed dispensing of a thimbleful.[1]

The question of agency produced similarly diverse views. Some courts maintained that agency had to be clearly established before a member could be unseated for an agent's act; at the other extreme, one judge held that every person attending a public meeting, the audience at which was given a general invitation by a candidate to work on his behalf, was an agent.[2] As late as 1905 an expert in election law declared that "it has never yet been distinctly and precisely defined what degree of evidence is required to establish such a relation . . . as to constitute agency;"[3] in 1915, the Minister of Justice refused to give the term "agent" a statutory definition.[4] This lack of clarity in the meaning of an important word was in part deliberate, as successive governments hesitated to define the term precisely lest too many loopholes be left in it. At the same time, the absence of exact definition produced the peculiar result that a member literally did not know when he might find his seat in the Commons threatened by an act committed by somebody of whom he had never heard. "It is, I am sure," a supporter wrote Sir John A. Macdonald in 1883 after a petition had been entered against the Prime Minister, "quite unnecessary for me to tell you how provoked I am at the conduct of some of our friends during the election, and that . . . Roe could have been so indiscreet, as sworn to, with a full knowledge of the consequences, does seem to me incredible. If the truth has been told you may well exclaim 'Save me from my friends!'"[5]

[1]*Debates*, 1879, p. 166.
[2]*Senate Debates*, 1900, p. 1083. See also *Debates*, 1879, p. 849.
[3]W. D. McPherson, *op. cit.*, p. 864.
[4]*Debates*, 1915, p. 2023. The latest instructions from the Chief Electoral Officer to election officials admit that "the definition of an agent is difficult to state at the same time briefly and comprehensively."
[5]M. W. Pruyer (?) to Sir John Macdonald, October 13, 1883. (Macdonald Papers, vol. 65, p. 147). In this particular instance, Sir John was out of pocket some $1,500 because of the petition. "Are the Lennox people going to let you pay all these things?" a supporter wrote, "From every point of view they are bound to defray all costs." (*Ibid.*, p. 221.)

The practice became established that the presiding judge in a trial would stop proceedings as soon as a single instance sufficient to void the election was established. This operation satisfied the petitioner, yet freed the respondent and the party organizations generally from any uncomfortable and widespread investigation of further corrupt practices.[1] A typical example occurred in the Ontario constituency of Kent in 1887, when a trial revealed a situation containing all the classic elements of a controverted election: doubtful agency; indirect bribery by the payment of excessive prices for goods; innocent candidates; drunken party stalwarts; workers with conveniently poor memories; an agent who found it expedient to leave the country; clever lawyers fishing for needed evidence they did not have; and bribed voters who took Liberal money and voted Conservative.[2] Despite these highly suggestive circumstances, the judge, having decided that the candidate himself was innocent of corrupt practices, merely observed that in "a trial of this kind it is not the duty of the judge to enter into a further enquiry; it is sufficient for him to dispose of the case. One case of bribery is established; therefore I must void the election." At the same time, in accordance with the Controverted Elections Act, he reported to the House that "there is reason to believe that corrupt practices have prevailed extensively at the said election. I am not, however, of opinion . . . that further enquiry as to whether corrupt practices have prevailed extensively is desirable, by which term I understand likely to prove useful or effectual."[3] The House of Commons— the "great uncontroverted," Grip called it[4]—needed little persuasion to refrain from the further enquiry mentioned by the judge, and accepted reports like this with respectful gratitude for the wisdom of the Bench.

The investigation of electoral corruption by the legislature, whether or not a candidate or member were involved, was a duty vaguely imposed by the Controverted Elections Act

[1]Debates, 1903, p. 891; The Week, December 28, 1894. These single instances of corruption were apparently often provided by collusion.
[2]The entire trial is given as Appendix No. 2 to the 1888 Journals. It is interesting also as a picture of how local organizations went to work at election time.
[3]Debates, 1888, p. 18.   [4]Grip, May 2, 1874.

of 1874. That statute allowed the House of Commons to take what action it saw fit if a judge reported widespread knavery at an election. For all practical purposes, this meant no action whatever; judges made reports implicating members in corrupt practices three times in the months immediately following the Act's passing, but the Commons made no move to investigate.[1] An attempt to facilitate inquiry into electoral malpractices was made in 1876, when it was enacted that any twenty-five voters could petition for an investigation if evidence of corruption existed and if no protest against the member concerned had been filed. (So frequent were protests that this second requirement stultified the new Act in many ridings). The House of Commons, on receiving such a request for an investigation, could then provide for a judicial commission to pursue the matter further.[2] In 1879 the electors of South Grenville filed the first petition of this kind, and the House was moved to immediate and decisive action.[3] The first step was to refer the petition to a committee which never mentioned it again. The second was to amend the Act so that all future petitioners had to deposit with the House accountant the sum of $1,000, from which all costs of an inquiry which proved to be based on an ill-founded petition were to be deducted before it was returned to the petitioners. This provision speedily gave the quietus to any more awkward petitions of that kind.

There is abundant evidence that an election during the first decades after 1867 was a rough game whose rules allowed ample scope for cheating, and to it substantial contributions were made by the wording of relevant laws and the nature of judicial decision. An independent newspaper recorded in 1883: "A mode of bringing the agents of corruption to public justice, irrespectively of any question as to the election itself, for an offence than which there can scarcely be one

[1]I have been unable to find any subsequent examples of the House making inquiry into electoral practices on a judge's report. In the 1887 case referred to above, a committee of the House merely recommended the filling of the vacant seat. In 1899, a committee took 500 pages of extraordinary evidence from 100 witnesses in connection with an election in West Huron, and came to no conclusion whatever. See *Journals*, 1899, Appendix No. 2.

[2]*Statutes*, 39 Vict., c. 10, s. 3. A commission could also issue following a judge's report.   [3]*Debates*, 1879, pp. 236-7.

either more injurious or less insulting to the nation, is what morality demands and politicians will never concede."[1]

One symptom of the looseness of the laws was the fact that the initiator of an election petition in any constituency did not need to be a resident of the district. Literally anybody could file a protest against an election, couched in general terms that the member must then disprove at his own expense.[2] The petitioners were thus often outsiders, sent into a constituency for the purpose of initiating a petition, and subsequently they quietly disappeared. This useful device, coupled with a saw-off, might result in a valid petition by an honest man against a dishonest one being conveniently cancelled out, so that neither side would press its suit. Again, there was nothing to require the courts to proceed with election trials at all, and since the judges were frequently overburdened with other cases it was often as convenient for the courts as for the members to allow petitions to lie dormant until a dissolution of Parliament abated them.[3] Saw-offs, although entirely illegal, were thus easily contrived, for the two parties had only to agree not to insist on a trial. In time, arrangements became even easier,[4] and by 1914 the Minister of Justice was able to comment on the fact that, considering the number of petitions that were started, remarkably few election cases ever came to trial. These conditions, he declared, constituted a public scandal.[5] For only one Parliament, that of 1891-6, did the total of unseatings approximate the record of forty-nine set during the halcyon days of 1875-8 when the Controverted Elections Act was having its initial work-out.[6]

[1]*The Week*, December 20, 1883. "No doubt," the same paper observed two years later, "we are governed largely by influences more or less corrupt." *Ibid.*, February 26, 1885.
[2]*Debates*, 1891, pp. 5357 ff., 5603 ff. One member here estimated that election trials cost as much as $3500 to the winning side, while the losers were in addition assessed for heavy costs.
[3]*Ibid.*, 1879, pp. 156, 233-5.
[4]By 1906, a new practice seems to have arisen whereby a counsel declared he had no evidence, and the case was consequently dismissed by the court. In addition, by this time a six months limit on petitions, originally intended to prevent the neglecting of petitions for indefinite periods, had been established. See *Debates*, 1906, pp. 235 ff.
[5]*Ibid.*, 1914, p. 910. Also *ibid.*, 1915, p. 2000.
[6]There were less than a dozen unseatings in the Parliament of 1878-82; slightly more during 1882-7; over twenty in 1887-91; forty in 1891-6.

The chief reason for this decline was clearly not a growth in electoral virtue but an increased use of the saw-off. Nor was the operation of this institution left to chance or the vagaries of local organizations; it was an important part of planned party warfare. J. W. Dafoe describes this procedure in his life of Sir Clifford Sifton:

A little later came the "saw-off" which in those times was an inevitable aftermath. . . . The pressure for these arrangements came, of course, from the elected members . . . but the actual arrangement had to be made by the leaders, since they alone had enough influence to get the consent of the local associations to these withdrawals. Mr. Sifton's correspondence shows that after the first session of the new Parliament the leaders got together at Ottawa and agreed that all the pending election petitions on both sides should be dropped. Sifton was charged with seeing that the arrangements west of Lake Superior were carried out; Hugh John Macdonald acted for the Conservatives.[1]

Sifton wrote to a colleague in 1900: "I have already given instructions to file petitions against all the Conservative members elected in the West . . . so that we will be in a position to protect our friends if necessary. One difficulty is that there are not quite enough Conservatives elected, but we cannot help that."[2]

All these arrangements were undoubtedly convenient for members, for the inclinations of these gentlemen to avoid an expensive court battle, with possibly a by-election to follow, can be understood if not condoned. On one occasion, for instance, a member feelingly explained in the House of Commons that a saw-off was the only way in which a man could hold a seat.[3] Unfortunately the convenience afforded by lax laws meant that the general picture of controverted elections and corrupt practices was for several decades after

[1]J. W. Dafoe, *Clifford Sifton in Relation to his Times* (Toronto, 1931), p. 196. Sifton ran into trouble in West Assiniboia because the local Liberals, who had been after the sitting Conservative for years and were sure they had him, declined to co-operate. Also P. Bilkey, *Persons, Papers, and Things* (Toronto, 1940), pp. 178-9.
[2]Sifton to W. Scott, December 17, 1900. (*Letters of Clifford Sifton*, Queen's University). A different type of consideration for a saw-off is found in a letter of Dalton McCarthy to Sir John Macdonald on September 12, 1888. "The Grits are willing to abandon the petition if their man is allowed to be elected by acclamation for the local." (Macdonald Papers, vol. 228.)
[3]*Debates*, 1900, pp. 7390-1.

Confederation unmarred by any serious attempts to brighten it.

A number of minor abuses may be listed for the extra light they shed on the whole situation. Thus it seems evident that in some instances a petition against a member was little more than a form of blackmail, the petitioner hoping to benefit financially by not proceeding with his case.[1] Another abuse arose from the fact that until 1891 the period within which a petition could be initiated ran from the date on which an election return was gazetted; the Government was thus able to prolong the exposure of its opponents to petitions by delaying the publication of election returns in the *Canada Gazette*.[2] Some time during the same period the practice began of breaking an election trial down into two separate actions, one on the petition itself, the other a preliminary trial of the right of the petitioner to petition, a device which the Prime Minister described in 1914 as occupying "months, sometimes years."[3] This comic opera procedure seems to have served no useful purpose beyond the gainful employment of lawyers, and it is worth noting that many a bright young lawyer entered politics via the revolving door of election trials.

The Controverted Elections Act thus became not so much an instrument for the suppression and punishment of corrupt practices as a means of providing new battlegrounds for party strife and party bargaining. The real purpose of the Act became lost in a maze of circumstances depending primarily on expediency; and corruption, far from being

---

[1]Petitions were described fairly frequently in debate as "blackmail." See *ibid.*, 1891, p. 5737; 1900, pp. 7375 ff. "Blackmailing" of members has been in the past (and still is) a game happily indulged in by many owners of vehicles, public halls, newspapers, and any other devices useful at election time. The standard practice is merely to raise rates to ridiculous heights. See *Debates*, 1900, p. 7387. In 1937, witnesses before the Special Committee on the Dominion Elections Act complained of these "hold-ups." See *Report*, pp. 115 ff., and *infra*, Chapter xv.

[2]For a typical complaint about this, see *Debates*, 1887, p. 142. *Sessional Paper* No. 27, 1891, gives the details of election returns and gazetting dates for the 1891 election, showing that the gazetting of returns was sometimes delayed several days.

[3]*Debates*, 1914, p. 918. This particular abuse was stopped in 1915. The practice had a statutory basis dating back to 1874, as the first Dominion Elections Act provided for a preliminary examination of petitioners.

252   THE CANADIAN HOUSE OF COMMONS

checked by the law, seems actually to have been promoted by its failure. The whole electoral system inevitably acquired a low reputation. Just as today many respectable citizens, who would not dream of robbing a bank, think nothing of juggling their income tax returns or smuggling items through the customs, so for several decades after Confederation otherwise honest men connived at the violation of election laws. In 1903 a frank member of Parliament declared:

So long as the candidates agree to suspend all ideas of morality during an election and go in for a general picnic, we shall continue to have all the expenditure of money that we have at the present time. Down in my part of the country we have the most moral people to be found in the world; but when an election comes around, they regard it as a splendid holiday. . . . They size up each candidate for what they can get out of him, and they generally run it up to the limit.[1]

Truly, as Sir Richard Cartwright observed on another occasion, elections were not "conducted on the principles of a boarding school for ladies."[2] The resulting situation must have kept many sensitive citizens from entering politics, with a consequent loss to Canadian public life that cannot be measured.

It is thus apparent that when Cabinet Ministers and party leaders informed the House of Commons from time to time that the controverted election laws seemed designed to *prevent* inquiry into corrupt practices[3] and that the law in general was practically a nullity,[4] there is no reason to assume that they were overstating the case. It was not that the House made no attempt whatever to improve the law; on the contrary, as a contemporary newspaper once remarked, there was a strong disposition to regard the disgraceful results of controverted election petitions as being caused largely by defects in the law,[5] and the law was tinkered with accordingly. Thus in 1891 it was declared that two

[1]*Debates*, 1903, p. 13616.
[2]Quoted in J. Cappon, "The Responsibility of Political Parties," *Queen's Quarterly*, vol. XII (1904-5), p. 311. This is an excellent descriptive article of corrupt practices in Ontario. Sir Richard Cartwright's knowledge of election frauds was more than academic, for he confessed on one occasion that in his unrepentant days he had twice purchased votes himself. Quoted by Sir Robert Borden in *Debates*, 1903, pp. 899-900.   [3]*Ibid.*, 1900, p. 7379.
[4]*Ibid.*, 1915, p. 1924.   [5]*The Week*, May 15, 1891.

judges instead of one should sit on election trials, a measure intended as much to protect individual judges from partisan attack as to reform the general system. Another important revision freed a candidate from responsibility for acts committed by agents contrary to the candidate's orders, and without his knowledge or consent,[1] thus removing from a candidate's friends "the wholesome restraint arising from the fear of depriving him of his election."[2] This statute is indicative of the fact that the general trend of both law and practice for many years after Confederation was in the direction of protecting candidates from the consequences of electoral malpractices by themselves and their friends, rather than of improving the techniques for investigating and punishing corruption.

No matter how stringent the law, there was of course no guarantee that electoral corruption would be reduced. The Commons was able to remind itself with a certain quiet satisfaction at all times that there would be no electoral corruption if there were no electors willing and even anxious to be corrupted, and this sort of thing could not be legislated out of existence.[3] As one veteran member said in 1938, harking back to the good old days, "I know it is within my memory—that people were literally bought on the market place, gangs of forty or fifty men actually sitting on the fence waiting until funds were provided so they could vote."[4]

Despite the ubiquity of the economic man in politics, it is a significant fact that not once did the House of Commons undertake a comprehensive investigation of electoral corruption; although petitions were at times arriving in such volume that the quorum in the legislature might have been threatened had the law not conveniently forbidden election trials while Parliament was in session. An order-in-council

[1]*Statutes*, 54-55 Vict., c. 20; *Debates*, 1891, *passim*. The proposal to use more than one judge was discussed as early as 1878, after Ontario had experimented successfully with it. (See *ibid.*, 1878, pp. 1454-5; 1879, pp. 164 ff. and pp. 849 ff.) The use of single judges, be it noted, not infrequently dragged the Bench into party warfare.

[2]*The Week*, July 24, 1891.

[3]See, for example, *Debates*, 1903, p. 13616, for a statement of this solacing thought by a member. Also *The Week*, September 22, 1887.

[4]*Debates*, 1938, p. 2026 (Mr. Power.) See also *ibid.*, 1900, pp. 7375 ff., for a graphic eye-witness account by a member of wholesale treating, and its results.

providing for a judicial investigation was passed in 1900, but the Commission which resulted made no report.[1]   In 1903 the topic was again given a general airing.   At this time the House gave serious consideration to compulsory voting as a means of rendering electoral corruption useless, but this particular remedy seems to have disturbed the members more than the condition it was to cure, and nothing was done.[2] A motion by the leader of the opposition requesting a general investigation in 1906 met a similar fate,[3] and it was not until 1914 that the Commons gave attention to needed improvements in the law.   In that year, with party leaders on both sides agreeing amicably that things were in a terrible state, a prominent Liberal member moved for the investigation of electoral frauds by a select committee and in 1915 a draft bill, which was the only significant report the Committee ever made, reached the Commons and passed with little opposition.[4]   The act made some admirable changes to expedite election trials by eliminating the useless preliminary examination of the right of petitioners to petition, and requiring the courts to proceed with trials promptly.   It also prevented the vague general petitions which had been lawful up to that time, and required that petitioners give "such particulars of the complaint set out in the petition as may be necessary to prevent surprise or unnecessary expense to the respondent and to ensure a fair and effectual trial."[5]

Exactly how this reformed act[6] affected corrupt practices is unfortunately impossible to determine, but it seems to have had the effect of virtually abolishing election trials, or at least contributing to their decline.   The number of trials reported to the House had dwindled steadily after the election of 1891, which had given rise to the astonishing total of over eighty controverted election cases, exclusive of appeals.

[1]The order itself is *Sessional Paper* no. 151. 1900.   See also *Debates*, 1900, pp. 6569 ff. and pp. 7082 ff., when the order was discussed.
[2]*Ibid.*, 1903, pp. 887 ff., 13581 ff.
[3]*Ibid.*, 1906, pp. 235 ff.
[4]*Ibid.*, 1914, pp. 900 ff.; 1915, *passim*.
[5]*Statutes*, 5 Geo. V, c. 13.
[6]Further changes of less significance were made in 1921.   *Statutes*, 11-12 Geo. V, c. 7.

Subsequent elections produced the following numbers of cases:[1]

1897–1900 inclusive	31
1901–1904	21
1905–1908	27
1909–1911	12
1912–1917	9
1918–1921	1
1922–1925	2

It is difficult to escape the conclusion that the changes of 1915 and 1921 were instrumental in eliminating the cases that could not be taken care of by saw-offs. Controverted election trials are today genuinely rare.

The entire credit for this improvement cannot be attributed to successive moves to make petitioning more difficult. Unquestionably, judging from the trend of development in the administration of elections generally, there has been since 1867 an enormous change in the attitude of members, parties, and the public towards improper manipulation of any part of the electoral machinery. It is a fair statement that most modern candidates for the House of Commons are careful to appoint conscientious agents, for self-protection if nothing else. Part of the change, again, is related to the appearance of what is loosely called the social conscience. But it is equally clear that part is the product of a mere growth in size of constituencies. When constituencies had small populations and the electorate was limited by sex and property qualifications, the purchase or importation of a mere forty or fifty voters might swing the election in any district. The modern electorate, whether more or less honest than its predecessors, is simply too large to manipulate voter by voter. "I do not believe," said Mr. C. G. Power in 1938, "that a wholesale purchase of votes is any longer

[1]These figures are approximate. Exact figures are impossible to obtain readily because of the haphazard way in which House documents are indexed, and because reports of cases to the Commons do not always distinguish between original trials and appeals. The given figures eliminate appeal cases as far as possible. See *Journals*, 1890-1926 inclusive.

either effective, practicable, or popular."[1] Strictly as a business proposition, honesty in elections is becoming compulsory in many parts of the country.

Attempts at manipulation, often successful, still occur, for as recently as 1934 Mr. Cahan complained in the legislature of organized personation in Montreal: "You must remember," he said, "in Montreal you can go to an association in New York who will supply you with 50 or 100 or 200 or 300 impersonators." In 1938 Hon. R. B. Bennett spoke of the continued existence of bribery and personation on "a very amazing scale."[2] Whole constituencies have been bought by judicious handling of the pork barrel or promises of its contents, a matter which the courts decided long since to be beyond the pale of their jurisdiction.[3] Finally, there are still frequent violations of the Controverted Elections Act, the most harmless of which concern those parts that forbid the employing of vehicles to take voters to the polls. This particular section has never been taken seriously; as a member observed amid choruses of agreement in 1920, it has been honoured more in the breach than in the observance.[4]

As the more interesting and spectacular phases of electoral corruption have declined to the point, at least, that they are rarely discovered, governmental machinery for the investigation and prosecution of individuals engaged in corrupt practices has made a belated and impressively inadequate appearance. In earlier days, when corruption was at its worst, the total absence of any centralized responsibility for checking corrupt practices naturally contributed to their prevalence; for while Canadian law early empowered the Government to appoint counsel for the prosecution of individual cases, there was no official akin to the English public prosecutor

[1]*Debates*, 1938, p. 2026.
[2]*Ibid.*, 1934, p. 4469; 1935, p. 1913; 1938, p. 2028. See also press reports of the Quebec provincial election of July, 1948.
[3]W. D. McPherson, *op. cit.*, p. 502. A judge is here quoted as saying, in regard to promises of the pork barrel: "Though by no means free from doubt, I do not feel warranted in setting aside the election in consequence of the speeches made, either by respondent or his agents." The main reason for this was the impossibility of proving that the promises had any corrupt influence, and the same would naturally be true of actual public works. In 1890, a motion to prevent this wholesale form of bribery was introduced in the House, and disposed of summarily.
[4]*Debates*, 1920, pp. 1160 ff. Also 1938, p. 2030.

who was specifically charged with the punishment of offenders.[1] On occasion, members on both sides spoke in favour of establishing such an office,[2] but neither party when in power seemed convinced of the need for it. Even the Chief Electoral Officer, when that position was created in 1920, was not charged with any definite responsibility in regard to electoral corruption. On the contrary, the duties of the Chief Electoral Officer were confined to the most routine aspects of operating the machinery. This situation was clearly exposed in 1926 when it was revealed that, although a case of corruption in a constituency was established, the administrator in charge of elections had not felt himself to have any responsibility. A committee of the House consequently suggested in 1928 that the Chief Electoral Officer should recommend prosecution when the circumstances seemed to warrant it,[3] and this was enacted in part in 1929, when he was given the same power as a commissioner under the Inquiries Act for certain defined purposes.[4]

These purposes are so limited that the general investigation of corrupt acts committed by anyone other than an election official remains untouched. It would be a serious error, therefore, to assume that the rarity of controverted election cases in recent years necessarily means that electoral corruption has disappeared.[5] Successive moves to protect members from "blackmailing" and merely vexatious petitions, and from responsibility for agents acting contrary to instructions and without the candidate's knowledge or consent, have inevitably placed greater difficulties in the way of honest petitioners, and today it is both difficult and expensive to charge a member or anybody else with corrupt practices. In 1938 R. B. Bennett, referring to a bill to limit candidates' election expenditures, said:

[1]*R.S. Can.*, 1886, c. 9, s. 73. See *Debates*, 1889, p. 427; 1891, p. 5750. This power was used on occasion; among other things it was a useful bit of patronage.

[2]E.g., *ibid.*, 1914, p. 904; 1915, p. 2025. Also *The Week*, December 28, 1894.

[3]See *Report of the Select Standing Committee on Privileges and Elections*, 1928 (*Journals*, 1928, pp. 485-6, and Appendix 6).

[4]*Statutes*, 19-20 Geo. V, c. 40, s. 5. In general these new powers granted to the Chief Electoral Officer referred to manipulations of lists, etc., rather than to such corrupt practices as personation and bribery.

[5]One controverted election trial followed the election of 1940, and one the election of 1949.

So long as we leave the corrupt elections act as it is today, we might as well conclude that we are wasting our time . . . if a thousand dollars has to be put up as a deposit, and all the machinery of the law resorted to, with all the technicalities which can be relied on by those who defend themselves against an attack on their seat.

There has grown up—not limited entirely to one party . . . a class of men whose one purpose in life is to flourish at election times and see how much they can get out of the candidate and the use they can put it to for the purpose of prostituting the electorate. . . . You have this type of person dealing with a situation about which he does not want the candidate to know anything, and about which the candidate does not want to know anything.[1]

The Prime Minister here revealed the great paradox of the law governing electoral corruption. On the one hand, no one is charged with its enforcement, and its effective operation, as the record shows, cannot safely be left to rival party organizations; if it is to function at all, it must do so on the initiative of members of the general public. But on the other hand, unlike almost all criminal matters, every conceivable difficulty exists to discourage the public from reporting violations of the law. The Controverted Elections Act has thus been stultified not merely by the practices which have grown up around it, but by some of its own terms.

---

[1]*Debates*, 1938, pp. 2028-32. Mr. C. G. Power entirely concurred in this general description (see p. 2026). See also *Report of Special Committee on Elections and Franchise Acts*, 1937, *passim*. Mr. Power made specific references to electoral corruption in his speech as a candidate for the party leadership before the Liberal convention of 1948.

CHAPTER XV

ELECTION EXPENSES

THERE are few more curious chapters in Canadian politics than that concerning the election expenses of candidates for the House of Commons,[1] for almost from the beginning the provisions of the law have been reasonably adequate, and have been uniformly disobeyed. The tale is one of quiet but thorough law-breaking in practice, and of genteel but persistent hypocrisy in utterance.

No one in Canada seems to have been greatly exercised over campaign contributions and expenditures until the Pacific Scandal of 1873, and the provincial laws which obtained in federal elections after Confederation were all silent on these topics. The disclosures of 1873, however, combined with the election of a somewhat puritanically minded Liberal Government in 1874, led to the enactment of provisions which were noteworthy not only for being the first of their kind in Canada, but also the best. Weak though they were, it must nevertheless be recorded that their subsequent development, both in law and in practice, has been one of fairly continual deterioration.

The main statutory requirements of 1874, incorporated in the first Dominion Elections Act, were as follows:

1. Except for a candidate's personal expenses, no payment of any kind could be made by or on behalf of any candidate before, during, or after an election, except through an authorized agent whose name and address were to be supplied to the returning officer.

2. All bills and claims for election expenses must be presented to the agent within one month after the election, and all claims could be paid only with the authority of both the agent and candidate.

[1]This chapter is not concerned with the larger problem of party campaign funds, except incidentally. This latter topic, however attractive, is more properly part of a study of Canadian political parties, and expediency dictates that this work be confined to the narrower question of election expenses as they concern candidatures for the Commons.

259

3. A detailed statement of all election expenses was to be made to the returning officer within two months after the election, and an abstract of the statement was to be published promptly by the election official.

4. Any agent or candidate who defaulted in supplying the statement of expenses was to incur a penalty of twenty dollars for every day of the default, and the filing of an untrue statement was a misdemeanour.[1]

The law, except for the addition in 1908 of a requirement that contributions to a candidate's election fund be published along with his expenses,[2] then remained unchanged until after the First World War. The absence of amendment to the law was no tribute to its excellence, for it was left without alteration precisely because it was not effective, and thus was eminently satisfactory to all concerned. Since no provisions were made to put responsibility anywhere for enforcement of its clearly worded terms, the statute was obeyed in practice only by those who chose to do so, and even then there was no way of ascertaining the accuracy of a published statement. Considering the prevalence of electoral corruption for several decades after 1867, there is every reason to suppose that the law was violated more often than not, for it is difficult to believe that a candidate or agent who fought an election with bribery and whiskey was going to be so short-sighted as to supply a returning officer with a detailed statement of his disbursements. "I think it is quite a stretch of credulity," a successful candidate remarked on one occasion, "to imagine that anyone who is so wickedly inclined as to commit a corrupt practice is going to write down on paper that he did so."[3] "The law in its present form," wrote another, "forces every live candidate to be a hypocrite on pain of having his election voided."[4]   In fairness

[1]*Statutes*, 37 Vict., c. 9, ss. 121-5. Macdonald had a general Dominion Elections Act ready in 1873 which included several clauses similar to the foregoing. See Macdonald Papers, vol. 73. Also *Debates*, 1870, pp. 363 ff., when Blake argued for supervision of election expenses.
[2]*Statutes*, 7-8 Edw. VII, c. 26, s. 23.
[3]*Debates*, 1907-8, p. 11887. On the rare occasions when the question of reporting election expenses has arisen in court cases, the courts have viewed a failure to report expenditures as a strong "presumption that corrupt practices have been resorted to." (See, e.g., *Belleau* v. *Dussault* [1885] 11 S.C.R. 133; *Larue* v. *Deslauriers* [1880] 5 S.C.R. 91.)   [4]*Canadian Magazine*, 1905, p. 318.

to the members, it must be admitted that they have seemed in the past to be more ready to accept accusations of unscrupulousness than of stupidity.

Candidates who were inclined to ignore the law soon found their consciences relieved by a custom to the effect that the law did not really mean what it said. To a layman, it might appear that the statement, "No payment . . . and no advance, loan or deposit shall be made by or on behalf of any candidate at any election . . . otherwise than through an agent" covered all conceivable expenditures by or on behalf of a candidate, and meant that all these were to be made through an agent. In practice this provision was interpreted (when it received any attention at all) as applying only to purely local expenditures; payments on behalf of candidates by party organizations, or indeed by anybody interested, were regarded as not coming within the purview of an agent's responsibility. This was so clear a violation of the law that it is difficult to believe it could come about except through a widespread willingness on the part of candidates that it should be so. So far as can be determined, the validity of this custom has never been tested in Canadian courts, nor is there an instance of the statutory penalty being imposed on anybody for failure to comply with the law.[1]

What this laxity meant in regard to electoral practices can be made clear by an example or two. The great "scandal sessions" of 1891-6, which produced some startling evidence of organized looting of the public treasury with a share of the profits finding its way into election funds, revealed clearly how casual an attitude towards election expenses was taken by many members. One man, for instance, filed a return of $384.30 when there existed receipts and other statements showing that he and his agent had received some $2,500 for election expenses from a party fund.[2] Again, published statements by two Cabinet Ministers showed expenses of less than $1,000 in each case, when there existed

[1]See W. D. McPherson, *The Law of Elections in Canada* (Toronto, 1905), pp. 973-86, for a detailed statement of the law concerning election expenses. The author cites very few cases to support his text, and a check of what citations are given reveals no instances of the foregoing. See p. 263, n. 1.
[2]*Debates*, 1892, p. 3743.

evidence that at least $16,000 had been spent in the two elections.[1] Significantly enough, neither of these two members denied that the money had been spent; they simply denied any knowledge that it had. "I take care," one of them said under oath, "when an election comes on to know nothing of the kind."[2] Taking a most charitable view of the circumstances, it was still true, as Sir Robert Borden remarked some years later, that "the candidates might be able very sincerely to make a statement of election expenses which would be a mere travesty of a statement of the whole expenses, because of the immense expenditures of . . . political organizations."[3] Even when candidates complied with the law and made a return, in short, the results in too many cases were meaningless.

They still are meaningless. To bring this particular point up to date, it is necessary only to quote two independent authorities. Thus Professor R. A. MacKay, in 1931, writes:

The four constituencies in which the writer sought to obtain information on campaign expenditure return five members to Parliament. The information was sought early in January, that is about five months after the election and three months after the return of accounts was required to be made by law. Only four of all ten candidates apparently made any return; these included three successful and one unsuccessful candidate. . . . Published returns were all in lump sums and virtually valueless. In every case, the writer was informed, no other request had been made to see the returns. [4]

Professor MacKay's statement was based on a small number of constituencies, but the Chief Electoral Officer stated in 1937, in regard to the whole country: "In my experience I do not think half of the defeated candidates file election returns. . . . [The] very severe penalty [on elected candidates] is never to my knowledge enforced. . . . During the last Parliament I have knowledge of two or three elected members who waited two or three years to make their returns,

[1]*Ibid.*, 1894, pp. 5179 ff.
[2]*Report of the Select Standing Committee on Privileges and Elections*, 1891 (Appendix No. 1 to *Journals*), p. 1136.
[3]*Debates*, 1908, p. 11888.
[4]R. A. MacKay, "After Beauharnois," *Maclean's Magazine*, Oct. 15, 1931. Quoted in full in R. MacG. Dawson, *Constitutional Issues in Canada, 1900-1931* (Oxford, 1932), pp. 208-18.

and sat in the House, and they were liable to a fine of $500 for every day they sat."[1]

This last glorious absurdity, it may be added, has never meant anything, primarily because when it was established the law was also changed to allow members to obtain permission from a court to file a belated return.[2] Permission is available on the flimsiest excuses, and my attention was drawn in interviews with members and public servants to more than one instance where an elected candidate successfully escaped the consequences of failure to make an expense return by speeding to the nearest judge to receive absolution.[3] The provision of a statutory way of evading a statute that was normally broken is surely the ultimate in legislative self-indulgence.

On this account, the existing provisions concerning election expenses are even weaker than the original enactment of 1874. On paper the law today remains remarkably clear, and human ingenuity could hardly devise a more exact statement of what is required. The continual violation of the law thus remains one of the most striking aspects of the whole electoral machinery. The fundamental problem, of course, is still the same: no intelligent provision whatever is made for law enforcement, and if a candidate or agent fails to file a statement, the returning officer is under no obligation to obtain one. The Chief Electoral Officer has no jurisdiction in the matter, for returns are made only to the election official in each separate constituency. Short of the equivalent of a court trial, there is no workable method of checking up on what returns are made; and even when returns are made and published, they usually appear as a small advertisement of interest to nobody. As a trustworthy deterrent to improper or excessive expenditure in elections, or as a mere method of publicizing the costs of an

---

[1]*Report of the Special Committee on Elections and Franchise Acts*, 1937, pp. 245-6. [2]*Statutes*, 10-11 Geo. V, c. 46, ss. 78-9.

[3]One member related a personal experience in which he had actually made his return, but inadvertently omitted a small sum paid to a supporter for a legitimate expense. The supporter, whose loyalty fell a victim to the possibilities of blackmailing the member because of this omission, threatened to take action to recover the $500 daily penalty provided by the law. The member rapidly interviewed the local judge, and filed a new election expense return.

election and the names of those who pay them, the law may be briefly summarized as a farce.

Quite apart from these legal deficiencies, there remains the dual problem of how much election campaigns do cost the candidates, and, what might be called its ethical aspect, how much campaigns should cost. To neither of these can a satisfactory answer be given, for the unreliability and even non-existence of data on the first, and the absence of any real criterion by which to judge the second, make definite comment difficult. It is at least clear that actual costs vary enormously; so trustworthy a member as Mr. J. S. Woodsworth once stated that he ran a federal election for $600; Mr. C. H. Cahan, with no particular reason for boasting, has confessed to election expenditures of $15,000, $25,000 and $75,000; and rumour has it that election charges for a single constituency have run as high as $100,000.[1] Even if Mr. Woodsworth's low costs of $600 were the average in each constituency, which could not be the case, it is tolerably clear that politics is not a poor man's game. As Professor MacKay says: "The poor man, even the man with a good income but dependent on his earnings for his living, can scarcely venture to serve his fellows in public life without risking his independence. Unable to finance his own campaign, he is in danger of becoming dependent on those who can and will—at a price."[2]

A most interesting question in regard to elections is why they should have to be so expensive. A great deal depends on the size and nature of the constituency, for a candidate could readily run up enormous transportation bills in some western ridings which are several thousand square miles in extent, while the similar charges in a compact urban constituency would be negligible. Similarly, the costs of a left-wing candidate in a labour district would not necessarily be large, nor would those of a representative of any party in a completely safe seat. Again, legitimate organization costs may be high. This is made clear by the following description by a candidate of a constituency machine:

[1]MacKay, op. cit.; R. MacG. Dawson, The Government of Canada (Toronto, 1947), p. 576; Report of Special Committee on Elections and Franchise Acts, 1937, p. 113.   [2]MacKay, op. cit.

There were in that constituency eleven divisions, each with a chairman, secretary, telephone man, clerks, caretaker of rooms, messengers. . . . At each poll was a captain, scrutineer, special constable, telephone man, and from four to ten "hustlers." Striking an average that means . . . 847 in the constituency. How much would it cost to pay those men a reasonable wage for a day's work? The usual tariff on both sides in Toronto is $4.00 per day . . . which means $3,388 for part of the work on election day. . . . [In addition], a cost for livery alone of $2,310. Thus the one final day of the election must with incidentals added have cost at least $6,000.

But that is only a fraction of the work or expense.' Firstly, there is the maintenance of a political club. . . . Then there is a thorough systematic canvass for eligible voters. . . . Then there is another canvass for the revision of lists. . . . Then the keeping of the lists up to date. . . . Then comes the preparation of hundreds of letters, pamphlets, circulars, editorials, identification cards, notices of meetings. . . . He will be a clever financier indeed who keeps within $10,000.[1]

Though forty years old, this description is still applicable to many urban ridings. A candidate's legitimate expenses, unless his supporters are so full of zeal for the cause that they will work without remuneration (as is the case with some of the new third parties), can obviously be enormous.

The possibility of illegitimate expenditure to swell the total still exists. The mere fact of excessive election expenditure, indeed, seems to carry with it the presumption that it could not possibly have been spent honestly, or even legally. This is not mere theory, for a prominent member told a House of Commons committee in 1937, "I was in charge of organization for the Liberal party in British Columbia for some years and Mr. Stevens was very high up in the Conservative party, and we knew then just as we know now that money was being expended in a way that was against the law. There is not any question about that."[2] That this situation is not confined to British Columbia has been made clear more than once in the House and before its committees.[3]

It must not be thought that excessive electoral expenditure, whether for honest or dishonest purposes, is necessarily the fault of the candidates. For one thing, many local party

[1]*Canadian Magazine*, 1905, p. 316. An interesting legitimate expense imposed on federal candidates in Nova Scotia in the 1867 election was the actual payment of returning officers and other election officials. See *Parliamentary Debates* (Scrapbook Hansard), December 11, 1867.

[2]*Report of Special Committee on Elections and Franchise Acts*, 1937, p. 122 (Mr. Turgeon).

[3]E.g., *ibid.*, *passim*, and *Debates*, 1938, pp. 2028 ff.

organizations seem to insist on as extravagant an outlay as possible; this point was established before a committee of the House in 1937 by a member who opposed legalizing certain types of election expenses "because if you open it up to allow for that, our organization would merely force us to do it." This would, he added, cause a large increase in the cost of elections.[1] Many sections of the community apart from party organizations exploit candidates at election time. "Let us," Mr. H. H. Stevens has said, "take large cities like Montreal, Toronto, Winnipeg, Vancouver or Hamilton ...; at election time owners of halls or large auditoriums usually hold up political parties. Practically there is double charge made in some cities, and newspapers charge a double rate per line for advertising. There are reasons for this no doubt, but it is merely part of the piracy that occurs in connection with election expense; they know that funds come fairly easily in some instances and therefore, they want to get their share."[2]

The pillaging of candidates is not confined to commercial organizations. Decades ago, a candidate recorded these experiences in terms that still have force today:

Every post brought an appeal for a subscription to aid some object or scheme which was threatened with extinction through want of funds to complete it. I was pathetically implored to remember that a few pounds now would complete some great and beneficent work, which, if those funds were denied, must perforce be abandoned and perish forever. Bazaars, bicycle clubs, tricycle clubs, boating clubs, skating clubs, football clubs, cricket clubs, and many other similar associations adjured me to become their patron and aid them with some slight pecuniary consideration. Wherever I turned it seemed that teetotal festivals were organized for my special delight which I was required to foster and attend. Friendly societies in scores showed an eager desire to record my honoured name upon their lists. Secretaries of chapel and school building funds poured exhortations upon me. ... So urgent and so minatory were some of these appeals that they looked to me to be almost a modern adaptation of the old system of blackmailing.[3]

There is ample evidence that parliamentary candidates still find their expenses increased by what a contemporary mem-

[1]*Report of Special Committee on Elections and Franchise Acts*, 1937, pp. 62-3. See also *Debates*, 1939, p. 1810 (Mr. Power).
[2]*Report of Special Committee on Elections and Franchise Acts*, 1937, p. 115. See also *Debates*, 1900, p. 7387.   [3]Quoted in *The Week*, January 28, 1886.

ber has called "innumerable good works which they are not in the habit of performing at any other time."[1]

Finally, unless several reputable members do a good deal of unnecessary prevaricating, the professional election agent does not always run his candidate's campaign as cheaply as possible. The most remarkable statement supporting this point was made before a committee in 1937 by a young Quebec member who, amid admiring cries from his colleagues, spoke his mind as follows:

In my constituency it used to cost $45,000 to run an election. I said to my people, "If you take me for a darned fool, I am going to stay home. I am not going to spend that amount of money to be elected as a member of Parliament; it is not worth it. . . " I pitched out the whole organization and ran the election myself. They used to have forty committee rooms. Every person who had a vacant room in his place would come to the agent and arrange to have it rented. Then they had clubs of bowlers and horseshoe pitching. There were a hundred clubs that had to be paid $100 each to get their support. . . .

I did not even open up the election laws. . . . The fellows that came to me with a little room about four feet wide that used to rent for $25.00 and $50.00 received the reply that it was none of my business. . . . Then, take the posters that are distributed around the city at an election time. I did not want any of them, as it is a very expensive form of advertising. The same applies to the high newspaper rates. . . . The law as it stands today puts you in the strange position of not knowing what your agent is doing. You give him a free hand and he runs up expenses that you know nothing about. When the election is over he comes and tells you that he did not want you to know such and such a thing because under the law you were not supposed to know it. He also says that he has a little account of some $600 or $700 which was incurred on behalf of some man who controlled some fifty voters in a certain part of the city, and he thought it was better to get him.[2]

Confessions such as these suggest that there is a great need in Canada for more rigorous supervision of election finances. One possible reform, the setting of a legal limit to the amount that can be spent in any one constituency, was suggested to the Commons in 1920, but it received very little attention, and the House revealed its general attitude to the problem

[1] *Debates*, 1938, p. 2026 (Mr. Power).
[2] *Report of the Special Committee on Elections and Franchise Acts*, 1937, pp. 117-18 (Mr. Parent). See also Mr. Stevens's remarks, *ibid.*, p. 119, and Hon. R. B. Bennett in *Debates*, 1938, pp. 2028 ff. Both these leaders corroborate Mr. Parent's statement.

by voting down a motion to limit the contribution that could be made to an election fund by any one individual.[1] (During the debate, it is interesting to note, Hon. W. S. Fielding observed that the only real solution to excessive and improper election expenditures was to make all such sums a charge on the federal treasury, and he prophesied rather wistfully that this utopian position might some day be reached.)[2] Again in 1937, the Special Committee on Elections and Franchise Acts negatived a proposal to limit election expenses.[3]

In the following year, however, a special committee approved a bill which reached the House as the Political Expenditures Bill of 1939,[4] and which reversed this stand. Its proposals were sweeping, requiring the publication of both the income and expenditure of parties and limiting the amount that could be spent in any one constituency to 20 cents per voter, plus $1000 for a candidate's personal expenses. In addition, it was proposed:

... to place the responsibility for enforcement on the Chief Electoral Officer instead of the local returning officer. Returns of receipts and expenditures were to be made to the Chief Electoral Officer and were to be published by him in the *Canada Gazette*; he was to have the power of inquiry following complaints filed by at least ten electors, who were required to deposit $200, which would be returned if the complaints were 'well-founded'; results of such inquiry were to be forwarded to the speaker of the House of Commons.[5]

Though by no means ideal—members would still have been allowed to make belated returns of expenses with a judge's certificate—it was an impressive group of proposals; "essentially," as Mr. Power described it, "a businesslike piece of legislation . . . so to modify the law that the candidates would be enabled to apply to election campaigns the same open, sane businesslike methods that they apply in their

[1]*Debates*, 1920, pp. 1171-3.   Long before this, *The Week* had urged limitation of election expenditures by law.   See *The Week*, June 28, 1889 and May 27, 1891.
[2]*Debates*, 1920, p. 1197.
[3]*Report*, p. 247.
[4]The draft bill appears in the *Journals*, 1939, pp. 407 ff.   See also *Debates*, 1939, pp. 1809 ff., 3552-3, 3871 ff.
[5]This summary is from R. MacG. Dawson, *The Government of Canada*, pp. 577-8.

own businesses."[1] Nonetheless, Mr. Power was obliged to admit in 1948 that the bill "was laughed at, and the objective ridiculed as purely academic and idealistic." Mr. Power's bill reappeared in 1949, when it passed second reading without debate and without a dissenting voice, but Parliament was dissolved before the bill progressed further.[2]

Some members in 1939 took the Political Expenditures Bill seriously, and the principle it involved seemed acceptable to at least a few. This was hardly surprising, since intelligent control of election expenses is as much in members' interests as in those of the general public. Unhappily, the objections of members, combined with the pressure of other business during the 1939 session of Parliament, necessitated that the bill be dropped then; and the two silent readings accorded the measure in 1949 did not even serve the purpose of drawing the public's attention to the problem of political expenditures. The special Committees of the House which considered the Dominion Elections Act in 1947 and 1948 regrettably showed no inclination to discuss the matter, so that, except for the admirable work of Mr. Power himself, election expenses have received little attention for nearly a decade. This is unfortunate, for the mere publicity that would of necessity attend a debate of the 1939 and 1949 proposals would be at least a beginning, and an aroused public opinion might conceivably reform a situation which has shown little or no improvement for three-quarters of a century.

[1]*Debates*, 1939, p. 1809.
[2]See Mr. Power's speech as a candidate for the leadership of the Liberal party in 1948; quoted in *Winnipeg Free Press*, August 12, 1948; *Debates*, 1949, (1st session), p. 2358; and especially an article written jointly by Mr. Power and Leslie Roberts for *Maclean's*, Feb. 1, 1949.

PART V

CONCLUSION

CHAPTER XVI

CONCLUSION

THE preceding pages have examined in detail the major aspects of representation in the Canadian House of Commons, from the first readjustment of constituency boundaries to the last post-election failure to file a statement of campaign expenditures. It has been shown that improvements have occurred in most parts of the representative system since 1867, but that much yet remains to be accomplished. In order to appraise the system as a whole, and to avoid a mere summary here of the main points brought forth in the text, it is now necessary to abandon the topical sequence followed in the first fourteen chapters.

The most obvious conclusion to be propounded is that the legislative record of the House of Commons on electoral and allied matters has been a remarkable mixture of competence and ineptitude. On the one hand, the great strides made in freeing the administration of elections from partisan interference cannot fail to impress. The judicious and serious attention which the House of Commons, ably advised by the Chief Electoral Officer, has given to the electoral machinery in the past three decades, is a far cry from the spirited bitterness which marked the debates of 1882, 1885, and 1908. Governments no longer introduce bills concerning representation which are thrust upon the Opposition regardless of protest; that proposed changes in any part of the electoral system are today discussed calmly by committees which represent all parties is symbolic of the progress that has been achieved. On the other hand, the continued incapacity of the legislature to devise rational schemes for the readjustment of constituency boundaries, the payment of members, and the control of electoral corruption and expenditure, throws a deep shadow which greatly obscures the truly admirable developments that have occurred.

There is no denying that the failures of the House of Commons have been at least as spectacular as the successes.

Through all the failures runs a common thread: the tender solicitude shown by members of Parliament for the interests of members of Parliament. Consideration for the welfare of the general public, for instance, has had little to do with the settlement of constituency boundaries, either in the adjustments themselves or the techniques employed to effect them. The extraordinary rules governing the payment of the sessional indemnity have been established by members of Parliament, acting in their public capacity as legislators, but hardly for public purposes. The chronicle of controverted elections and electoral expenses has been partly one of evasion of the country's laws by those who enacted them, and who might on that account, one would think, properly be found among the laws' foremost champions. That so many of the regrettable aspects of Canadian politics have been made possible by legal procedures and devices suggests that the preponderance of lawyers in the House of Commons has not been an unmixed blessing. But it would be unfair to leave the impression that the legal profession alone has been blameworthy; the self-indulgence which marks the legislative record on these topics has arisen from normal human failings, and it would require a gross perversion of logic to conclude that members of Parliament were on that account inferior to ordinary men. On the contrary, as all the preceding pages testify, too many general elections in the past have returned a fair proportion of very ordinary men indeed.

The manner in which legislators manage laws closely related to their own personal welfare is a valid criterion by which to measure the quality of the men concerned. Despite the incapacities already cited, a justifiable deduction is that contemporary members of Parliament are better men than their predecessors. Modern representatives, despite the loopholes which still exist in the Independence of Parliament Act, do not loot the public domain and public treasury as did their counterparts in the eighties; they no longer exploit for partisan purposes the laws which govern such matters as candidates' qualifications and the procedure for nominating and voting; nor do they readily tolerate corrupt methods of campaigning on so generous a scale as in years gone by.

They still bungle the decennial redistribution of seats, but not with the high-handed malice so conspicuous before 1903. They still pay themselves handsomely for not attending in their places, but today they have at least the excuse that sessions are both long and arduous. When seen in their proper perspective, the legislative failures recorded in this volume lessen in significance if the tremendous improvements both in the representative system and the attitudes of members towards it are given full consideration. This survey of merely one part of the House of Commons' history since 1867 makes one suspect that the nostalgic yearnings for the parliamentary giants of yesteryear, which sometimes appear in the memoirs of journalists and politicians, have little basis in fact.[1]

It must nevertheless be admitted that the positive achievements of the House of Commons took their own time in coming, and were often the result of circumstances beyond the reach of the legislature. The manipulation of the whole electoral system for partisan purposes was regarded as a legitimate tactic by a majority of both Houses of Parliament as recently as 1917. Not until 1920, when the same Government which countenanced the overt tricks of 1917 established a Chief Electoral Officer to oversee the administration of elections, can it be said that the system had attained a status reasonably free of the suspicion that it could be distorted to one party's advantage. Even then, the Chief Electoral Officer was confined to recommending changes in only the most routine administrative aspects of the Dominion Elections Act, and his responsibility for the machinery ended with his annual report.[2] "I do not conceive," he has reported more than once, "that the intention . . . was to require, or indeed to permit me to put forward suggestions for the alteration in its essentials of the election machinery prescribed by the Act."[3]

The Chief Electoral Officer, although he enjoys the rank of a deputy minister and the tenure of a judge, thus has in regard to policy an official position inferior to almost any

[1]See, e.g., P. Bilkey, *Persons, Papers, and Things* (Toronto, 1940), pp. 179 ff.
[2]See *Report of Select Standing Committee on Privileges and Elections*, 1928, which examined the Officer on these points.
[3]*Report of the Chief Electoral Officer to the Speaker*, 1936, p. 5.

other deputy minister in the public service. Many topics connected with representation, such as the adjustment of constituency boundaries and the general investigation of electoral corruption, are entirely outside his jurisdiction. Yet his real influence as the expert advisor of members and committees on electoral matters is very substantial; he holds a monopoly in his field, and his work is respected by the legislature whose servant he is. The natural trend of his proposed alterations in the electoral machinery, because of his peculiarly vulnerable position as an executive whose activity is closely allied to that of political parties, has been in the direction of reducing to the utmost the discretionary power he may be called upon to exercise in an emergency. An unavoidable tendency towards increasing complexity in the electoral system has thus occurred, accompanied by a growing reliance on rigid legalistic procedure. This has been offset by the fact that the Chief Electoral Officer for over twenty years has not been a trained lawyer.[1]

The improvement made in 1920 by the establishment of the position of Chief Electoral Officer was deliberately brought about by the legislature. But statutory reform would not have been possible had not other circumstances connected with elections made it so. Manipulation of the representative system and the use of corrupt campaign tactics have become increasingly difficult, not primarily because of legislative enactment, but because of two factors with which the House of Commons had little to do. One of these has been the development of a public opinion which is severely critical of improper electioneering methods. This first became noticeable around the turn of the century in the changed attitudes of members towards the electoral machinery, and affords some proof of the generalization that the public gets the kind of representation it deserves. The other factor has been the enormous growth in size of constituencies since 1867, brought about by an expanding

[1]Mr. Jules Castonguay, who was Chief Electoral Officer until 1949, completed in 1948 forty years of service as an administrator of elections. Before the office of Chief Electoral Officer was established, he was in the office of the Clerk of the Crown in Chancery. Mr. Castonguay was succeeded in 1949 by his son, who had been his executive assistant.

population and a widening franchise; this has simply made manipulation and corruption impracticable.

Another development which has assisted in the rise of an impartial electoral administration, and one for which the House of Commons may fairly be given some credit, has been the improvement of the public service generally. The history of representation in Canada, when not dominated by party spirit, has been featured partly by honest trial-and-error methods of legislation, the inefficacy of which frequently reflected nothing more than weakness in administrative techniques. This weakness actually contributed to the manipulation of the electoral machinery for partisan purposes; for when it was virtually impossible to establish an efficient system which reached down into every section of the country yet operated for only a few weeks every four or five years, the easy solution to the problem was to leave the election in each constituency completely in the hands of local partisans.

Considering the magnitude of the task which the electoral machine must accomplish, it is therefore at least doubtful if a fair, comprehensive, and efficient administration could have been created until great improvements had been made in communications and a number of allied matters. A significant statement that supports this suggestion was made by the Chief Electoral Officer in one of his reports:

I should like . . . to make due acknowledgment of the sympathetic co-operation of all the Departments of the Government to which requests for cooperation were transmitted. . . . The Department of National Defence placed its aeroplanes at the disposition of returning officers. . . . The Department of Fisheries . . . put fishing boats. . . . The Department of Public Works arranged for office accommodation in public buildings. . . . The Department of Public Printing and Stationery provided a very efficient service. . . . The Post Office rendered invaluable services. . . .[1]

The successful management of a modern general election, in short, is an administrative task of huge proportions, and the development of a trustworthy machine had to wait upon progress in many apparently unrelated fields. Not the least of these was the franchise, for the simplicity of a system

[1]*Report of Chief Electoral Officer to the Speaker*, 1936.

that includes almost everybody, as compared with a complicated suffrage that varied according to province, sex, income,
or possessions, has greatly facilitated the entire operation of
a general election.

The development of a genuine electoral administration
has brought under governmental authority a great deal of
work formerly performed by party organizations. The
electoral system and the party system were two parts of the
same thing for several decades after 1867; with the passage
of time, the two have become separated. The process has
greatly affected the nature of political organization in
Canada. The periodic battles to have constituency boundaries altered to the advantage of local partisans, the com-
petitive compilation of voters' lists, the fighting of elections,
the unseating of members and the consequent frequency of
by-elections, provided for many years after Confederation
ample work to employ an active group of party workers in
every district. At times, indeed, the local supporters were
too active. "After three elections in this riding and a protest
inside of nine months and another protest entered," a follower
wrote Sir John A. Macdonald in 1891, "our friends are
exhausted and sick of the contests."[1]

The decline in such local party activity, and the developments in the public service which have decreased the
patronage available to constituency partisans, have removed
several of the conditions which make party organization
necessary at all. This is not to say that parties today have
little work in each electoral district; they still provide several
score of enumerators for a week or two at each election,
and supply the fighting forces which use the electoral machine.
But between elections there is far less to do than formerly,
so that the difficulty of maintaining an organization as
such as necessarily increased. It follows that improvement
in one fundamental aspect of Canadian democracy, the
electoral system, has certainly weakened another, the local
party unit.

An increasing divergence from provincial politics has been
another important trend in federal election practices. For

[1]S. R. Hesson to Macdonald, March 7, 1891 (Macdonald Papers, vol. 72).

prolonged periods, federal and provincial activities were almost identical; the same election officials and voters' lists were used, and the same individuals took leading roles in both. For a few years after 1867, the same person (in the two largest provinces) could be simultaneously a member of a federal and a provincial legislature, and so close was the connection between the two fields that Sir John A. Macdonald was for a time able to exercise a degree of supervision over electoral matters in Ontario.[1] For a time, provincial assemblies provided a fair proportion of the recruits for the House of Commons, but in most parts of Canada this trend has been declining steadily for decades. It is impossible to believe that this separation of provincial and federal politics into two separate compartments has not added to the complications of federal-provincial relations.

The attitude of the two major parties towards the use of provincial electoral machinery for federal purposes naturally varied with each party's position at Ottawa, and the political complexion of the provincial governments. Neither party has been able to pursue consistently a particular policy towards the electoral system. Thus the Liberals, largely in self-defence, were strong proponents of provincial rights from 1867 to 1896; but on their accession to power in 1896 they accepted only a partial return to provincial machinery, and it was they who took the final steps in the establishment of a completely federal electoral system in 1929. The Conservatives, on the other hand, favoured a centralized electoral system from the beginning; yet when in Opposition, as from 1896 to 1911, the Conservatives have on occasion been forced to champion the provinces. Both parties have introduced into federal politics electoral techniques which had been successfully used in local affairs, and indeed almost all the major reforms effected in the national system since 1867 had their origins in the provinces. The ballot, one-day voting, the trial of controverted election cases by the

[1]"Your Election Law is all right," he informed the Premier of Ontario in 1869, "I do not remember now why I held it over." Macdonald to J. Sandfield Macdonald, October 29, 1869 (J. Sandfield Macdonald Papers). Another letter dated February 20, 1871, reveals Sir John giving the Ontario leader advice on his election campaign and allied matters.

courts, and manhood and female suffrage, are a few important examples.

The Bench is another important part of the community which was at first closely connected with electoral matters, and which has been greatly strengthened by the developments which have freed the representative system of partisan interference. The general temper of Canadian politics during the first decades after 1867 was such that any electoral device which involved the judiciary was certain to bring to that institution a degree of disrepute. The use of the courts for controverted election cases after 1874, and the employment of judges to compile voters' lists after 1885, thus on occasion forced the judiciary into the hurly-burly of political strife. More than once, judges were savagely attacked by partisan newspapers for decisions in election trials; and since judges were an integral part of the machinery established by the Franchise Act of 1885, critical discussion of that Act in the legislature inevitably involved the Bench. A few electoral functions are still performed by judges, in the revision of voters' lists and the trial of controverted elections, and the fact that these activities never result in criticism of the judiciary today is not merely a tribute to the Bench, but to the whole representative system.

The concentration of control over all aspects of the electoral system in federal hands, and the development of the administrative machine to a high point of efficiency, have thus been accompanied by advantages for other parts of the government. But, as has been shown, the improvement of the electoral administration has not been entirely beneficial: the local party organizations have been weakened by the decline in their activities; and a division of the two fields of provincial and federal politics has been facilitated. Further, there is no evidence that the process of development has increased the representative nature of the House of Commons. In a narrow sense, there is today a virtual guarantee that the winner of an election in any constituency is an honestly chosen representative elected by qualified electors who cast their votes properly. But in a broader sense, almost every aspect of parliamentary representation which can be seen to be biased at all is biased in favour of the same regions and groups.

The system by which members are paid is in effect heavily weighted in favour of representatives from Ontario and Quebec. A statistical analysis of membership in the legislature reveals a similar bias. Even the statute which protects the independence of Parliament is open to an analogous prejudice, for it freely allows directors and controlling shareholders of corporations having government contracts to sit in the Commons, and most of these individuals come from central Canada. The House of Commons, notwithstanding the adoption of universal suffrage and the perfection of an impressive electoral administration, has continued to be recruited from the same groups, and in this sense has remained singularly under-representative of many important sections of the whole community. To the multitude of circumstances which give central Canada the preponderance of advantage in the national economy, the representative system, broadly viewed, must be added. While the techniques by which members are chosen have undergone revolutionary changes since 1867, the House of Commons in important aspects has stayed very much the same.

APPENDIXES

APPENDIX A. Relevant Sections of the British North America Acts.

APPENDIX B. Dates and Results of General Elections since 1867.

APPENDIX C. A Note on the Statistics on Representation.

APPENDIX A

SECTIONS OF THE BRITISH NORTH AMERICA ACTS OF
1867, 1915, AND 1946,
RELATING TO REPRESENTATION IN THE
HOUSE OF COMMONS OF CANADA

I. SECTIONS OF THE BRITISH NORTH AMERICA ACT, 1867.

17. There shall be One Parliament for Canada, consisting of the Queen, an Upper House styled the Senate, and the House of Commons.

37. The House of Commons shall, subject to the Provisions of this Act, consist of One hundred and eighty-one Members, of whom Eighty-two shall be elected for Ontario, Sixty-five for Quebec, Nineteen for Nova Scotia, and Fifteen for New Brunswick.

39. A Senator shall not be capable of being elected or of sitting or voting as a Member of the House of Commons.

40. Until the Parliament of Canada otherwise provides, Ontario, Quebec, Nova Scotia, and New Brunswick shall, for the Purposes of the Election of Members to serve in the House of Commons, be divided into Electoral Districts as follows:—

1. ONTARIO

Ontario shall be divided into the Counties, Ridings of Counties, Cities, Parts of Cities, and Towns enumerated in the First Schedule to this Act, each whereof shall be an Electoral District, each such District as numbered in that Schedule being entitled to return One Member.

2. QUEBEC

Quebec shall be divided into Sixty-five Electoral Districts, composed of the Sixty-five Electoral Divisions into which Lower Canada is at the passing of this Act divided under

285

Chapter Two of the Consolidated Statutes of Canada, Chapter Seventy-five of the Consolidated Statutes for Lower Canada, and the Act of the Province of Canada of the Twenty-third Year of the Queen, Chapter One, or any other Act amending the same in force at the Union, so that each such Electoral Division shall be for the Purposes of this Act an Electoral District entitled to return One Member.

3. NOVA SCOTIA

Each of the Eighteen Counties of Nova Scotia shall be an Electoral District. The County of Halifax shall be entitled to return Two Members, and each of the other Counties One Member.

4. NEW BRUNSWICK

Each of the Fourteen Counties into which New Brunswick is divided, including the City and County of St. John, shall be an Electoral District. The City of St. John shall also be a separate Electoral District. Each of those Fifteen Electoral Districts shall be entitled to return One Member.

41. Until the Parliament of Canada otherwise provides, all Laws in force in the several Provinces at the Union relative to the following Matters or any of them, namely,—the Qualifications and Disqualifications of Persons to be elected or to sit or vote as Members of the House of Assembly or Legislative Assembly in the several Provinces, the Voters at Elections of such Members, the Oaths to be taken by Voters, the Returning Officers, their Powers and Duties, the Proceedings at Elections, the Periods during which Elections may be continued, the Trial of Controverted Elections, and Proceedings incident thereto, the vacating of Seats of Members, and the Execution of new Writs in case of Seats vacated otherwise than by Dissolution— shall respectively apply to Elections of Members to serve in the House of Commons for the same several Provinces.

Provided that, until the Parliament of Canada otherwise provides, at any Election for a Member of the House of Commons for the District of Algoma, in addition to Persons qualified by the Law of the Province of Canada to vote, every male

British Subject, aged Twenty-one Years or upwards, being a Householder, shall have a Vote.

42. For the First Election of Members to serve in the House of Commons the Governor General shall cause Writs to be issued by such Person, in such Form, and addressed to such Returning Officers as he thinks fit.

The Person issuing Writs under this Section shall have the like Powers as are possessed at the Union by the Officers charged with the issuing of Writs for the Election of Members to serve in the respective House of Assembly or Legislative Assembly of the Province of Canada, Nova Scotia, or New Brunswick; and the Returning Officers to whom Writs are directed under this Section shall have the like Powers as are possessed at the Union by the Officers charged with the returning of Writs for the Election of Members to serve in the same respective House of Assembly or Legislative Assembly.

43. In case a Vacancy in the Representation in the House of Commons of any Electoral District happens before the Meeting of the Parliament, or after the Meeting of the Parliament before Provision is made by the Parliament in this Behalf, the Provisions of the last foregoing Section of this Act shall extend and apply to the issuing and returning of a Writ in respect of such Vacant District.

51. On the Completion of the Census in the Year One thousand eight hundred and seventy-one, and of each subsequent decennial Census, the Representation of the Four Provinces shall be readjusted by such Authority, in such Manner, and from such Time, as the Parliament of Canada from Time to Time provides, subject and according to the following Rules:—

(1) Quebec shall have the fixed Number of Sixty-five Members:

(2) There shall be assigned to each of the other Provinces such a Number of Members as will bear the same Proportion to the Number of its Population (ascertained at such Census) as the Number Sixty-five bears to the Number of the Population of Quebec (so ascertained):

(3) In the Computation of the Number of Members for a Province a fractional Part not exceeding One Half the whole Number requisite for entitling the Province to a Member shall be disregarded; but a fractional Part exceeding One Half of that Number shall be equivalent to the whole Number.

(4) On any such Re-adjustment the Number of Members for a Province shall not be reduced unless the Proportion which the Number of the Population of the Province bore to the Number of the aggregate Population of Canada at the then last preceding Re-adjustment of the Number of Members for the Province is ascertained at the then latest Census to be diminished by One Twentieth Part or upwards:

(5) Such Re-adjustment shall not take effect until the Termination of the then existing Parliament.

52. The Number of Members of the House of Commons may be from Time to Time increased by the Parliament of Canada, provided the proportionate Representation of the Provinces prescribed by this Act is not thereby disturbed.

147. In case of the Admission of Newfoundland and Prince Edward Island, or either of them, each shall be entitled to a Representation in the Senate of Canada of Four Members, and (notwithstanding anything in this Act) in case of the Admission of Newfoundland the normal Number of Senators shall be Seventy-six and their maximum Number shall be Eighty-two; but Prince Edward Island when admitted shall be deemed to be comprised in the third of the Three Divisions into which Canada is, in relation to the Constitution of the Senate, divided by this Act, and accordingly, after the Admission of Prince Edward Island, whether Newfoundland is admitted or not, the Representation of Nova Scotia and New Brunswick in the Senate shall, as Vacancies occur, be reduced from Twelve to Ten Members respectively, and the Representation of each of those Provinces shall not be increased at any Time beyond Ten, except under the Provision of this Act for the Appointment of Three or Six additional Senators under the Direction of the Queen.

II. SECTION 2 OF THE BRITISH NORTH AMERICA ACT, 1915.

The British North America Act, 1867, is amended by adding thereto the following section immediately after section fifty-one of the said Act:—

"51A. Notwithstanding anything in this Act a province shall always be entitled to a number of members in the House of Commons not less than the number of Senators representing such province."

III. SECTION 1 OF THE BRITISH NORTH AMERICA ACT, 1946.

1. Section fifty-one of the British North America Act, 1867, is hereby repealed and the following substituted therefor:

"51. (1) The number of members of the House of Commons shall be two hundred and fifty-five and the representation of the provinces therein shall forthwith upon the coming into force of this section and thereafter on the completion of each decennial census be readjusted by such authority, in such manner, and from such time as the Parliament of Canada from time to time provides, subject and according to the following rules:—

1. Subject as hereinafter provided, there shall be assigned to each of the provinces a number of members computed by dividing the total population of the provinces by two hundred and fifty-four and by dividing the population of each province by the quotient so obtained, disregarding, except as hereinafter in this section provided, the remainder, if any, after the said process of division.

2. If the total number of members assigned to all the provinces pursuant to rule one is less than two hundred and fifty-four, additional members shall be assigned to the provinces (one to a province) having remainders in the computation under rule one, commencing with the province having the largest remainder and continuing with the other provinces in the order of the magnitude

of their respective remainders until the total number of members assigned is two hundred and fifty-four.

3. Notwithstanding anything in this section, if upon completion of a computation under rules one and two, the number of members to be assigned to a province is less than the number of senators representing the said province, rules one and two shall cease to apply in respect of the said province, and there shall be assigned to the said province a number of members equal to the said number of senators.

4. In the event that rules one and two cease to apply in respect of a province then, for the purpose of computing the number of members to be assigned to the provinces in respect of which rules one and two continue to apply, the total population of the provinces shall be reduced by the number of the population of the province in respect of which rules one and two have ceased to apply and the number two hundred and fifty-four shall be reduced by the number of members assigned to such province pursuant to rule three.

5. Such readjustment shall not take effect until the termination of the then existing Parliament.

(2) The Yukon Territory as constituted by Chapter forty-one of the Statutes of Canada, 1901, together with any Part of Canada not comprised within a province which may from time to time be included therein by the Parliament of Canada for the purposes of representation in Parliament, shall be entitled to one member."

APPENDIX B

DATES AND RESULTS OF GENERAL ELECTIONS SINCE 1867

| Year | Date | Party Forming Government | Party Standings | | | | |
			LIB.	CONS.	PROG.	C.C.F.	SOC. CR.	OTHER
1867	Aug. 7-Sept. 20	Conservative	80	101				
1872	July 20-Oct. 12	Conservative	97	103				
1874	Jan. 22	Liberal	133	73				
1878	Sept. 17	Conservative	69	137				
1882	June 20	Conservative	71	139				
1887	Feb. 22	Conservative	92	123				
1891	Mar. 5	Conservative	92	123				
1896	June 23	Liberal	117	89				7
1900	Nov. 7	Liberal	128	78				8
1904	Nov. 3	Liberal	139	75				
1908	Oct. 26	Liberal	133	85				3
1911	Sept. 21	Conservative	86	133				2
1917	Dec. 17	Unionist	82	153 (Unionist)				
1921	Dec. 6	Liberal	117	50	64			4
1925	Oct. 29	Liberal	101	116	24			4
1926	Sept. 14	Liberal	116	91	13			25
1930	July 28	Conservative	88	137	2			18
1935	Oct. 14	Liberal	171	39		7	17	11
1940	Mar. 26	Liberal	178	39		8	10	10
1945	June 11	Liberal	125	67		28	13	12
1949	June 27	Liberal	193	42		12	10	5

APPENDIX C

A Note on the Statistics on Representation

THE statistical analyses of representation in the Canadian House of Commons given in Chapter VII of the text are part of a comprehensive unpublished study, and are based on a file of approximately 2,200 cards, each card representing a Canadian Member of Parliament. The file covers the entire period from 1867 to the election of 1945, the following information being sought in each case: name; date and place of birth; party affiliation and electoral record; constituencies represented; occupation or economic interests; religion; education; previous experience in municipal or provincial politics; and career after leaving the House of Commons. Some of this information, such as names and constituencies represented, was readily obtainable from official sources, and much of the rest was equally accessible in such reference books as the *Canadian Parliamentary Guide*, *Who's Who*, etc. Some of it, however, such as the "post-M. P." career of a man who did not attain the Elysian fields of the Senate or the Bench, was difficult and often impossible to secure, for most reference books of biography show a regrettable tendency to drop names from their pages unless the man concerned is continuously successful in his career. Defeated or retired members are for this reason often hard to trace, unless there is some justification for their prominence as a citizen other than their political undertakings. Another point on which it has been impossible to find satisfactory data is that of members' education, although it seems a fair statement that an overwhelming majority of members receive a better-than-average education.

A large number of sources were useful, ranging from annual civil service lists to the daily press. The backbone of the file, however, depends on a comparatively few major sources of reference:

Canada: *Sessional Papers* (Civil Service Lists, Annual Reports, etc.)

Morgan: *Canadian Men and Women of the Time* (2 vols. 1896 and 1912.)

Côté: *Political Appointments, Parliaments, and the Judicial Bench in Canada* (2 vols. 1896 and 1917.)

Canada Year Book
Canadian Almanac
Canadian Parliamentary Guide
Canadian Parliamentary Companion
Who's Who in Canada
The Canadian Who's Who
National Reference Book of Canadian Men and Women
Encyclopaedia of Canada
Prominent Men of Canada
Canadian Who Was Who
Cyclopedia of Canadian Biography
Canadian Biography

Many of these works duplicate others on the list, so that the systematic use of several such books in turn provided a useful check on the accuracy and completeness of the data extracted from them. There are at least two reasons for being slightly suspicious of standard collections of biographies. The facts about any one individual are nearly always provided by the man himself (or, in a few obstinate cases, *not* provided), so that the usual human tendency to draw the long bow, even within the meagre scope of *Who's Who* items, is always a threat to truth, perhaps especially so in the case of politicians. Secondly, there is always the chance that some reference book has merely copied a particular item from another, so that one is no check whatever on the other. These two points, combined with the fact that the editors of many collections of biographies seem to be guided by sheer caprice in the determination of which individuals are, and which are not, qualified to grace their pages, impose certain unavoidable limitations on many of the sources I have used.

Certain aspects of the work presented particular problems. Some of the statistics, for example, are more complete than others. Several of the data used are of a more definite nature than others, so that certain of the conclusions which follow are more precisely formulated. The exact age of a member, for example, can usually be ascertained without difficulty. On the other hand, such descriptive terms as "agriculturalist" cannot be used with any great precision in analysing the interests of members, since full-time farmers, officials of such organizations as the Grain Growers' Association, and well-to-do financiers who live on farms can all claim to have agricultural interests.   Making allowance for circumstances such as these, I think there is enough information in these statistics to give at least a clearer view of Canadian parliamentary representation than has hitherto been obtainable.   As J. F. S. Ross says in his comprehensive study of parliamentary representation in Great Britain, "Gaps there are and, it is to be feared, errors; but I am satisfied that they are not so extensive, nor of such a character, as to impair the general accuracy of the conclusions reached."[1]   Nevertheless, and at the risk of repetition, it must be emphasized that the statistics must be used with great caution.

[1] J. F. S. Ross, *Parliamentary Representation*, (Yale, 1944) p. 15.

INDEX

INDEX

and disfranchisement, 236; and election expenses, 259, 265; and election officials, 172–82, 185–6; and electoral corruption, 242n, 243, 244, 250, 254; and franchise, 211–32; and independence of Parliament, 85, 89, 95–7; and nominating procedure, 155–6; and payment of members, 100n; and qualifications of members, 64–6, 69, 72, 73–5, 78, 81; and redistribution, 24, 27, 29, 30, 33, 34, 36–46; representation from, 115–49, 291; and voters' lists, 190–204; and voting procedures, 158–60, 164–6, 167–8

Lieutenant-Governors, 143–9, 242

Listener, 6n

Local politics, members' experience in, 121–4

London, 215

Lower Canada, 20, 21, 63, 79n, 83, 84, 98–9

Luce, R., 5n, 6n, 63n, 64n

Lunatics, disqualified for House of Commons, 75–6; disfranchised, 234–5

MACDONALD, A. L., 79

Macdonald, H. J., 250

Macdonald, John A., 8, 278, 279; and disfranchisement, 235n; and election expenses, 260n; and election officials, 172, 174, 175, 177, 179, 180; and electoral corruption, 242–3, 246, 250n; and franchise, 211–16, 217–18, 222, 224n; and independence of Parliament, 87, 89, 91, 92–4; and qualifications of members, 61, 67, 68, 78, 80, 81; and redistribution, 20, 21, 22, 28, 29, 30; and voters' lists, 190, 191, 192, 194, 197n; and voting procedures, 158, 168

Macdonald, J. Sandfield, 279n

Macdonnell, J. A., 197n

MacKay, R. A., 262, 264

Mackenzie District, 54, 55, 56

MacIver, R. M., 4, 5n

Maclean's Magazine, 262n, 269n

MacNicol, J. R., 164n

Macphail, A., 106n

Maisonneuve, 81, 82

Manhood suffrage, 214–15, 223–6, 232, 233, 280

Manitoba, and disfranchisement, 238; and election officials, 179; and electoral corruption, 241; and franchise, 214–15, 221–2, 224n, 225, 230; and qualifications of members, 65n, 66, 78; and redistribution, 23–4, 25, 26, 49n, 53, 55, 56; representation from, 115–49, 291; and voters' lists, 193, 200; and voting procedures, 166

Manufacturers in politics, 131–6

Maritime Provinces, 15, 23, 39–42, 43, 58, 65, 124, 128, 130–1, 177, 199, 219; *see also* provinces by name

Marquette, 81, 240n

Marvell, A., 98n

McCallum, R. B., 163n

McCarthy, Dalton, 78, 196–7, 250n

McCuaig, J. S., 78

McDonald, Judge, 194n

McGee, D'Arcy, 167

McGreevy, T., 71–2

McKechnie, L. M., 111n

McPherson, W. D., 62n, 76n, 244n, 246n, 256n, 261n

Meighen, A., 48n, 94–6, 179, 202n, 228

Members, House of Commons, Canada, ages of, 118–21, 128–31, 293; attendance of, 8, 107n; birthplaces of, 124–8, 292; 'blackmailing' of, 251, 257, 263n, 266–8; and constituencies, 9–14; disqualifications of, 9, 76; dying in office, 143–9; expulsion of, 62, 69–75; holding more than one seat, 80–2; illness of, 103–4; membership in assemblies, 65–9; and natural resources, 89–90; and oath of allegiance of, 77; and offices of emolument, 80, 83–97; payment of, 98–114, 273–4, 275, 281; privileges of, 8, 69–75; property qualification of, 61, 63–65; qualifications of, 61–82; quality of, 274–5; recall of, 9–10, 79, 80; religious qualification of, 79; residence requirement for, 77–9; resignation of, 9, 79, 80; statistics of, 115–49, 292–4; and theories of representation, 9–16; unseating of, 8, 76, 240–58; and *passim*

Mennonites, 227

Merchants in politics, 131–6

Mileage allowance, members', 101, 102

Military Voters' Act, 227–9

Mill, J. S., 3, 4, 99

Mills, D., 38n, 174

Miners in politics, 131–6

Ministers, in House of Commons, 83, 84, 92–7, 109, 252, 261; M. of Justice, 246, 249; Secretary of State, 182

Minors, eligibility for House of Commons, 61–2; ineligibility as voters, 235

Mongolians, 220, 235

Montmagny, 196n

Montreal, 34–5, 47, 215, 222, 256, 266

Moore, G., 194n

Morgan, H. J., 292

Mowat, O., 215–16

Murphy, C., 229n

Muskoka, 172n

NATIONAL DEFENCE, Department of, 277

National Reference Book of Canadian Men and Women, 293

National Resources Mobilization Act, 11–13, 14

Native Canadians in politics, 124–8

Natural resources, 89–90

New Brunswick, and disfranchisement, 233, 235, 238; and election officials, 177; and electoral corruption,

241; and franchise, 212, 214–16, 221–3, 224n, 225, 230; and independence of Parliament, 84; and nominating procedure, 154; payment of members, 98; qualifications of members, 63, 66; redistribution, 21, 39–42, 44n, 53, 55, 56, 57; representation from, 115–49, 291; voters' lists, 189, 193; voting procedures, 157

Newfoundland, 54, 55, 56, 291

New Glasgow, 155

New Zealand, 49, 50, 204n

Nipissing, 155n

Nominating procedure, 153–7, 206, 274

Non-voters, 238–9

North West Council, 68; Territories, 26, 200n

Nova Scotia, 10; and disfranchisement, 233, 235, 238; and election expenses, 265n; and electoral corruption, 241; and franchise, 211–16, 221–2, 223, 224n, 225, 226, 230, 232; and independence of Parliament, 84; and nominating procedure, 154; and qualifications of members, 63, 65, 68, 69, 77n, 79; and redistribution, 21, 33n, 39–42, 53, 55, 56, 57; representation from, 115–49, 291; and voters' lists, 189, 193; and voting procedure, 157, 167

OCCUPATIONS OF MEMBERS, 111–12, 131–6, 292–4

Offices of emolument, 244; *see also* Independence of Parliament

'One-twentieth clause', see redistribution

Onslow, A., 5

Ontario, and disfranchisement, 235, 236, 238; and electoral corruption, 241n, 253; and franchise, 211–16, 220, 221, 222, 225, 229, 230; and independence of Parliament, 83; and nominating procedure, 154; and payment of members, 101,